Financial Simulation Modeling in Excel

Financial Simulation Modeling in Excel

A Step-by-Step Guide

KEITH ALLMAN
JOSH LAURITO
MICHAEL LOH

WILEY

John Wiley & Sons, Inc.

Published by John Wiley & Sons, Inc., Hoboken, New Jersey.
Published simultaneously in Canada.

For general information on our other products and services or for technical support, please contact our Customer Care Department within the United States at (800) 762–2974, outside the United States at (317) 572–3993 or fax (317) 572–4002.

Wiley also publishes its books in a variety of electronic formats. Some content that appears in print may not be available in electronic books. For more information about Wiley products, visit our website at www.wiley.com.

Library of Congress Cataloging-in-Publication Data:

Allman, Keith A., 1977–
    Financial simulation modeling in Excel : a step-by-step guide / Keith Allman, Josh Laurito, and Michael Loh.
        p. cm. – (Wiley finance series; 18)
    Includes bibliographical references and index.
    ISBN 978-0-470-93122-6 (pbk); ISBN 978-1-118-13720-8 (ebk);
ISBN 978-1-118-13721-5 (ebk); ISBN 978-1-118-13722-2 (ebk)
    1. Finance–Mathematical models–Computer programs. 2. Microsoft Excel (Computer file)
I. Laurito, Josh, 1981– II. Loh, Michael, 1977– III. Title.
    HG173A437 2011
    332.0285′554–dc23

                                                                                2011017551

Printed in the United States of America.

10 9 8 7 6 5 4 3 2 1

Contents

APPENDIX A

APPENDIX B

Regardless of where I work, simulation has crept into my financial career. After nearly a decade of working with it in many capacities I've found it to be a mixed blessing. In many investment companies when the term *simulation* is simply brought up there are a variety of reactions. The two most visible camps of thought seem to be the utilizers, who think the results of a simulation have value and the skeptics, who think simulation overcomplicates analyses.

The utilizers believe that when a concept or instrument is researched correctly, information parsed and calculated properly, and a simulation constructed in a statistically correct manner, the results can be used to make decisions. I tend to fall into this camp, with a few caveats I will mention later, because I have seen its utility in a variety of settings. Infrastructure deals that I saw early in my career that involved vehicular traffic, trade, or passenger flows, made more sense through simulation results given the wide variety of scenarios that could play out over time. A commodity company investment that I worked on at Citigroup involving soybeans seemed more appropriate after seeing the historic volatility of soybean prices and how their expected evolution might affect our exposure. In my structured finance career, the value of simulation on a very granular level for distressed mortgage-backed securities provided insight into obligor delinquency, default, and eventually expected security value loss. More recently, as I moved into private equity, simulating pools of corporate exposures and fund performance has become an important tool in assessing portfolio risk.

With all of these positives, there are some valid criticisms of simulation that are espoused by the skeptics. Relating to the overcomplication arguments is the thought that simulation is complex and that many mistakes can be made. I agree with this criticism, and one of the caveats that I alluded to earlier is that simulation must be implemented correctly for it to be useful and productive. I have seen simulations fail for a number of reasons, but most relate to poor implementation. In one transaction that I saw taken to a credit committee, the simulation implemented was purely derived from Excel's random number generator creating numbers based on a uniform distribution. No analysis was done around the appropriate distribution, and the CEO, who had an actuary background, instantly criticized the presentation.

In another transaction at an investment bank, a transaction specialist asked me to use a third-party simulation program to assist in modeling a structured product. I used the model exactly as it was intended and provided the results to the specialist. I knew that the time frame for the transaction was limited, but I was surprised that later in the day the specialist was preparing the results to use for the investment committee. The results that he had were a simulation of the asset side only and had no bearing on the liability structure being implemented. Trying to use such results in the manner he intended would have been erroneous. Luckily, the problem was caught in time and the proper analysis later done.

Even worse are systemic failures of simulation that we have recently seen. Before the 2007/2008 global financial crisis, the market assumed a lower correlation level for mortgage-backed securities than was actually intrinsic to the system. Simulations were run, and securities were poorly sized against default partly relating to this correlation underestimation. As the crisis evolved, the correlations were rerun and noticeably higher, meaning that the securities structured via simulations using lower correlations were much riskier than originally thought.

The intent of exposing my negative experiences with simulation is by no means to dissuade readers from using it and therefore throwing into question what the many pages that follow this preface could possibly be about. The purpose is to show that many of the problems related to financial simulation are caused by improper construction, use, or interpretation. Historical data that provides probabilities, volatility, or correlations might not be scrubbed and analyzed correctly, the implementation of simulation methods might be against the wrong distribution or structurally incorrect, and interpretation of results could be construed to arrive at fallacious conclusions.

The problems seem surmountable when enough time is taken to use simulation correctly. To be able to do this in a financial context, many people encounter difficulties because the bulk of the texts that explain simulation methodologies are extremely dense and theoretical. Few try to distill the important concepts into a readily accessible format with meaningful and practical examples. Like the other books in my step-by-step series, this book attempts to bridge the gap between basic technical implementation and purely theoretical explanations.

A noticeable difference with this book compared to my others is the appearance of two other names on the cover: Michael Loh and Josh Laurito. Simulation is a highly complex topic, and to thoroughly dig into the details their unique experiences and abilities were absolutely necessary. Michael's technical background in physics and finance brings a high mathematical acumen, which is reflected in the most difficult Model Builders seen on the website and throughout many sections of the text. Josh has deep industry experience and firsthand experience using simulation in a variety of contexts on Wall Street. Frequently we will use the terms "I" and "we" throughout the book. In both cases we are referring to all three of us from a collective perspective.

It's my belief that the combination of our skills and experience has been conveyed in an approachable, unintimidating, and clear manner. I hope that the pedagogical approach allows readers to walk away with a new tool in their analytical skill set and a feeling of personal value addition. If readers feel that something is still not clear or that they have found a possible typo or error, I encourage them to check the book's website for errata or to contact me personally at keith.allman@enstructcorp.com.

KEITH ALLMAN

Acknowledgments

I can definitively state that this book would not have been possible without my coauthors, Michael Loh and Josh Laurito. At times it was difficult, but both persisted through complex Excel/VBA work, tedious explanations, and long nights writing. Thank you, Mike and Josh. I must also thank the staff at John Wiley & Sons once again for allowing me the opportunity to add to the body of financial knowledge that the Wiley Finance series offers. Specifically, Bill Falloon, Jennifer MacDonald, and Tiffany Charbonier were critical to this book printing.

—Keith Allman

I would like to thank Keith Allman for providing me with this opportunity to help him write this book. Working with my coauthors on this project has been an amazing and enlightening experience for me. I am grateful, especially to Josh Laurito, for the patience my coauthors have shown me and for all the fantastic work that they have put into this book. I would also like to thank our publisher, John Wiley & Sons, because without their support none of this would have been possible.

—Michael Loh

Writing a book under almost any circumstances is a time-consuming endeavor. But writing one with three authors, on two continents, across eight time zones involves an extraordinary amount of dedication and patience. Mike and Keith were fantastic through the entire process, and I want to thank them for all the time and expertise they devoted to putting together the best text possible. I also want to thank the people at Wiley for their guidance and openness through the process of writing this book. In addition, special thanks to my partners, Gregg and Tim, as well as the whole team at Lumesis: Abdullah, Alex, Chong, Jacob, Justin, Lev, and Louis, for supporting me and our vision despite the hours this project took away from our venture. Most importantly, I want to thank my family and friends for their encouragement and patience as I disappeared for weeks at a time to work through what seemed like an endless project. Mom, Dad, Aaron, Becca, Jess, Shruti, and everyone else: thank you so much for your love and support.

—Josh Laurito

About the Authors

KEITH ALLMAN is an investment manager at Bamboo Finance, a private equity fund that invests in for-profit, commercially viable companies that provide a good or service that beneficially impacts the lives of low-income individuals. Mr. Allman is primarily responsible for generating new investment opportunities and managing existing investments. In addition, he manages the risk-monitoring process of the portfolio. Previously, Mr. Allman was the director of analytics and modeling at Pearl Street Capital Group, where he focused on private equity fund of funds, capital relief transactions, and venture debt funds. He also founded Enstruct, which services clients worldwide in capital markets and equity valuation, distressed valuation, and quantitative-based training. His analytical training originated at Citigroup, where he modeled structured products for their conduits and eventually emerging market transactions for its Principal Finance group. He has published three books with John Wiley & Sons, including *Modeling Structured Finance Cash Flows in Excel: A Step-by-Step Guide, Reverse Engineering Deals on Wall Street: A Step-by-Step Guide,* and *Corporate Valuation Modeling: A Step-by-Step Guide.* He is also an active volunteer for Relief International, for which he provided on-the-ground training for credit analysts at microfinance institutions in the Middle East. He is currently a director on Relief International's board. He holds bachelor's degrees from UCLA and a master's degree from Columbia University.

JOSHUA LAURITO, CFA, is a cofounder and principal of Lumesis, a leading provider of credit-analysis software and solutions to the municipal finance market. He also heads the analytics and data science divisions at CrowdTwist. Previously, he directed corporate modeling for Hexagon Securities, a boutique merchant bank that advises and invests in banks and specialty finance companies. Mr. Laurito held a managing directorship at RangeMark Financial Services, a credit-risk management and capital-markets firm specializing in structured finance. At RangeMark, he headed analysis of structured-asset resecuritizations and esoteric interest rate products, as well as municipal and financial institution credits and derivatives. He started his career in finance as part of the Global Structured Credit Products group at Merrill Lynch, where he assisted in the underwriting and modeling of securities backed by corporate and structured credits. Mr. Laurito is a CFA charterholder and holds a degree in chemistry and mathematics from Columbia University.

MICHAEL LOH is a software developer at Tech-X Corporation in Boulder, Colorado. He is working on electrostatic and electromagnetic particle-in-cell simulation code with applications in particle-beam physics, plasma fusion, and electron-hole transport in semiconducting detectors. Before joining Tech-X, he was a software developer and quantitative analyst at RangeMark Financial Services, where he developed the theory and application software to simulate the performance of residential and commercial mortgage-backed securities. Mr. Loh has a background in physics and was engaged in a Ph.D. program at the University of Chicago before joining RangeMark. His research focused on determining the evolution of matter distribution throughout the universe from observations of galaxy clusters at high redshifts. He left with a masters in physics. He also has a bachelor's degree in physics from UCLA.

Financial Simulation Modeling in Excel

CHAPTER 1

Introduction

P rojecting future performance in finance is rarely an endeavor that will lead to results that exactly mimic reality. Equity products vary as the market evolves, seemingly simple fixed-income products may fluctuate in value due to changing interest rates, and overall most financial products have an ebb and flow of value. None of this is shocking, since much of finance is about the risk of the unknown. Understanding, measuring, and making decisions with future performance risk in mind is the focus of most financial professionals' day-to-day jobs. To understand this risk, models can be built to project what would happen given a set of certain circumstances. Depending on the sophistication of the financial analyst and the level of detail justified for a transaction, a range of techniques are available. The most basic isolated calculations form the starting point for these techniques, which then become more complicated when interconnected concepts are tied together in a deterministic model, and eventually a simulation may be constructed when a simple closed form solution is not appropriate or even possible. This book intends to focus on the last of those three methods, simulation, by taking readers through basic theory and techniques that can be instantly applied to a variety of financial products.

WHAT IS SIMULATION?

In general, simulation is typically a process that attempts to imitate how events might take place in real life. Simulations can be extraordinarily simple, such as conducting a mock interview with a peer, or incredibly complex, such as using a flight simulator to mimic a Mars landing. A simulation can also be for a tangible real-life process or for something abstract. For instance, the military often engages in simulations that try to replicate real-life war scenarios. Soldiers storm faux buildings with people playing different roles in accordance with situations they would expect in a real war. However, there are also abstract simulations such as those conducted in finance.

Even though simulations in finance may be somewhat intangible, the events that we worry about are very real. Perhaps a fund manager has a portfolio of corporate exposures. The most obvious real-life event that would be of concern is the default of one or more of these corporate exposures. Simulating defaults would be an important exercise for the fund manager to undertake. Similarly, a fixed-income specialist might invest in fixed-rate products; however, the specialist might be funded by floating rate debt returns. Basis risk exists in such a system, and the evolution of interest rates is the real-life event that the specialist would worry about. A simulation of interest rates could greatly help the specialist design a portfolio to reduce risk.

CHARACTERISTICS OF A SIMULATION

Regardless if one is entering into a military simulation or creating a code-based simulation, there are similarities. The starting point for most simulations is the assumptions that go into it. For a military simulation that is preparing for urban warfare, this might include the number of soldiers per unit, the weapons and supplies that each solider carries, the standard and unique training of the soldiers, and the possible buildings, enemies, weather, and so forth that they could encounter. In a financial simulation, such as the corporate default example, you might have characteristics of the companies, such as the industry, regional operating location, historical asset levels, historical liability levels, and so forth.

Once the assumptions of the topic that we are trying to simulate are understood, a method for assembling the system and rules for how the system works are required. In our military simulation example, we would have a training area where the soldiers arrive with all of the training and gear one would expect, and then have an area with buildings and enemies they would expect to face. A mission with an objective would be established, and certain rules might be integrated to help make the simulation as real as possible. For instance, even though a soldier could theoretically leave the simulation area to get around an obstacle, a rule could define the simulation area and state that soldiers are not allowed to go beyond its perimeter. Similarly, in a financial simulation we would need a medium in which to conduct the simulation, which in modern times is done within the confines of a computer application. We program rules to guide our assumptions' behavior through processes that simulate how real-life events might unfold.

Another characteristic of simulations is that they may be repeated to determine varying outcomes. In the military situation, soldiers may choose one path through the buildings in one iteration of the simulation and then choose a different path in another iteration. The outcomes in both scenarios could be markedly different. Similarly, in a financial simulation asset levels for the same company in a future period could be assumed to be different from one simulation iteration to the next. This could mean that the default outcomes are also different.

At the end of the simulation, there should always be an analysis. Multiple aspects of the military simulation would be analyzed, such as speed of completion of the simulation, effectiveness at achieving the mission objective, supplies used,

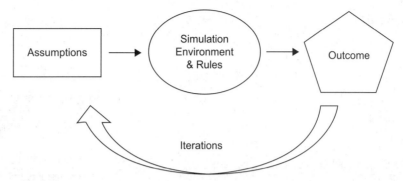

FIGURE 1.1 Most simulations will follow a similar process of selecting or creating assumptions, constructing a simulation environment with rules, analyzing the outcome, and possibly repeating the process.

and so forth. In the financial simulation, we would want to see the frequency of companies defaulting, which types of companies defaulted, the characteristics of those companies, the balance of exposures for the ones defaulting, the time at which they defaulted in the future, and so forth.

Finally, we should be concerned about the validity of our results. Numerous flaws could occur in the construction of the military simulation. Perhaps the individuals posing as enemy soldiers are not as aggressive as in real life or the equipment used is different. In the financial simulation, perhaps we assumed lower correlation than really exists or measured historical volatility wrong. All of these could lead to error that should be taken into account. See Figure 1.1.

INSTRUCTIONAL METHODOLOGY

Financial simulation can be a tricky subject for readers and authors since people have a multitude of reasons for using simulation in finance. To approach this unique issue, the book is laid out in a specific manner. Chapters 2 and 3 are what I would call "tool set" chapters. They focus on core elements of simulations that are inherent to most financial simulations (and to many simulations in other fields as well). Chapter 2 works through random number generation and eventually to explaining a common term heard in finance, Brownian motion. After that, in Chapter 3, correlation between variables is explained with examples on how correlated random numbers are generated. These tools are invaluable for constructing simulations and require a thorough understanding. For instance, one of the most common errors I have noticed financial analysts make when implementing simulations for the first time is an incorrect method of generating random numbers. Similarly, incorrectly accounting for correlation can lead to massive problems in a simulation.

Tools	Processes	Review

- Random Number
  Generation
- Correlation

- Black Scholes
- Hull White Interest
  Rates and Pricing
- Structural and
  Reduced Form
  Models
- Simulating Pools of
  Assets

- Data Deficiencies
- Understanding Error
  and the Limitations of
  Simulation

FIGURE 1.2   The chapters in this book follow a logical and intended order.

Once the tools are developed, readers begin to use them for different purposes. Chapter 4 takes readers through simulating interest rate paths to price bonds using methods credited to Hull and White. Chapter 5 expands the reader's knowledge of simulation by creating a corporate default simulation based on structural and reduced form models. Default is taken further in Chapter 6 with a thorough look at simulating pools of assets. Clearly, as authors, we cannot anticipate every reader's specific need, but the topics we have chosen reflect the most frequent and current topics related to simulation.

Finally, integrated throughout the chapters, but also a focus of chapters themselves is analysis, interpretation, and advanced thoughts on the simulation process. Chapter 7 shows readers data deficiencies and how to manage data as it relates to a simulation. Exercises, in the form of Model Builder examples, are used to help demonstrate these concepts. Although not as technically demanding, these sections should not be skipped over since they focus on the proper use of simulation; which is just as important as implementing it correctly. See Figure 1.2.

HOW THIS BOOK WORKS

There are notable differences and many similarities between this book and the others in my Step-by-Step Guide series. All rely on theory and practical exercises to transform financial concepts into dynamic, usable models. A common theme to the other books is that they work through individual "modules" that culminate in a single complete model. While this book has readers work through similar "modules," chapter after chapter, instead of creating a single unified model the Model Builders produce multiple, smaller models. This is not to say that they are less complex; in fact, many of the models in this book are technically and mathematically more complex than the other books. The use of multiple models is necessary because simulation has its place in many parts of finance, and using a single unified model would be illogical and inappropriate.

Whether you are familiar with the other books or new to the series, you will find that each section begins with a discussion of theory and then moves on to a Model Builder exercise, where the theory is transferred to an application in Excel. Eventually as all theoretical concepts are read and Model Builder steps completed the reader should have operational examples that are identical to the ones included on the website that accompanies this book. Readers should make every attempt at constructing the models themselves, since this is the best way to learn and understand every aspect of the models. If any part of the text seems unclear a reader should leverage the completed models on the website to understand every section.

While financial theory and implementation are two critical elements in learning proper modeling techniques, one of the biggest challenges of creating an instructional book is the different skill levels of readers. Some readers have a deep understanding of the theory and are really searching for practical techniques to create usable Excel/Visual Basic Applications (VBA) based solutions, while others may come from a very technical background and understand the mechanics of Excel/VBA but are more interested in learning what body of knowledge exists and how it ties into finance. For this reason, readers will notice various attempts at making the text applicable for the widest possible audience.

A balance has been attempted on both the theoretical and technical level. For the theory sections, enough background and mathematical formulas are provided to introduce, elucidate, and reinforce the section we are focusing on. However, this book is purposely not set up to list out and derive all formulas, nor does it intend to explicate in detail the origination of every concept. Enough theory is provided to understand what it is we are discussing, why it is important in finance, and how the analytical method that is provided can be used.

The technical level of this book starts out fairly simple, but it gets more complex in later chapters. For each chapter we strive to demonstrate the theory behind what we are discussing by first using Model Builder examples that operate entirely on the sheet without the use of VBA. However, Excel is a poor medium for simulation and VBA used within Excel's provided Visual Basic Editor (VBE) is a better environment to practically implement simulations. With this in mind we have provided VBA-based examples to many of the most important sections. We have tried to keep the coding straightforward for those who may be new to or at a beginner level of the VBA language.

Given that some readers will be on an extreme end of the spectrum, either completely new to financial simulation or advanced in the field, we have created an appendix to prevent the burden of too much off-topic or advanced information for the average reader. For instance, background mathematical concepts may be necessary for some readers, while some advanced topics discussed may pique advanced readers' interest. Rather than leave such readers without a resource or with the thought that some sections ended too quickly, we have included background mathematics and more advanced implementations in the Appendix. The complementary, completed Excel/VBA files related to these discussions are available on the book's website.

ABOUT THE COMPANION WEBSITE

It is clear that technology is changing how we take in information. You may be reading this book in digital form via an e-reader of some type. As digital media becomes a larger market, technical books like this have to adapt to provide all of the information necessary for readers. The previous Step-by-Step books included CD-ROMs to deliver the electronic information, such as the Model Builder files. Now we are moving to a web-based solution where users can download the files wherever they have an Internet connection.

Since my training website Enstruct, www.enstructcorp.com, is already established with errata for the previous books and additional financial modeling exercises, the files for this book can be downloaded from the site. To go to the secure file directory for this book, go to www.wiley.com/go/financialsimulationmodeling and enter the following:

Password: fsm2012

If there are any technical issues with the website, please e-mail: info@enstructcorp.com.

EXCEL 2003 AND EARLIER VERSUS EXCEL 2007/2010

We are at a time when there are many users who have switched to Excel 2007 or Excel 2010 and a few who are still using Excel 2003. While the powerful differences between 2003 and 2007/2010 versions of Excel are related to memory accessibility and usage, there are major shifts in the menus. This text will provide instructions assuming the reader is using Excel 2007/2010. If any users of 2003 or earlier encounter problems, they should contact the authors for assistance.

More important for this book are the differences between Excel versions in respect to VBA. There are differences between 2003 and 2007/2010, particularly since Add-In files, extension names, and references may be slightly different. For instance, 2007/2010 macro-enabled files end in .xlsm rather than .xls. Similarly, Add-Ins end in .xlam in 2007/2010 rather than .xla. Another critical difference is that Excel 2007/2010 provides readers the option to save their file in a macro-free workbook. Users of this book should be careful of this option when creating

FIGURE 1.3   Be careful of the differences in file saving between Excel 2003 and Excel 2007/2010.

code or using downloaded files from the website. If a file with VBA code is saved as a macro-free workbook, then all of the code is removed and the code functionality lost.

Another key caveat is that users who are using Excel 1997 or earlier may encounter serious problems since there were many updates to VBA after that version. If there are any Excel error problems, I will once again reiterate to check the complete Model Builder files on the website, and if the solution is not clear to contact the authors. See Figure 1.3.

A final word about Excel versions relates to Mac users. The Excel 2008 version on Mac does not allow for the use of VBA. However, the 2011 version does. Mac users running Excel 2008 should be careful when opening Excel files with VBA from the website.

A FEW WORDS ABOUT SEMANTICS

Learning about financial modeling can be tricky in written instructional form since words translate into commands, which can be very specific for computer programs. To avoid confusion, the following is a quick guide to the words that are used in this text and how they translate into the required actions the reader must perform. The key is to understand that there are four main operations we will perform on a cell and a fifth word to be aware of:

Enter a value. When the Model Builder exercises ask for a value to be entered, this will be a number, date, or Boolean (TRUE or FALSE) value. These are values that will be referenced for some type of calculation purpose.

Enter a label. A label is text in a cell to help the model operator understand values and formulas in relative proximity. Note that I use the word as a verb as well. For example, I may say label A1, "Project Basic Cash Flow". This means that the text "Project Basic Cash Flow" should be entered into A1. Also, there are times when I will use the word label with a number. This means that a number will be used as a label and not referenced in the actual calculation on the sheet or be used by the VBA code. Mostly these types of numbers will be used to describe time periods.

Name a cell or range of cells. Not to be confused with labeling, naming is a specific technique that converts the reference of a cell or range to a user defined name. This is done using the Name Box in the upper left corner of the Excel application or by selecting the Formulas tab and selecting the Name Manager button. In the Name Manager dialogue boxes, you can create, edit, and/or delete named references. It is particularly important to name a cell or range of cells as commanded if VBA code is being used for the Model Builder. This is because the name will be used in the code to reference the cell or range on the sheet. If the name does not exist the code will break down with an error.

Enter a formula. The core reason we are using Excel is for calculation purposes. A formula is initiated in Excel with the "=" sign. When I state to enter a formula, I will provide the cell it should be entered in and the exact formula that should be entered. Often I have copied the formulas from the Excel models themselves to ensure that the text exactly corresponds to the example models provided on the website.

Function. Be careful with the difference between a formula and function, as some people are used to hearing "Look at the function in A2" or "Enter the function there." The word *function* in this book can be used in a few ways. The most common way is when readers are instructed to use a pre-defined Excel function such as SUM, NORMSDIST, AVERAGE, and so forth. These are functions that are already created in the Excel Worksheet Function library and require the user to type only the name with parameters in parentheses to return a value. You will also hear the word *function* used when we describe the theoretical formulas that underpin the topics being taught. Readers should be aware that the use of the word

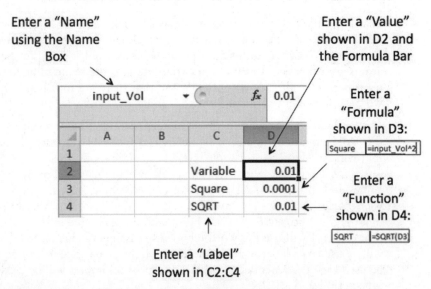

FIGURE 1.4 Commands in this book should be followed as described in the figure and in the text preceding it.

is to help explain the formula at hand. Finally, the word *function* may show up in certain sections where VBA is used. In VBA, users can use functions from many precreated libraries or create their own functions for use on the sheet or within VBA modules. If we use the word *function* in that context, it means we are most likely talking about a function that returns a value in the code. See Figure 1.4.

MODEL BUILDER 1.1: Initial Settings

With the first Model Builder, we should take a moment to understand how the Model Builder sections differ from other parts of the book. Each Model Builder is an instructional section that should be completed with the use of a computer running Excel. It should be followed step-by-step using the instructions. Each Model Builder assumes that each step in the Model Builder was read and implemented. The eventual result of the Model Builder sections is a complete version of the model we are discussing. Versions completed by the authors reside on the book's companion website. If at any point you find yourself lost you should open the corresponding completed file on the website to see how the relevant section should be completed.

This first Model Builder is to make sure that our versions of Excel are all set to identical settings. Depending how you installed Microsoft Excel or Office you may need the installation disc to enable all of these settings.

First, we will be using a few functions and tools that require the Analysis Tool Pak, Analysis Tool Pak VBA, and Solver Add-Ins to be installed. To do this:

For Excel 2007: Select the Office button, select Excel Options, select Add-Ins, and then select the Go button, which is to the right of Manage and a box that should default to Excel Add-Ins. This will bring up the same box as in Figure 1.5. Check the boxes for Analysis Tool Pak, Analysis Tool Pak VBA, and Solver. Select OK. If the Add-Ins are not installed it may prompt you with a few messages stating that Excel will need to install them. Depending on how Excel was initially installed, you may need the installation disc to complete the install.

For Excel 2003 and earlier: Select Tools, select Add-Ins, and check the boxes for Analysis Tool Pak, Analysis Tool Pak VBA, and Solver. Typically the Analysis Tool Pak and the Analysis Tool Pak VBA are the first two Add-Ins on the Add-Ins list. Solver is usually at the bottom. Select OK. If the Add-Ins are not installed, it may prompt you with a few messages stating that Excel will need to install them. Depending on how Excel was initially installed, you may need the installation disc to complete the install. Figure 1.5 depicts the Add-In selection box.

The next setting we should set is the ability to run macros. We will add significant functionality through the use of VBA. If you would like to take advantage of this you will need to continue on to step 3.

For Excel 2007: Excel 2007 requires a bit more setup to work with macros. Select the Office button, and select Excel Options. On the default tab, the Popular tab, check the third check box down, "Show the Developer tab in the Ribbon." Press OK. Once the Developer tab is visible, select it and then select Macro Security. In Excel 2007 you have four options for Macro settings, three of which are similar to Excel 2003. The only exception is that you can disable all macros except ones with a digital signature. Since hardly anyone has taken Microsoft up on its security measures and people rarely use digital signatures for Excel files, we will ignore that option. We can safely set it to disable all macros with notification. The notification will occur when the workbook is opened and will be a button with "Options…" in it at the top of the sheet or through a dialogue box asking you

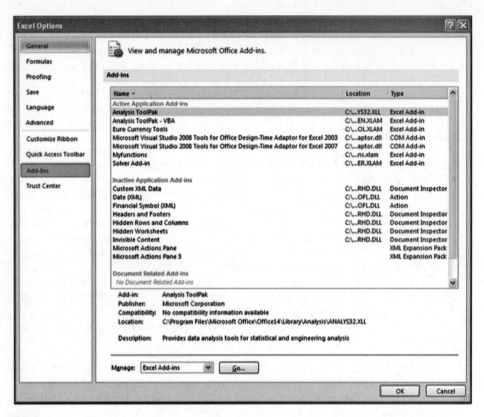

FIGURE 1.5   The Add-In selection box allows users to install precreated or user-created Add-Ins.

to enable macros. All workbooks from this book's website can be accepted, as they are virus-free. An example of one of these dialogue boxes is shown in Figure 1.6. In Excel 2007 you should not have to restart Excel for this to take effect.

For Excel 2003 or earlier: Select Tools, select Macros, select Security. You have the choice of either Low, Medium, or High. Low will allow macros without prompting, Medium will prompt you to enable or disable macros within a workbook when it is opened, and High disables macros in a workbook. The main concern is that viruses can be built into macros, which can cause significant damage or security concerns. All VBA subroutines and functions in this book contain no viruses and can safely be opened with macros enabled. You may want to set your computer to medium security so that you enable only trusted workbooks. For the changes to take effect, you must shut down Excel and reopen it. When prompted, enable macros for each file by selecting Enable.

Once the Add-Ins are installed and the macro security is set, we can actually start constructing our models. At this point we should go over repetitive processes for the remaining Model Builders. For many of the new Model Builders that are constructed, you will be asked to create a new Excel

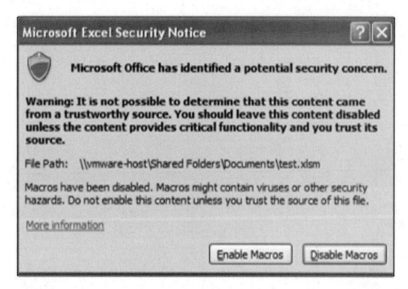

FIGURE 1.6 Once the macro security setting is set to "Disable All Macros with Notification," the following "Options . . ." button appears when workbooks with macros are opened.

workbook. It is recommended to get in the habit of using the naming convention we recommend. This normally follows MBX.Y_User.xlsm. This will let you quickly identify which ones you worked on and put them in order for later reference. It also means that completed versions on the website will be filed similarly, since they are named MBX.Y_Completed.xlsm.

FINAL REMINDERS

This is a complex book, perhaps more so than some of the earlier ones in this series. For each chapter read the theory section carefully, follow the Model Builder instructions in order (skipping ahead can cause multiple errors), and check the complete files on the website when lost or simply to compare your version. If you require more background information or are looking for more advanced implementations do not forget to read the Appendix and check the corresponding files on the website. Finally, if you are looking for a deeper discussion on certain topics there are multiple books that we have recommended throughout this text. With this in mind, we will move on to Chapter 2 to start developing our skills in financial simulation.

Random Numbers, Distributions, and Basic Simulation Setup

When I teach financial modeling courses and introduce simulation methodologies, I often poll the class to see what people already know about simulation. Responses vary from dazed, completely blank looks, to terms such as "stochastic," "Monte Carlo," or "random walk." It's the last statement, "random walk," that seems to generate the most discussion. I suspect that this could be due to a popular book, *A Random Walk Down Wall Street,* in which Burton Malkiel suggests that asset prices show signs of random processes. Since a random walk or more basically, a random element, is a fundamental part of many types of financial simulations, I find it critical to start any discussion with a definition of what a random element is and how it is properly used in a financial simulation.

SEED VARIABLES AND RANDOM NUMBER GENERATION

At the most basic level, the random element in a financial simulation model is a random variable, which is a quantification that can change. How a random variable is first established and how it changes each time is critical. The first and most obvious characteristic of a random variable is that it is random, meaning that the random variables created should not evolve and repeat in a pattern. The two key elements to preventing repetition are the initial starting point or seed state and the algorithm used to create the random variables.

Prior to explaining the details of a seed variable and random number generation algorithms, we should pause a moment to reflect that the mere mention of using a seed variable suggests that the numbers are not truly random. The proper terminology for random numbers that have deterministic attributes is pseudorandom numbers. More advanced methods of creating random numbers use observable real-world phenomena that can be detected and converted numerically. For example, low-level thermal or voltage change can be measured and converted to a numeric value. I once read that the decay of radioactive material would be one of the best random number generators. I could just picture a junior analyst at an investment bank with his computer hooked up to a protective, radiation-proof box containing uranium, explaining to his boss that he needs it to run his simulations. For practical computational purposes in finance, we will be creating and working with pseudorandom numbers.

The first critical part of generating pseudorandom numbers is determining how to select a seed state. As its name suggests, it is the beginning or first growth point of a series of pseudorandom variables. If the same pseudorandom number generation algorithm were applied to the same seed state, the same series of pseudorandom numbers should be produced. Since the evolution of the pseudorandom numbers is predicated on the value of the seed state, seed states themselves should be as random as possible. Many pseudorandom functions use the precise time the random variable is initiated as the seed state. In other cases some analysts want to be able to repeat the chain of pseudorandom numbers that were generated, and they have systems that allow them to enter a specific seed state.

Once a seed state is selected, an algorithm is required to create pseudorandom variables at future time steps. Such algorithms have evolved over the last few decades, constantly improving to eliminate repetitive elements. For the purposes of this book we will be relying on Excel's algorithm to generate a pseudorandom number, which has been a bit controversial. The pseudorandom number generator in versions of Excel prior to 2003 is problematic when used with millions of iterations. For these reasons Microsoft changed the pseudorandom number generator in 2003. Microsoft states that its new pseudorandom number generator passes a series of professional standard tests:

> The battery of tests is named Diehard. The algorithm that is implemented in Excel 2003 was developed by B.A. Wichman and I.D. Hill. This random number generator is also used in the RAT-STATS software package that is provided by the Office of the Inspector General, U.S. Department of Health and Human Services. It has been shown by Rotz et al. to pass the DIEHARD tests and additional tests developed by the National Institute of Standards and Technology (NIST, formerly National Bureau of Standards).

For most users' purposes, this level of sophistication is sufficient. For those who seek further advancement in pseudorandom number generation, there are third-party add-ins such as ZRandom, which uses the Mersenne Twister algorithm.

DISTRIBUTIONS

Once pseudorandom numbers are generated, the most common error I see when I look at finance students who are starting to implement simulations into their analysis is for them to generate a series of pseudorandom numbers using Excel's prebuilt functions and assume that those numbers can be directly used to test the probability of events taking place. We will delve into working with probabilities in simulations later in this chapter, but for now what we have to realize is that a pseudorandom number can be generated from differing numerical distributions.

The best way to understand what it means to generate a pseudorandom number from different numerical distributions is to start with the outputs from the series of pseudorandom numbers and create a histogram with the numbers. In the Model Builder sections in this chapter, we will look at how to create these outputs, but for now we should understand that pseudorandom numbers generated assuming different distributions will have very different characteristics. Figure 2.1 shows three histograms generated from uniform, normal, and lognormal distributions, as labeled.

MODEL BUILDER 2.1: How to Implement Uniform Pseudorandom Number Generation in Excel

As was just shown in Figure 2.1, a pseudorandom number can take many forms depending on the distribution assumed. In this Model Builder exercise we will start with the most basic pseudorandom generation on the Excel sheet using the RAND function and show how to create a histogram to demonstrate that the RAND function draws numbers between 0 and 1 from a uniform distribution. Note that the file MB2.0 will be used for this Model Builder exercise, but only one sheet is dedicated to it.

1. Open a new workbook in Excel and save it as MB2_User. With all of the future Model Builder exercises, it is preferable that you create your own version and use the book's website versions only when necessary or to check your work. The reference sheet for this exercise in the MB2.0 file is named "Uniform Pseudorandoms from Sht".

2. On your version of the Model Builder exercise, in C5 enter the following: "=RAND()". As stated in Chapter 1, enter only the characters you see between the double apostrophes. Notice that this function does not accept any parameters between the parentheses and that when any item on the sheet or workbook is calculated a new value is shown. The value is a uniform pseudorandom number between 0 and 1. Every time F9 is pressed, if Excel is in manual calculation mode or when a calculation takes place, this pseudorandom number will be regenerated. Copy or drag the function down to C104 to create 100 pseudorandom numbers.

3. Next we are going to create a histogram to visually see the distribution of random numbers. We will create "buckets" or intervals and see how many of the pseudorandom numbers fall within each interval. To do this, enter 0 in E6, .1 in F6, and continue entering values increasing by .1 in each successive cell in row 6 until 1 is reached in O6. If this does not make sense refer to the complete electronic files on the website.

4. There are multiple methods in Excel to count the number of pseudorandom numbers that fall within each bucket. We will take a look at three ways, one of which requires Excel 2007 or later. The first method that is backward compatible with versions of Excel prior to Excel 2007 is to use a formula with two COUNTIF functions. Enter the following formula in F7:

$$=COUNTIF(\$C\$5:\$C\$104,">"\&E6)-COUNTIF(\$C\$5:\$C\$104,">"\&F6)$$

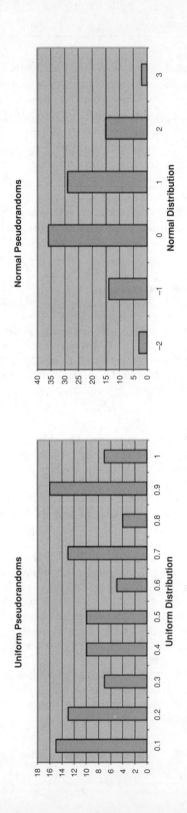

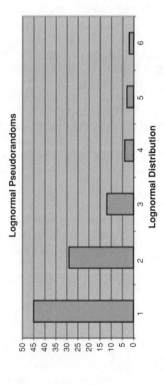

FIGURE 2.1 Three histograms depicting a uniform, normal, and lognormal distribution.

Histogram Data										
0	0.1	0.2	0.3	0.4	0.5	0.6	0.7	0.8	0.9	1
	14	15	5	15	5	7	7	11	8	13

FIGURE 2.2 A histogram in Excel, such as this one, helps summarize large data sets

The COUNTIF function counts the number of cells that meet a certain criteria. The criteria parameter can be any logical statement, but it is tricky to enter. If we want to say greater than a referenced value then we have to put the "greater than" symbol (>) in double quote marks and then use the ampersand to connect the greater than symbol to a referenced cell, which contains a value. The first part of the formula above counts the number of cells that are absolutely greater than the first bucket value (0 in this case). To find out the number of cells that are WITHIN the next bucket range we subtract out the number of cells that are greater than the next interval in the bucket range. Copy and paste this formula over the range F7:O7. Also, we may want to check to make sure we are counting all 100 cells and should put a quick sum check in place. Enter "=SUM(F7:O7)" in Q7. Figure 2.2 shows the area that should be created.

5. Next we should create a chart to see what the histogram distribution looks like. Create a column chart using F7:O7 as the only y series and the bucket range as the x series. Once this is created, you may notice a particular distribution. However, press F9 and it should change. Keep pressing F9, and you should see no discernible pattern for the distribution, since the pseudorandom numbers are being drawn from a uniform distribution. We are seeing some variance from a complete set of identical column sizes because we are only using 100 pseudorandom variables. If we extend the random number generation to include more and more numbers we would see the columns start to equalize in size and be more consistent between calculation (i.e., pseudorandom number regeneration). The sheet should look like Figure 2.3. You may also want to name the sheet "Uniform Pseudorandoms from Sht" to distinguish between the upcoming sections.

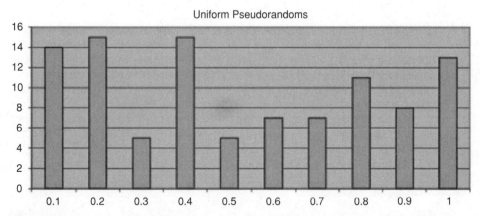

FIGURE 2.3 Charting the summarized histogram data makes it easy to visualize the results of a simulation.

MODEL BUILDER 2.2: How to Implement Uniform Pseudorandom Number Generation in VBA

Since it is impractical to implement simulation directly on the Excel sheet and since many examples in this book will use VBA, we should also cover how pseudorandom numbers are generated in VBA. Beyond a difference in the function spelling, there are additional steps and nuances regarding the seed state we should be aware of in VBA. To understand these differences, Model Builder 2.2 will recreate the first two steps of Model Builder 2.1 in VBA. The histogram and chart creation are best done on the Excel sheet.

1. In the same workbook as Model Builder 2.1, open the Visual Basic Editor and insert a new module, also insert a new sheet named "Uniform Randoms from VBA".
2. Start the module with some basic variable declaration and array dimensioning code as follows:

```
Sub UniformRandGen()
 Dim rCt As Integer, rMax As Integer
  rMax = 100
 ReDim uArray(1 To rMax, 0)
```

3. The next part of code is one of the important sections that implements the pseudorandom generator:

```
Randomize
```

The Randomize statement initializes the pseudorandom number generator in VBA. If it is used on it is own as in the example code then the system timer is set as the seed state.
4. Next enter the following code:

```
For rCt = 1 To rMax
    uArray(rCt, 0) = Rnd()
Next rCt
```

This code starts a For Loop that will run for 100 loops (given the value set for rMax). Within the For Loop the array, uArray, is filled with a value provided by the Rnd function. The Rnd function creates a pseudorandom number from a uniform distribution. If it is entered with no parameters after it, as in the example code, Rnd generates the next pseudorandom number in the sequence. While there are a few combinations of using Randomize and Rnd with and without parameters, the way it is set up currently is probably the most useful.

The second most useful option would be to have the same set of pseudorandom numbers repeat. This can be done using a negative number parameter in the Rnd function. Replace the following line of code:

```
uArray(rCt, 0) = Rnd()
```

with:

```
uArray(rCt, 0) = Rnd(-rCt)
```

5. The final piece of code exports the array we filled to the Excel worksheet so we can quickly see the results. Prior to entering this final piece of code, go back to the worksheet that you created in this Model Builder and name the range C5:C104, "rng_VBAuRnd". Now you can go back to the VBE and enter the following code in the same subroutine where you left off:

```
Range("rng_VBAuRnd") = uArray
End Sub
```

NORMAL PSEUDORANDOM NUMBERS

Creating uniform pseudorandom numbers is an excellent starting point, but often doesn't take us far enough in finance, where normal distributions are often assumed. Common errors can occur when people new to financial simulation try either using uniform pseudorandom numbers where normal pseudorandom numbers should be used or incorrectly transform uniform pseudorandom numbers. Fortunately there are prebuilt functions in Excel and established methods such as Box-Muller that allow us to quickly transform uniform pseudorandom numbers to normal pseudorandom numbers.

Although we can quickly transform uniform pseudorandom numbers to normal pseudorandom numbers, we should take a moment to understand what this actually means. With a uniform distribution there is no propensity for the numbers toward a mean or a variance around the mean to give the distribution "shape." A normal distribution will exhibit a mean and a symmetrical distribution of numbers around that mean depending on the variance.

A good example of the difference between a uniform distribution and a normal distribution is shown by creating a coin toss simulation. In such a simulation we would draw a uniform pseudorandom variable from our computer, perhaps using RAND on the sheet or Rnd in VBA, and then check to see if that number is greater than or equal to .5 (indicating a head) or less than .5 (indicating a tail). We could then run one simulation for hundreds of iterations and then count to see the number of heads and tails for that single simulation. If we ran 30 simulations, each with 200 iterations, we could then see the histogram of "heads" results for all of the simulations. This should not be uniform and should exhibit normal qualities with .5 as an approximate mean. See Figure 2.4.

MODEL BUILDER 2.3: Understanding Normal Distributions through a Coin Toss Example

1. Create a new worksheet in the same MB2 workbook that you have been working in. Name this sheet "Coin Toss Example".
2. In A8:A207 create a list of ascending numbers starting from 1 and incrementing by 1. This will provide a count for the iterations.

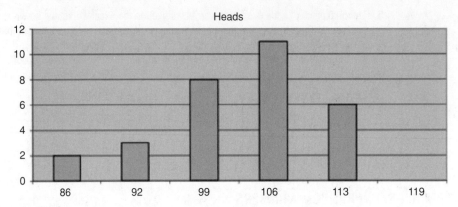

FIGURE 2.4 Counting the number of times "heads" is drawn from a
series of coin toss examples produces a normal distribution

3. Enter the text "Coin Toss x" in C4:AF4, replacing "x" with 1 for the first cell and incrementing it by 1 until it reaches 30 in AF4.

4. Each column in the range C:AF can be thought of as an individual simulation. Each iteration for each simulation will contain a uniform pseudorandom number. Let's quickly generate this by entering

$$=RAND()$$

in C4:AF207.

5. We now need to summarize the results of each column. Create labels by entering the text "Heads" and "Tails" in B6 and B7 respectively.

6. Count the number of heads by entering the following formula in C6:

$$=COUNTIF(C\$8:C\$207; ">="\&0.5)$$

Copy and paste this formula over the range C6:AF6.

7. Count the number of tails by entering the following formula in C7:

$$=COUNTIF(C\$8:C\$207; "<"\&0.5)$$

Copy and paste this formula over the range C7:AF7.

8. We can view an example uniform distribution by charting all of an individual simulation's iteration values. In order to view the normal distribution of results we should create a histogram. In AH24 and AH25 enter the following labels respectively: "Mean" and "Std Dev".

9. In AI24 enter the following formula:

$$=AVERAGE(C6:AF6).$$

Also, in AI25 enter the following formula:

$$=STDEV(C6:AF6)$$

10. The next step is to create a histogram based on the mean and standard deviations. First we will have labels starting in AI27 with −3, −2 in AJ27, and continuing to increment by 1 until AO27 has a 3 in it.
11. In AL28 reference the mean that was just calculated by entering the formula: "=AI24"

    We now need to reduce the histogram buckets by a standard deviation. To do this enter the following formula in AK28:

$$=AL28-\$AI\$25$$

12. Copy and paste this formula over the range AI28:AK28.
13. The opposite should be done for the other side of the distribution. Enter the following formula in AM28 to increase the mean by a standard deviation:

$$=AL28 + \$AI\$25$$

    Copy and paste this formula over the range AM28:AO28.
14. The final steps are to create the histogram count data. In AJ29 enter the following formula in order to count the number of Heads occurrences that are between −3 and −2 standard deviations from the mean:

$$=COUNTIF(\$C\$6:\$AF\$6, ">="\&AI28)-COUNTIF(\$C\$6:\$AF\$6, "="\&AJ28)$$

    Copy and paste this formula over the range AJ29:AO29. It is important to keep track of what the histogram formula is doing. In this case it is counting the "Heads" results that fall BETWEEN standard deviations. Charting the data will help visualize the resulting normal distribution.

QUICKLY GENERATING NORMAL PSEUDORANDOM NUMBERS USING PREBUILT EXCEL FUNCTIONS

The fastest method to create a normal pseudorandom number in Excel is to leverage Excel's prebuilt functions. Learning the RAND function, which creates a uniform pseudorandom number, is the first step, while understanding the NORMSINV function is the second. The NORMSINV function returns the inverse of the normal distribution, when provided with a probability. The question, "What is the inverse of the normal distribution?" often follows the introduction of the NORMSINV function. To help explain the function we will look at a more intuitive distribution function and use a tangible example to explain how both functions work.

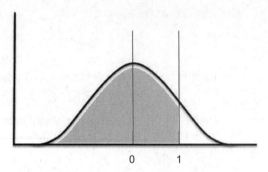

FIGURE 2.5 The NORMSDIST function provides the value under the curve given a point on the distribution. Here the value under the curve for 1 is visually shown.

The easier normal distribution function to learn first is the NORMSDIST function. If one were to enter "=NORMSDIST(1)" in a cell and press ENTER, the value .84135 would be returned. The NORMSDIST function returns the cumulative area under a normal distribution curve, up to the standard deviation value selected, assuming a distribution with a mean of 0 and a standard deviation of 1. Thus putting a 1 in the parameter for the function returns .84135, meaning that .84135 of the area under the curve is captured up to the first standard deviation. This is visualized in Figure 2.5.

To further explain this, enter "=NORMSDIST(-1)" in a cell and press ENTER. The value .15865 is returned because the area under the normal distribution curve to -1 is .15865. See Figure 2.6.

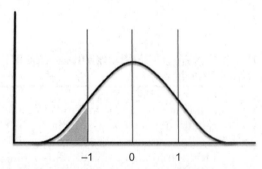

FIGURE 2.6 Notice that the function is cumulative in nature starting with lower bounds. Here, when −1 is used as the parameter the area returned only goes up to where −1 would fall on the normal distribution.

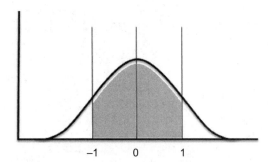

FIGURE 2.7 A figure that might be familiar from statistics classes is returned when we look at the probability of being within two numbers on the normal distribution.

Notice that if we add the two values we just calculated we get 1, which is always the total value of the area under the normal distribution. Now, given the symmetrical nature of the normal distribution, most people talk about probability in regards to the normal distribution by saying, "What is the probability of being WITHIN "x" standard deviations of the mean?" NORMSDIST can provide this by subtracting the function return with a parameter of –1 from the function return with a parameter of 1. If you do this in Excel you will get a value of .68268, meaning that there is a 68.268 percent chance of being within one standard deviation for a sample value drawn from a population exhibiting a normal distribution with a mean of 0 and a standard deviation of 1. See Figure 2.7.

In the series of previous examples we provided a data point on the normal distribution and had the NORMSDIST function return the cumulative probability. In a more tangible example we could have been talking about heights and wanted to know the probability that a certain height is exhibited out of a population of heights. In our example earlier we would have been providing the heights and getting the probability returned from the function. However, what if we wanted to the opposite, that is, provide the probability and have the height returned? We can do this using the NORMSINV function. Test this out by entering "=NORMSINV(.84135)" in a cell. The returned value will be very close to 1, which was the parameter we used earlier with NORMSDIST to get the .84135 value.

MODEL BUILDER 2.4: Creating Normal Pseudorandom Numbers Using Excel Functions

---

1. In the Model Builder file that you have been creating, insert a new worksheet and label it "Normal Pseudorandoms from Sht".
2. In cell C5 enter "=NORMSINV(RAND())". Notice that earlier we had said that NORMSINV returns the value on the normal distribution given a probability. RAND provides a pseudorandom

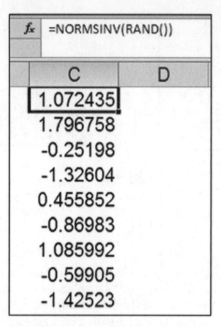

FIGURE 2.8 The NORMSINV function combined with the RAND function can quickly produce a set of normal pseudorandom numbers.

number between 0 and 1, which can be thought of as a random probability. This produces a normal pseudorandom number. Copy and paste the formula over the range C5:C104.

3. As with the Uniform Pseudorandoms from Sht sheet make a histogram to summarize the data. To do this we should check the minimum and maximum of the data set returned from the newly entered functions. Generally the minimum and maximum should be around −3 and 3 respectively. In E6 enter −3 and grow it by 1 in each successive cell to the right until it reaches 3.

4. Use the same formulas as the "Uniform Pseudorandoms from Sht" sheet to count the number of data points in the data set that fall within the buckets created in step 3. The sheet should look like Figure 2.8 thus far.

OTHER METHODS OF GENERATING NORMAL PSEUDORANDOM NUMBERS

Earlier in this chapter we discussed the merits of using different methods and algorithms to generate uniform pseudorandom numbers and found the RAND function to be suitable in many financial situations. Further transforming the uniform pseudorandom numbers can be done quite easily using the NORMSINV function, but as we get more advanced and possibly switch entirely to a code-based solution, we may want to explore more computationally efficient methods of transformation.

The Box-Muller transformation is a widely accepted method of taking uniform pseudorandom numbers and creating normal pseudorandom numbers. The Box-Muller transformation uses the trigonometric functions SIN and COS. If a simulation were being done in VBA, using this transformation would be more efficient than using NORMSINV, since NORMSINV would have to be called from the WorksheetFunction library, while SIN and COS are contained in the VBA library. Code that is written with references to the WorksheetFunction library is generally slower than code using the VBA library.

Implementing the Box-Muller transformation is relatively simple and can be done on the sheet as shown in the following Model Builder.

MODEL BUILDER 2.5: Creating Normal Pseudorandom Numbers Using the Box-Muller Transformation

1. Insert a new sheet in the Model Builder 2 workbook that you have been working in. Name this sheet "Box-Muller".
2. Label the following cells:

> C5: "Uniform 1"
> D5: "Uniform 2"
> E5: "Normal 1"
> F5: "Normal 2"

3. Insert an increasing row of numbers, starting with 1 and ending with 100, in B6 to B105.
4. In C6 enter =RAND() and copy and paste this across the range C6:D105.
5. In E6 enter the following formula:

$$=SQRT(-2*LN(C6))*COS(2*PI()*D6)$$

The Box-Muller transformation is using the Cartesian system, which in the current implementation is two dimensional and will therefore be able to generate two normal pseudorandom numbers. In the first number transformation it uses the cosine function. Copy and paste this formula over the range E6:E105.

6. Now we can create a second normal pseudorandom number using the sine function. Enter the following formula in F6:

$$=SQRT(-2*LN(C6))*SIN(2*PI()*D6)$$

Copy and paste this formula over the range F6:F105.

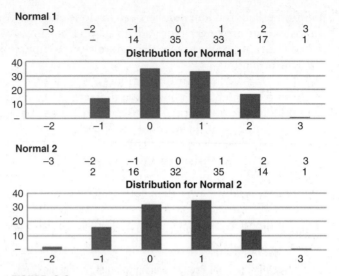

FIGURE 2.9 The Box-Muller transformation takes the uniform pseudorandom numbers created by the RAND function and returns a set of two normal pseudorandom numbers. The resulting histograms for each set of normal pseudorandom numbers are shown here.

7. We can check the results of our number generation by building two histograms as we have done in the previous Model Builder exercises in this chapter. Figure 2.9 shows the normal results of those histograms.

PUTTING TOGETHER A MORE DEVELOPED SIMULATION USING THE FUNDAMENTAL COMPONENTS

Thus far we have looked at individual components to a simulation, heavily focusing on critical basic elements such as pseudorandom number generation. While these concepts are extremely important as the basic building blocks for a simulation, we should review in more detail a few additional elementary concepts, namely iterations and sampling.

Iterations are the number of times the simulation runs. One complete cycle of the simulation is one iteration. When a low number of iterations is used there can be a large variance in the error from the simulation. In general a large number of iterations should be used to reduce such variance. What number is the right number of iterations? This is definitely project dependent and by no means definitive, but in finance you will often see Monte Carlo simulations running a minimum of

10,000 to 20,000 iterations. In some cases there have been models that we have worked on with up to 1,000,000 iterations assumed.

In certain situations we may only be able to sample from a population to infer results. We have already seen this with the coin toss example, where we know that the probability of getting a heads or tails is $1/2$ or .5. We ran a simulation of tossing a coin and came up with probability results that were close to what is expected. The more samples that are included in a simulation, the closer we can estimate the actual probability. In summary, increasing the sampling gives more accurate results, while increasing the number of iterations decreases the variance on the results.

MODEL BUILDER 2.6: The N-sided Die Example

To help piece together all of the basic elements, we are going to run a more sophisticated simulation. This simulation is done using both the Excel sheet and VBA code. While simulations in finance can be done on the sheet, it is important to understand code-based solutions because as we move on to more advanced concepts through this book there are sections that will simply be far too inefficient to be done on the sheet. If you are struggling with any of the code, refer to the completed version of the Model Builder available on the website.

1. Open a new workbook, save and name it MB2.6_User.xls.
2. Name the first sheet "UserSimulate" and enter the following labels in the corresponding cells:

```
B3: "Number of Sides"
B4: "Iterations"
B5: "Sample Size"
E3: "Simulated Probability"
E4: "Error of Probability"
E5: "Actual Probability"
```

3. Enter the following initial values in the corresponding cells:

```
C3: 6
C4: 1000
C5: 50
```

4. Since we will be using VBA, we should name the inputs and certain output cells on the UserSimulate sheet. Name the following cells with the corresponding names:

```
C3: nSides
C4: iterations
C5: numOfRolls
F3: expectedProb
F4: errOfProb
```

5. Figure 2.10 shows how the sheet should look thus far. Open the Visual Basic Editor and insert a module. Name the module "SimFunctions".

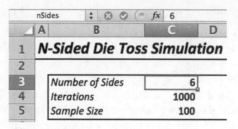

FIGURE 2.10   Building out the inputs with proper naming is important for the VBA code later.

6. In the SimFunctions module we will create a few subroutines and functions. We will start with the first main subroutine and as we come to additional functions and subroutines that are required we will note them and come back to them later in this Model Builder. The first subroutine we will create is called GenRndNumDist. Initialize a subroutine with this name.

7. Next declare the following variables:

```
Dim iNSides As Integer
Dim dProb As Double, adSimProb() As Double
Dim lIterations As Long, lNumOfRolls As Long, lI As Long, lJ As Long,
alResult() As Long
Dim scratch As Range
```

   Notice that we have created variables and arrays (denoted by the () after the name).

8. The next piece of code is for error handling, in case a user forgets to put in valid assumptions. This is a particularly important habit to get into for simulation models since we don't want to set off a simulation for thousands of iterations with invalid inputs. Enter the following code for the error handling:

```
If Not (CheckInputs) Then
    Exit Sub
End If
```

9. Turn off screen updating to save time. In some cases we may leave this on to show the results of a simulation via a chart, but for the most part we should always turn it off for any subroutine:

```
Application.ScreenUpdating = False
```

10. Like error handling, we should get in the habit of clearing any Excel workspace that is filled by VBA. This prevents latent information from previous simulations from being incorporated incorrectly into a new analysis:

```
Range(Range("BinStart"), Range("BinStart").Offset(150, 3)).Clear
```

11. We should now assign user-entered values from the Excel sheet:

```
iNSides = Range("nSides").Value
lIterations = Range("iterations").Value
lNumOfRolls = Range("numOfRolls").Value
```

12. Once we have values drawn in from the Excel sheet, we can resize our arrays so they fit the input data for the simulation:

```
ReDim alResult(1 To lIterations)
ReDim adSimProb(1 To lIterations)
```

13. Specific to this simulation is the fact that we know what the probability of an n-sided die roll should be. It is simply 1 divided by the number of sides:

```
dProb = 1 / iNSides
```

14. Code is extremely conducive to simulation, particularly with functionality such as looping. The completion of a loop in itself is an iteration. However, in this example we actually have more than one loop in each iteration due to the possibility of rolling the die multiple times each iteration. For this example we will have two loops, one nested within another. The outer loop is the iteration loop, while each completion of the inner loop is a simulated roll of the die. In general (and there can be exceptions), the outermost loop of a simulation will be an iteration:

```
For lI = 1 To lIterations
   For lJ = 1 To lNumOfRolls
```

15. Within each loop we generate a uniform pseudorandom number and compare it to the probability that is expected. If the number is less than or equal to the probability, then we log a value of 1, if not, nothing is logged. This is repeated for each roll of the die.

```
  If (Rnd <= dProb) Then
     alResult(lI) = alResult(lI) + 1
End If
 Next lJ
```

16. For each iteration we need to figure out the simulated probability. Since this is dependent on the sample size or the number of rolls of the die, we must enter the following code:

```
 adSimProb(lI) = alResult(lI) / lNumOfRolls
Next lI
```

17. Once the loops are complete and our arrays are filled, we need to export the results to the Excel sheet:

```
Range("expectedProb").Value = MyMean(adSimProb)
Range("errOfProb").Value = Sqr(MyVar(adSimProb))
```

18. Two additional subroutines help us visualize the information:

```
Call CopySimResultsToScratch(adSimProb, lIterations)
Call SetupHistogramBins
```

These two subroutines export the iteration results to a scratch sheet so we can create a histogram. The second subroutine listed (SetupHistogramBins) creates the bins for the histogram. This can be done on the sheet or in code depending on the functionality that the user desires.

	A	B
1		
2	0.15	0
3	0.15	0.01
4	0.17	0.02
5	0.2	0.03
6	0.09	0.04
7	0.19	0.05
8	0.19	0.06
9	0.18	0.07
10	0.11	0.08
11	0.23	0.09
12	0.13	0.1
13	0.2	0.11
14	0.16	0.12
15	0.18	0.13

FIGURE 2.11 The Excel sheet is populated with results from the CopySimResultsToScratch subroutine.

19. Finally, we wrap up the code by turning screen updating back on and selecting the active sheet that we want to view after the simulation runs.

```
Range("nSides").Select
Application.ScreenUpdating = True
End Sub
```

20. The main subroutine in steps 1 to 19 requires two additional subroutines that were called in step 18. The first one of these subroutines, CopySimResultsToScratch, is an interesting one to learn from because it shows a method of exporting simulation data based on the number of iterations (which can be different from simulation to simulation). Figure 2.11 depicts the output range. Since this is a supplementary and relatively simplistic subroutine, the entire uncommented code is shown here, rather than going through it in sections:

```
Private Sub CopySimResultsToScratch(adSimProb() As Double,
lIterations As Long)
  Dim scratch As Range
  Dim lI As Long
```

```
   Worksheets("scratch").Range(Range("start"), Range("start")
   .End(xlDown)).Clear

   Set scratch = Worksheets("scratch").Range(Range("start"),
   Range("start").Offset(lIterations-1))

   scratch = Application.WorksheetFunction.Transpose(adSimProb)
End Sub
```

The interesting part to this subroutine is that it accepts the number of iterations and the probability that we are trying to return for each iteration as a parameter. The subroutine then clears the export area, sets a range based on the number of iterations and writes out the probability array to that range.

21. An additional subroutine that is used, which is an optional code-based solution to creating histogram bins, is called SetupHistogramBins. Like CopySimResultsToScratch, this subroutine is simple and is provided in its entirety here:

```
Private Sub SetupHistogramBins()
   Dim i As Integer
   Dim binRng As Range

   Worksheets("scratch").Range("$B$1:$B$101").ClearContents
   Set binRng = Worksheets("scratch").Range("bins")

   For i = 0 To 100
     binRng.Offset(i).Value = i * 0.01
   Next i
End Sub
```

The key to this subroutine is that it makes 100 bins at increments of .01 in the For Next loop. The .01 hardcoded figure could be replaced by a variable that is assigned from the Excel sheet inputs section if a user wanted flexibility in changing this.

22. Finally there are three custom functions; two used for calculation purposes and the third for the error handling. The first one in order of the provided Excel workbook is the error-handling function called CheckInputs (the commenting has been left in to explain each section of code):

```
Private Function CheckInputs() As Boolean

   ' Check to make sure that the number of dice sides is greater
   than 0.
   If Not (Range("nSides").Value > 0) Then
       MsgBox Prompt:="Please enter a nonzero positive value for N
       Sides"
       CheckInputs = False
       Exit Function
   End If
```

```
' Check to make sure that the number of iterations sides is greater
than 0.
If Not (Range("iterations").Value > 0) Then
    MsgBox Prompt:="Please enter a nonzero positive value for the
    number iterations"
    CheckInputs = False
    Exit Function
End If

' Check to make sure that the number of rolls is greater than 0.
If Not (Range("numOfRolls").Value > 0) Then
    MsgBox Prompt:="Please enter a nonzero positive value for
    number
    of rolls per iteration"
    CheckInputs = False
    Exit Function
End If

    CheckInputs = True
End Function
```

The first calculation function is MyMean:

```
Function MyMean(ByRef avInput() As Double) As Double

    Dim dSum As Double
    Dim lCnt As Long
    Dim lJ As Long

    dSum = 0
    lCnt = 0

    For lJ = LBound(avInput) To UBound(avInput)
        If IsNumeric(avInput(lJ)) Then
            dSum = dSum + avInput(lJ)
            lCnt = lCnt + 1
        End If
    Next lJ

    If lCnt = 0 Then
        Exit Function
    End If

    MyMean = dSum / lCnt
End Function
```

This function is essentially an average function that takes the simulation probabilities from the main subroutine and averages them out by summing them and dividing by the count. The interesting part of this function is the use of LBound and UBound to define the number of loops for the For Next loop. This technique is useful because when we are running simulations we are going to want to be efficient in our looping.

The final function is MyVar, which is essentially the same as MyMean, but it calculates the variance:

```
Function MyVar(ByRef avInput() As Double) As Double

    Dim dMean As Double
    Dim lJ As Long
    Dim lCnt As Long
    dMean = MyMean(avInput)

    MyVar = 0
    lCnt = 0

    For lJ = LBound(avInput) To UBound(avInput)
        If IsNumeric(avInput(lJ)) Then
            MyVar = MyVar + (avInput(lJ)-dMean) ^ 2
            lCnt = lCnt + 1
        End If
    Next lJ

    If lCnt = 0 Then
        Exit Function
    End If

    MyVar = MyVar / lCnt
End Function
```

The main difference between MyVar and MyMean function is the calculation that is done in the For Next Loop. In MyVar the variance is being captured, while in MyMean the mean is recorded.

23. As a final step you may want to create a button on the Excel sheet and assign the GenRnd-NumDist subroutine to it so you can quickly run the simulation from the Excel sheet.

While this Model Builder is simple, it is a good example of the basic inputs and outputs seen in many simulations. This Model Builder also exemplifies a few thoughts we should have in efficiency:

■ For Excel-based systems it is easy to store the inputs on the sheet, draw them all into VBA, process the results in VBA, and then export them back to the sheet for easy viewing. Figure 2.12 exemplifies proper setup. It is incredibly inefficient to do everything on the sheet or to use VBA to loop through sheet-based calculations.

■ Since the number of iterations can frequently change, it is useful to work with dynamic arrays that are cleared and resized based on the number of iterations.

■ User-defined functions process faster than calling functions from the WorksheetFunction library. Learning how to create user-defined functions is also important because in more advanced simulations there are often complex calculations that have not been created in predefined functions.

The other important take away from this Model Builder is an initial understanding of the statistical foundations of simulations. Take some time to run the subroutine by changing the inputs and looking at the resulting histogram. The first change you should try is lowering the number of iterations. Change it from 1000 to 50 and run the simulation. Looking at the histogram chart you will see the distribution is very choppy. With lower iterations there is higher variance in the results and what should be a smooth normal distribution is all over the place. Using data parsed by confidence intervals from such a result could be misleading.

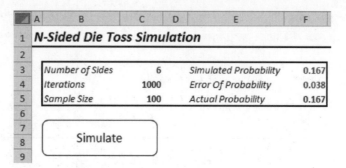

FIGURE 2.12 An efficient simulation draws all inputs into code for calculation and exports results back to the sheet for easy interpretation and analysis.

Alternatively, reset the iterations to 1000 and this time lower the sample size to an extreme level such as 5. Notice now that the distribution looks off because of a small sample, but also look at the error (range errOfProb on sheet). The difference in the error is much higher with a smaller sample size. This similarly will lead to misleading results.

BROWNIAN MOTION AND WIENER PROCESSES

With a solid understanding of random numbers in mind, we can delve deeper into how these topics evolved in finance. The term *Brownian motion* is often heard in financial classrooms and occasionally in jobs that involve securities analysis. In fact the first time I thoroughly went through Brownian motion was when a managing director at my first job after graduate school was introducing his method for analyzing credit default swaps. Brownian motion is named after the 19th-century Scottish botanist Robert Brown. Brown noticed that when pollen grains were suspended in water they jiggled and moved about in seemingly random fashion. Today, this random motion is known as a Wiener process and is used as a foundation to model many financial products and attributes of financial products, the most common being stock prices and interest rates. Since most of us are comfortable with the idea that prices and rates do not fluctuate in a purely random fashion, we must first assert a few stipulations, which we will discuss later in the section, to make this framework more representative of real-world observables.

Wiener Process

Formally a Wiener process $(W_n(t))$, otherwise known as a random walk, is defined as follows: at any given time t_i a binomial process, a process by which there are only two possible outcomes, will take either a step forward or a step backward with a step size of 1/sqrt(n), where n is the total number of steps taken. Thus the outcome at t_{i+1} will depend only on that of the prior state, namely at t_i. Therefore the value of W_n at any time t can be computed by equation 2.1:

$$W_n(t_i) = W_n(t_{i+1}) + \frac{X_i}{\sqrt{n}} \tag{2.1}$$

where X_i is a random variable that is defined to be either 1 or –1 with equal probability. We can easily deduce from the above equation that generally the value of a Wiener process at any time t can be computed as equation 2.2:

$$W_T(t) = \sqrt{\frac{t}{T}} \left(\frac{\sum_{i}^{t} X_i}{\sqrt{t}} \right) \tag{2.2}$$

Here we replaced n with T, the total time, and where we are assuming that time is measured in integral time periods such as days, months, or years. If T is large enough, the Central Limit Theorem tells us that $W_T(t)$ is a normally distributed random variable with mean 0 and standard deviation of sqrt(t/T), that is $N(0, \text{sqrt}(t/T))$.

MODEL BUILDER 2.7: Basic Brownian Motion

1. This Model Builder will take readers through a simple setup for implementing Brownian motion and allowing users to see the results of as many time steps as desired (within a reasonable limit for Excel/VBA). First, we should create a new workbook since this represents a distinctly different setup than before. Name the workbook MB_2.7_User.xls.
2. For labeling purposes enter the following labels in the corresponding cells:

   A1: "Brownian Motion"
   A3: "N – Steps"

3. Next enter a value of 100 in B3 and name the same cell nsteps.
4. Switch over to the Visual Basic editor, insert a new module, and then enter the following code to create the function BinaryStepSelection:

```
Function BinaryStepSelection() As Double
    If (Rnd() < 0.5) Then
        BinaryStepSelection = 1
    Else
        BinaryStepSelection = -1
    End If
End Function
```

This function has a familiar element from prior sections of this chapter: the syntax Rnd. In this situation we are creating a function that returns either a 1 or –1 depending on whether a uniform random variable is greater than or equal to .5 or less than .5.

5. The function we just created is used in the following subroutine RandomWalk(), which takes in the user desired number of time steps and runs a basic random walk. Enter the following code in the same module where the BinaryStepSelection function was entered:

```
Sub RandomWalk()
    Dim walk() As Double
    Dim stepSize As Double
    Dim steps, i As Long

    steps = Range("nsteps").Value
    stepSize = 1 / steps

    ReDim walk(1 To steps)

    walk(1) =BinaryStepSelection() * stepSize
    For i = 2 To UBound(walk)
        walk(i) = walk(i-1) + BinaryStepSelection() * stepSize
    Next i
    Call CopySimResultsToScratch(walk)
    Call PlotRandomWalk(steps)
End Sub
```

You will notice that the code is quite simple and involves declaring variables, assigning values from the sheet and with basic math, creating an array to store the results, and then looping through each time step and filling the array with the calculated values. Note that two other subroutines are used in the workbook, but these are purely for output purposes. In order to make the best use of text space the code for these subroutines is contained in the completed MB_2.7_Complete.xls workbook on the website.

6. Viewing the complete version we can view a random walk from the VBA code on a line graph, which is shown in Figure 2.13.

FIGURE 2.13   A random walk with 1000 steps.

Brownian Motion as a Stochastic Process in the Real World

As mentioned in the start of this section, we can use Brownian motion to represent the fluctuations typically seen in the stock market. Very naively we could assume the stock price, S, with some initial value S_o, to be purely Brownian with variance, σ. This would give the relation in equation 2.3,

$$S = S_o + \sigma W_T \qquad (2.3)$$

Note that this behaves exactly as the process shown in Figure 2.10 but with an offset of S_o. Immediately we can see a few drawbacks to this direct approach. First and foremost it should be clear to most readers that a stock price cannot go negative. A second more subtle issue is that financial observables will tend to drift and not simply oscillate around the mean.

Let's try to resolve the first issue by coming up with a scheme in which the stock price is never negative. The following, equation 2.4, would be a simple but effective guess:

$$S = S_o \exp(\sigma W_T) \qquad (2.4)$$

By encapsulating the stochastic element as a power of an exponential function, the result will always be positive even if the exponent itself is negative. You may now be wondering why we chose in particular the exponential function. After all any positive number taken to the nth power will always return a value between 0 and infinity. The reason why this is a good choice will soon become evident.

Now we're making progress, but we're still not done. Recall that a Wiener process has a mean of 0 with some constant variance. This means the stock price will simply fluctuate about $S_o \exp(0) = S_o$. What we need to do here is to introduce a drift term, μ, that scales with time. This would force a movement in future stock prices by shifting the mean at each time step (equation 2.5).

$$S = S_o \exp(\sigma W_T + \mu t) \qquad (2.5)$$

Does this really work? We can prove to ourselves that it does work by computing the expectation value of the exponent (equation 2.6).

$$\langle \sigma W_T + \mu t \rangle = \sigma \langle W_T \rangle + \mu \langle t \rangle = \mu t \qquad (2.6)$$

since $<W_T> = 0$ and $[\mu,\sigma]$ are constants.

Our simple guesses have taken us quite far. But you may have noticed that while we solved two problems, we have now introduced another, namely that the price is now unbounded and will eventually drift toward infinity. All the issues we have discussed so far are problems from a purely mathematical standpoint. However, in practice it can be overlooked as long as the modeler is aware of their pitfalls. Models with these attributes are popular primarily because they are *simple* and the solutions to these models are easily tractable and faster to implement. The Black-Scholes model is an example of a popular implementation that is subject to these types of pitfalls. The initial stochastic process from which the solutions are derived may not go negative but it will converge toward infinity. Of course, more complicated models are designed to specifically address these issues, such as the Hull-White model we will go through in Chapter 4. The drawback for the increased accuracy, as you will see, is a far more complicated implementation.

Pricing Derivatives

Now let's explore why we chose the exponential in the first place. For those who have taken finance courses you may recall that the return of a bond that matures with constant interest rate, r, at time, T, is determined by the relation (equation 2.7),

$$B(T) = B_o \exp(rT) \tag{2.7}$$

Does this look familiar? If we took the rate as the observable for our stochastic process, then this equation, rewritten as equation 2.8, would look a lot like what we discussed in the last section.

$$r(t) = r_o + \sigma W_T + \mu t \tag{2.8}$$

The bond price won't have such a simple form anymore, but that is not the point. What we have just developed is a foundation on which we can build interest rate models that can be used to price various types of financial derivatives.

Brownian Motion as a Differential Process

To further develop our tool sets for simulation, we will introduce Brownian motion as a differential process. Please refer to Appendix A if you are not familiar with partial differential equations or require additional mathematical background. Many physical processes, including those in finance, behave according to slight changes in the underlying variables. For example, interest rates are in reality a continuous process and to properly characterize processes dependent on the rate and time, we have to formulate that process as dependent on the differential change in the rate. With this in mind, we can rewrite equation 2.8 as a differential process (equation 2.9)

$$dr = \sigma dW + \mu dt \tag{2.9}$$

Now making generalized statements about r, like the expected value, is a little more difficult because the solution to the equation would have r be dependent on two variables, W and t. Fortunately we can do a basic integration to find the function $r(t, W)$ that satisfies equation 2.9 because each of the dependent variables, t and W, are completely separable. For the case of the regular Brownian motion, we see that equation 2.8 exactly meets our requirements. We would then expect r to be normally distributed with standard deviation σ and mean μt.

Geometric Brownian Motion

While values such as interest rates can be assumed to follow a Brownian motion, other quantities, such as stock prices or asset values, are typically assumed to follow a geometric Brownian motion (GBM), equation 2.10.

$$dS = \sigma S dW + \mu S dt \qquad (2.10)$$

It may seem equation 2.10 is very similar to equation 2.9, but the solution and overall implications are very different. The dependent variables are not separable anymore as there is an extra S term in the equation. Fortunately, in this scenario we can use Ito's Lemma to help solve our stochastic differential equation (SDE). The lemma states that the differential for a multivariable function, $f(t, r)$, can be approximated by equation 2.11,

$$df(t, S) = \frac{\partial f}{\partial S} dS + \frac{\partial f}{\partial t} dt + \frac{1}{2} \frac{\partial^2 f}{\partial S^2} dS^2 \qquad (2.11)$$

If we were to replace S with r, set $f(r) = r$, and substitute equation 2.9 for dr, you will see that equation 2.9 is recovered. This result should be somewhat expected since we stated beforehand that equation 2.9 can be directly integrated to produce equation 2.8. However, what should f be for a geometric Brownian motion depicted in equation 2.10?

As a starting point, note that if we divide both sides of equation 2.10 by S, we get a term dS/S, which, when integrated, gives us a natural logarithm and a natural starting point for our guess, that is $f(S) = ln(S)$. Before we continue further we should mention that the differential of a variable, say dt, means we are looking at very small changes in the quantities. As a consequence, the square of a very small number, either dt^2 or $dtdW$, can be assumed for all practical purposes to be zero and freely ignored. The only difference in this particular example (a proof will not be given here) is that dW^2 tends toward dt. If we apply $f(S) = ln(S)$ along with our assertions to equation 2.10, we get the following (equations 2.12 and 2.13),

$$d\ln(S) = \sigma dW + \mu dt - \frac{1}{2}\left(\sigma^2 dW^2 + \mu^2 dt^2 + \sigma \mu dt dW\right) \qquad (2.12)$$

$$d\ln(S) = \sigma dW + \left(\mu - \frac{1}{2}\sigma^2\right) dt \qquad (2.13)$$

Now we are free to integrate equation 2.14 much like we did with equation 2.10 (see equation 2.14).

$$\ln(S) = \ln(S_o) + \sigma\, W + \left(\mu - \frac{1}{2}\sigma^2\right)t \qquad (2.14)$$

In light of this new equation we can say the *log* of the variable S is now normally distributed with standard deviation of σ and mean of $(\mu$-$\sigma^2/2)t$. Or more succinctly, a variable S that follows a geometric Brownian motion is said to be *lognormally* distributed. In finance you routinely hear the term phrase, "we expect this result to be lognormally distributed." When somebody assumes this, they are not stating a law or fact that something *has* to be distributed this way. They are merely making a statement that they believe the underlying process is GBM.

Before we close our discussion on GBM processes, we must discuss one more issue because it will be useful when building the Merton-KMV model in Chapter 5. Given that we assume a variable follows a GBM process, how does one compute its volatility or standard deviation? One might be tempted to use Excel's STDEV function on the series of numbers produced from $ln(S_i)$-$ln(S_o)$. This however will not work even though we *expect* it be true. The reason for this is because the time term is constantly growing, which results in a larger and larger difference that will severely bias the STDEV result. The key to making a technique like this work is to examine the differential, which is the difference between neighboring points (equation 2.15).

$$\ln\left(\frac{S_i}{S_{i-1}}\right) = \ln(S_i) - \ln(S_{i-1}) = \sigma\,\Delta W + \left(\mu - \frac{1}{2}\sigma^2\right)\Delta t \qquad (2.15)$$

We mentioned earlier in this chapter that the expected value of a Wiener process, W, is normally distributed. We also stated that the expected value of ΔW is *also* normally distributed. Therefore the relation in equation 2.15 is also normally distributed but without the bias imposed by an increasing time term. This is exactly what we need. Furthermore, this line of reasoning would also apply to regular Brownian motions discussed earlier.

UNDERSTANDING SIMULATION RESULTS

Now that we have the tools to *run* simulations and had practice in specific situations, we need some rudimentary understanding of how to interpret our results. As we talked about earlier in Chapter 1, the need to perform a simulation could arise from the fact that the result cannot be explicitly determined. However once the simulation is performed, we need to ask ourselves, "How much can we trust the outcome?" It would be rather irresponsible for the practitioner to run a simulation without any thought given to the accuracy or trustworthiness of the result and then present the outcome as a statement of fact. First we must understand what an error is and the various types that we can encounter throughout our analysis.

Statistical Error

Earlier in this chapter we introduced the N-Sided Die example. While the result of the exercise might seem trivial, it presents many useful concepts that are applicable to all simulations in general when discussing errors. When dealing with random processes such as rolling a die, the main source of error is statistical. Imagine for a moment we flip a coin once and it lands on heads. That one sample tells us that the probability of landing on heads is 100 percent; however, this is clearly wrong since, as we all know, the probability is 50 percent. After five such flips we may get a set of results that may look like the following {H, H, T, H, T}, which implies that the probability of landing heads is now 60 percent. As we increase the sample size the probability we measure will slowly converge toward 50 percent.

Increasing the sample size seems like a simple solution, but now you may be wondering what if for our particular application we are restricted to a sample size and can only flip the coin five times per *iteration*? How confident are we of our results? Essentially this question is asking how much can that 60 percent change if we were to flip the coin five times again. Naturally one would not necessarily expect the same pattern to show up for each iteration. For example, the next iteration may produce the following pattern {H, T, T, T, T}, which gives a probability of 20 percent. The only way to find out is to do multiple iterations with five samples each and use statistics to examine the results. At this point we should mention that the iterative process is only necessary if we don't know the probability ahead of time. In the case of the coin we *know* the probability so we can actually use the binomial distribution to explicitly compute our confidence.

Once we iterate N times, we would have N probability measurements. Now we can make a statement about what we expect the probability to be and how confident we are of this probability. The *expected* value would just be the average of our N measurements. Determining the confidence is conceptually a little trickier. When we ask about the confidence interval, what we are essentially asking is, "How many of our points falls within a certain interval?" How would we compute confidence bounds if we wished to be confident to 68 percent? Notice that the probabilistic outcome of a coin flip with a certain sample size is a random normal process. The properties of a normal process are such that it is symmetric about the mean, and the area under the curve one standard deviation out on each side is roughly 68 percent of the total area under the curve. Therefore, the standard deviation of our N measurements would give us our error, or expected confidence, in our final measurement. In terms of notation it is written as the following (equation 2.16):

$$P \pm \Delta P \tag{2.16}$$

Normal distributions are a special case due its symmetrical properties about the mean, which means the error bars are also symmetric. However, what happens when we try to characterize processes that are not symmetric, like one that obeys a lognormal distribution? See Figure 2.14a and 2.14b.

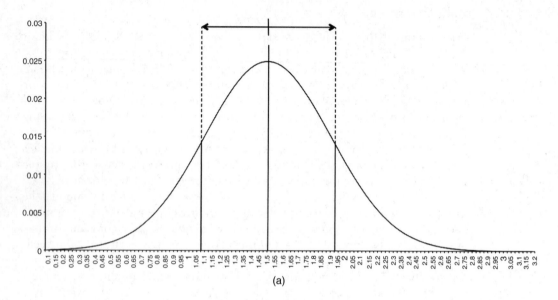

(a)

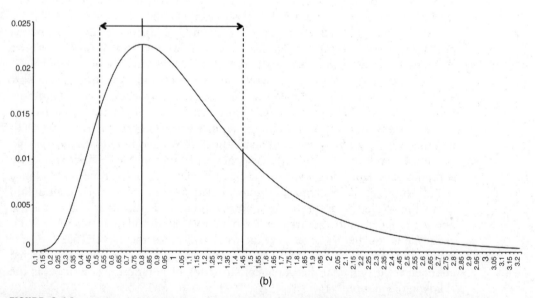

(b)

FIGURE 2.14 (a) Normal distribution with symmetric confidence intervals to 68 percent. (b) Log normal distribution with skewed confidence intervals to 68 percent.

In this case to properly characterize the nature of your statistical errors, each domain (+) and (–) must be analyzed separately. In statistical terms, this asymmetric property is known as *skewness*.

Sometimes the model that must be simulated is highly nonlinear, and it would be impossible to guess at the underlying distribution. For example when determining the cash flow from a mortgage default model, the underlying monthly payments would not exhibit normal characteristics. This may not seem obvious at first, but consider that as you try to predict cash flow 20 years into the future, you would expect the values to be highly uncertain with correspondingly large error bars. But you also know that the actual balance, and thus the actual dollar value, would need to decrease as people either default or pay down their loans. If the modeler just simply takes the standard deviation in this case and imposes symmetric bounds, the error bars will most likely encapsulate negative dollar values. In reality this cannot possibly be true. In situations like this, the only way of resolving this issue is to plot the histogram of the results itself to see what the underlying distribution looks like.

Systematic Error

The second type of error, or uncertainty, is the one that we are most familiar with. This error is caused by the limitation inherent in our tools of measurement. Tools in this case can mean a physical instrument, like a ruler, or a mathematical model that is known to be inaccurate due to certain levels of approximation that had to be made for solvability. Whatever that tool may be, systematic error is always present in our measurement and cannot be suppressed simply by doing more and more trials.

Let us take the ruler as an example to see what we mean. Imagine this ruler has 1/16-inch tick marks. Let us take this one step further and also imagine these tick marks to be rather thick, enough so such that it is difficult to tell which 1/16th segment begins and the other ends. When using this ruler to measure something that is 1–1/32″ long, it would be really difficult to resolve the difference between 1″ and 1–1/16″. Thus the measurer could say either one is valid but with a certainty that the *real* answer is most probably within a 1/16″ range about the quoted amount. Obviously this error will stay with you each time you use the ruler because the tick marks will never spontaneously get thinner.

Another example that is more applicable to finance is the mathematical approximations used to solve complicated problems. Typically in finance, this level of approximation is applied within the time domain of the problem. For example, the equations that describe option prices or default probabilities are usually based on the fact that time is continuous. In reality, however, it would be impossible to simulate with time steps so small as to be meaningfully continuous when compared to the properties of the underlying assets. More realistically the time interval under consideration is usually along the order of a day, week, month, or even year. As with the ruler example, the process of making time discrete will induce an error that cannot be suppressed by simply increasing the number of trials. Even if the simulation was statistically sound and strongly converges toward a definite answer, that answer will have an inherent and inescapable bias or uncertainty to it.

Accumulating Errors

Once we have established that our measurements have errors associated with them, what happens when we need to try to add or subtract our results? How does the error of two independent measurements combine to give the error of the new value? For example, imagine if we want to invest our money by buying many options. If the price of each option has an uncertainty—let this not be confused with the uncertainty of payout, but rather the uncertainty in the price itself—what is the uncertainty of the price our portfolio?

If option A has price $a \pm \Delta a$ and option B has price $b \pm \Delta b$, and the two are added we should expect to get $c \pm \Delta c$ where c is simply $a + b$. One would naively guess that the error in c, Δc, is also the sum of the errors in a and b, that is, $\Delta c = \Delta a + \Delta b$. In fact this is actually a very reasonable guess as it represents the *maximum* possible error that c can have. Furthermore, it can also be shown that if the values of A and B were subtracted, the maximum error remains the same. While there may be some sense in this definition, we can see that it is a rather pessimistic outlook on the situation. Each individual error in a and b merely states that there is a certain chance that the *actual* value is somewhere between the error bounds. When adding the values together there is a chance that the errors can cancel each other out! By simply adding the errors together we are in effect overestimating our uncertainty. The standard method of adding errors is by adding them in quadrature, also known as taking a quadratic mean, which is calculated using equation 2.17:

$$\Delta c = \sqrt{\Delta a^2 + \Delta b^2} \tag{2.17}$$

We have just figured out a way of accumulating errors when we perform a simple operation like adding or subtracting two numbers with a certain level of uncertainty to them. However, what happens when we try to do something more complicated like dividing and multiplying? Or what happens when we try to generalize it to any possible relationship, $f(x,y)$? Here the methodology gets slightly more complicated and can be stated as equation 2.18:

$$\Delta f = \sqrt{\left(\frac{\partial f}{\partial x}\Delta x\right)^2 + \left(\frac{\partial f}{\partial y}\Delta y\right)^2} \tag{2.18}$$

There is a short introduction to partial derivatives in Appendix A if you are unfamiliar with the concept. We will leave it as an exercise to the reader, but please note that if $f(a,b) = a + b$, then equation 2.18 exactly reduces to equation 2.17.

In the above discussion, we mentioned only an example with two variables, that is, two options. If there were more variables, or options in the portfolio, the errors will accumulate in a similar manner. Instead of having only *a* and *b* in the square root of equation 2.17, you would simply add the squares of all your terms, and take the square root of the final sum.

THIS IS JUST THE BEGINNING

In this chapter we introduced many of the basic components of simulations and led up to how they begin to translate into financial implementations. The focus has been on correctly generating pseudorandom numbers, understanding the distributions that we use to transform pseudorandom numbers, showing examples of how to construct a simulation using Excel and VBA as the medium, and eventually how randomness appears in finance via Brownian motion and Wiener processes. Although we have yet to discuss deeper financial applications of the concepts learned in this chapter, the importance of each of these items cannot be understated. No matter how sophisticated and unique the financial simulation being implemented is, if the random number generation algorithm is flawed the results of the simulation will be wrong. Similarly if the wrong distribution is being used the results will also be flawed.

In Chapter 3 we will take the tools and techniques that we have just learned and expand upon them with more complex statistical concepts. The examples will begin to be illustrated through more financially related Model Builders and eventually in later chapters, the concepts will be entirely financially based with supporting Model Builder examples.

Correlation

Once we understand the basics of random number generation, its applications in light of varying distributions, and basic examples of simulations, we should think more toward applications of these tools to finance. The most immediate applications relate to default, options, and commodity and interest rate projection. For each of these topics we have learned that there are more complex interactions at work than just generating a random number and assuming a certain distribution. Correlation between price movements or default status is perhaps the most important interaction that we need to be aware of. The financial crisis that began in 2007 has shown us the importance of estimating correlation correctly; one of the key failures in risk management and rating agency methodology going into the crisis was an underestimation of correlation within mortgage and structured debt default risk.

THE BASIC IDEA OF CORRELATION

The basic idea of correlation is how sensitive the value of one entity or metric is to the change in another value of an entity or metric. Let's take a very simple, tangible example as a starting point. There is usually an observable correlation between a person's income level and their education. Census data in the United States typically shows that more educated people earn more money. Look at the data set plotted in Figure 3.1.

The first thing to realize is that a scatter plot best shows correlation visually, between two sets of variables. Here we can see that there is a positive correlation, that is, one where as the value of one variable increases there is an increase in the value of another variable. The correlation is actually quite strong in this case (mainly because I made up the data set). When we work through Model Builder 3.1 we will see that there is a .87 correlation between education level and income in this example. Another way of thinking about what this means is to use extreme cases. If the correlation is equal to 1, the two variables are completely linked, and for every unit of increase in one of the variables there will be a proportional increase in the other variable. Conversely, if the correlation is equal to 0, it means

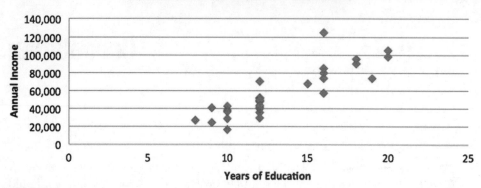

FIGURE 3.1 Income levels are shown on the y-axis and show a distinct positive correlation with education levels on the x-axis.

that for every unit of increase in one of the variables there should be no expectation of proportional movement in the other variable.

The formula for correlation (usually represented by r) is shown in equation 3.1:

$$r_{x,y} = \frac{\sum (X - \mu_x)(y - \mu_Y)}{\sigma_X \sigma_Y} \qquad (3.1)$$

In this equation, σ_x represents the standard deviation of the X values and μ_x represents the mean of the X values (careful: μ has different meanings elsewhere in this text and in finance: it is often used to represent a "drift" return for assets).

It is crucial to keep in mind that correlation measures only the linear relationship between two variables. Quadratic and other "power" relationships between variables may give results indicating no correlation between data sets. When beginning initial research on the relationship between different variables, it is a good idea to graph the scatter-plots and inspect them to see if the graph "looks like" a quadratic relationship. If so, performing regressions of one variable against the root of another may be appropriate.

MODEL BUILDER 3.1: Basic Correlation Calculations

1. This Model Builder examines the fundamental correlation calculations using mathematics on the sheet and prebuilt Excel functions. It will be useful since the correlation calculations here are the underpinnings for correlation calculated using matrix mathematics and eventually in the corporate default simulation. The first step is to create a new workbook and save it as "MB_3_User.xls".

2. Next we need to import data from the complete Model Builder file located on the website. Open MB_3_Complete.xls and copy the data from B3:D33. Paste the values of this data over the same range on your newly created sheet.

3. To understand the underlying meaning of the correlation coefficient calculation we will first calculate the coefficient using basic math functions. The first part of this calculation is measuring how each of the samples, for each variable, deviate from the mean of each variable's sample data set. This can be done by entering the following equation in E4:

$$=(C4-AVERAGE(\$C\$4:\$C\$33))*(D4-AVERAGE(\$D\$4:\$D\$33))$$

Copy and paste this over the range E4:E33. Also, we should label E3 "Numerator" since the prior calculation is part of a larger calculation.

4. Next we should calculate the deviations and square them for each variable. Enter the following equation in F4 and copy and paste it over the range F4:F33:

$$=(C4-AVERAGE(\$C\$4:\$C\$33))^2$$

5. Similarly we should do the same for the other variable. Enter the following equation in G4 and copy and paste it over the range G4:G33:

$$=(D4-AVERAGE(\$D\$4:\$D\$33))^2$$

Also, label both columns with "Denominator 1" in F3 and "Denominator 2" in G3. So far the sheet should look like Figure 3.2.

MB 3.1: *Calculating the Correlation Coefficient*

Subject	Education Level	Income	Numerator	Denominator 1	Denominator 2
1	12	52,000	6,734	1.60	28,266,944
2	10	43,000	46,768	10.67	204,966,944
3	16	57,000	(866)	7.47	100,278
4	20	98,000	273,934	45.34	1,655,133,611
5	8	27,000	159,668	27.74	919,100,278
6	12	36,000	27,001	1.60	454,400,278
7	12	40,000	21,934	1.60	299,866,944
8	16	125,000	185,001	7.47	4,581,033,611
9	16	80,000	62,001	7.47	514,533,611
10	18	90,000	154,701	22.40	1,068,200,278
11	18	95,000	178,368	22.40	1,420,033,611
12	10	38,000	63,101	10.67	373,133,611
13	20	105,000	321,068	45.34	2,273,700,278
14	12	51,000	8,001	1.60	39,900,278
15	12	48,000	11,801	1.60	86,800,278

FIGURE 3.2 The sheet should develop calculations for each sample.

◢	B	C	D	E	F	G
34						
35	Sums			2,328,967	343.87	20,969,241,667
36	Equation			2,685,260		
37						
38	Function/Math Equation:		0.8673	0.8673		

FIGURE 3.3   The correlation coefficient can be calculated in multiple ways.

6. Sum each of the Numerator, Denominator 1, and Denominator 2 columns in E35, F35, and G35, respectively, using the SUM function.

7. The denominators need to be multiplied and the square root taken of that product. To do this, enter the following equation in E36:

$$=SQRT(F35*G35)$$

8. Finally, the correlation coefficient is calculated by dividing the numerator by the equation calculated in step 7. Enter the following equation in E38 to get this result:

$$=E35/E36$$

9. Alternatively we can do this calculation using the CORREL function in D38:

$$=CORREL(C4:C33,D4:D33)$$

The final calculations should look the same as Figure 3.3.

CORRELATION IN A FINANCIAL CONTEXT

We have just looked at how correlation is calculated using an easy to understand example, provided historical data, but what is important to simulation is how correlation is used for future projections. If we believe there is a correlation between items that we are simulating, we will have to account for it in our simulation; otherwise the end results can be very different.

The two most common areas that correlation enters into financial simulations are industry- and regional-based correlations. For instance, if we are invested in a telecommunications company and the telecommunications industry as a whole is in decline, we would expect a correlation in the performance of our individual telecommunication company investment. Likewise, if we are invested in a company that services Asian markets and Asian markets are in decline, we might expect our individual invested company to experience decline because of the regional correlation. Let's take a look at a simple simulation of 10 corporate loans with a single correlation factor and see how the correlation affects the expected default of the basket of loans.

MODEL BUILDER 3.2: Introducing Correlation in a Basic Corporate Default Model

1. This Model Builder expands off of our basic correlation coefficient calculation and shows how correlation can affect the results of a simulation. In this example there are 10 assumed exposures that are from different companies, but all maintain the same risk profile in regards to par amount, tenor, and risk rating. In the same workbook, MB_3_User.xls, insert a new worksheet and name it "MB 3.2".

2. We can save time by importing assumption data from the completed MB_3_Complete.xls workbook on the website. Copy the data from B6:D16 on the MB3.2 sheet of MB_3_Complete.xls and paste it into the same location on your workbook. This data is shown in Figure 3.4 and shows the 10 separate investments, the identical par amounts, and the default probabilities. We will discuss default probabilities in further detail later in Chapter 5, but for now we should understand that these percentages are generated from historical default data of similar companies. The main nationally recognized statistical rating organizations typically produce annual default studies that show the updated default probabilities of various company and security types.

3. Ultimately a default probability is a percentage between 0 and 1. As we saw from the previous section on distributions, if we assume a normal distribution we cannot simply work with the default probability. In fact we do not want the probability, but the inverse of the distribution it is related to. This provides us a number that can be thought of as the default threshold. If we imagined a normal distribution this would be the z value or the actual point on the normal distribution. When we create normal random numbers in the upcoming simulation, we

Assumed Correlation Coefficient: 20.00%

Loan #	Par Balance	Default Probability	Default Thresh
1	10,000,000	45.00%	-0.12566
2	10,000,000	45.00%	-0.12566
3	10,000,000	45.00%	-0.12566
4	10,000,000	45.00%	-0.12566
5	10,000,000	45.00%	-0.12566
6	10,000,000	45.00%	-0.12566
7	10,000,000	45.00%	-0.12566
8	10,000,000	45.00%	-0.12566
9	10,000,000	45.00%	-0.12566
10	10,000,000	45.00%	-0.12566

FIGURE 3.4 In this example we will take a theoretical basket of 10 exposures.

will test whether we went below the default threshold, indicating default. Convert the default probabilities to thresholds by entering the following formula in F7:

$$=NORMSINV(D7)$$

Copy and paste this formula over the range F7:F16. You should also label F6 with the title "Default Threshold".

4. Before we run multiple iterations to see the aggregate results, let's look at what the default test might look like for just one iteration. To do this, we already should be able to set up the first part, which is the noncorrelated component. This is done by generating a normal random variable and testing whether it is less than the default threshold. Notice that for each of the ten exposures this is a unique figure and requires the formula NORMSINV(RAND()) for each company. So what exactly is the noncorrelated component of a corporate default simulation? The intent is to try to integrate factors that could affect default that are unique to each company. This could be concepts such as management capability, fraud, or other unique circumstances that we would not expect to affect another company if it affected one of the companies in our basket.

The opposite of the noncorrelated component to corporate defaults are concepts that might affect the other companies if it occurred in one of our ten exposures. Earlier we mentioned examples that could include industry or regional problems. Keep in mind there can always be other correlations beyond these two. To account for this, we create one normal random variable that is the same for each of the 10 entities.

The way we induce correlation then is to use a certain percentage of the noncorrelated normal random variable versus the correlated normal random variable, depending on the assumed level of correlation. This can be implemented using the following formula:

$$=(Correlation\ Coefficient)*Correlated\ Normal\ Random+((1\text{-}Correlation$$

$$Coefficient^2))^{0.5}*Non\text{-}Correlated\ Normal\ Random$$

Let's piece these concepts together by first entering the following labels in the corresponding cells:

I6: "Non-Corr Component"	K6: "Combined Test Value"
J6: "Corr Component"	L6: "Default Test"

5. In I7 enter the following formula:

$$=NORMSINV(RAND())$$

Copy and paste this across the range I7:I16. This is the noncorrelated component, which is demonstrated by the fact that every time the sheet is calculated there will be a unique normal random number for each exposure.

6. In J7 enter the following formula to create the correlated component:

$$=NORMSINV(RAND())$$

Rather than copying this formula down over a similar range as in step 5, enter the following formula in J8:

$$=J7$$

Now copy this formula over the range J8:J16. Notice that we created the same normal random number for each exposure.

7. Now we are going to implement correlation. Prior to doing this we should put in an assumed correlation coefficient. Label B4 "Assumed Correlation Coefficient" and enter the value "20%" in E4 for now.

8. Go back over to the area we were working in during step 6 and enter the following formula in K7:

$$=\$E\$4*J7+((1-\$E\$4^2)^0.5)*I7$$

Copy and paste this formula over the range K7:K16. Notice that this formula takes the correlated component and multiplies it by the correlation coefficient and adds to it the noncorrelated component multiplied by the square root of one minus the correlation coefficient squared (the non-correlated factor).

9. Our default test in L7 is now ready. Enter the following formula in L7:

$$=IF(K7<F7,1,0)$$

This simulates whether a default occurred against the distribution formed by the exposure's default probability by entering a 1 if a default occurred and a 0 if it did not. Copy and paste this formula over the range L7:L16.

10. We may want to visualize this in a more obvious way with the following formula in M7:

$$=IF(L7=1,\text{"Default"},\text{"No Default"})$$

Copy and paste this formula over the range M7:M16.

11. In L17 we should sum the total number of defaults for all exposures. Enter the formula =SUM(L7:L16) in L17. Thus far the sheet should be developing like Figure 3.5. Note that the actual numbers could be different from the Excel work you are developing.

12. So far we have completed one iteration. If we push F9 to calculate the sheet, the random numbers will be regenerated and we should see a different default pattern among the 10 (there is the chance that the default pattern could be identical since it is random, but this will occur very infrequently). We should next expand our analysis to multiple iterations. Ideally this is done in VBA for efficiency, but we can show how it can be done directly on the sheet. All we need to do is consolidate the prior calculations into a single row; each row will then represent an iteration. Start this by creating the labels "Exposure Number" in B32 and "Iterations" in B33. Enter the values 1 to 10 in C32:L32. These will label the area for each exposure's test that we will soon create.

13. In B34:B5033 enter 1 to 5000 to label each row that represents an iteration.

	I	J	K	L	M
6	**Non-Corr Component**	**Corr Component**	**Combined Test Value**	**Default Test**	
7	-1.4606	0.4321	-134%	1	Default
8	0.2708	0.4321	35%	0	No Default
9	0.2578	0.4321	34%	0	No Default
10	0.3899	0.4321	47%	0	No Default
11	0.1731	0.4321	26%	0	No Default
12	-1.7279	0.4321	-161%	1	Default
13	-0.0088	0.4321	8%	0	No Default
14	-0.2837	0.4321	-19%	1	Default
15	-0.3859	0.4321	-29%	1	Default
16	0.2211	0.4321	30%	0	No Default
17				4	

FIGURE 3.5   A single iteration default test for 10 entities.

14. M33 should be labeled "Corr Component", with M34 containing the following formula:

$$=\text{NORMSINV(RAND())}$$

Copy and paste this over the range M33:M5033. This is the correlated component that will be the same for all 10 exposures during a single iteration. Notice that it will change for each iteration though.

15. Next enter the following formula into C34:

$$=\text{IF}(((\$E\$4)*\$M34+((1-\$E\$4\^2))\^0.5*\text{NORMSINV(RAND())})$$

$$<\text{OFFSET}(\$F\$6,C\$32,0),1,0)$$

While this formula looks complicated it is actually a condensed version of the calculations we did in steps 1 to 9. For each exposure this formula takes the correlation coefficient and multiplies it by the same normal random number (representing the correlated component) and adds this to the product of the square root of one minus the correlation coefficient squared multiplied by a unique normal random number. The sum of these two calculations is then tested against the default thresholds from the tabled data starting in F7. Note that an OFFSET function is used to look up the default threshold for each exposure. If the calculation is less than the default threshold a 1 is returned; otherwise a zero is returned. Copy and paste this over the range C34:L34.

16. Next we should sum up the number of defaults in each iteration or row. Do this by entering the following formula in O34:

$$=\text{SUM(C34:L34)}$$

Copy and paste this formula over the range O34:O5033.

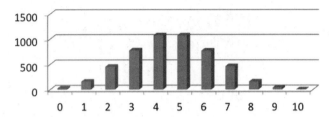

FIGURE 3.6 With a low correlation coefficient, the distribution from the simulation should look relatively normal.

17. We now need a method of visualizing the large data set that we have created. In Chapter 2 we introduced the idea of a histogram as a useful tool for visualizing simulation results. We can implement this again by counting the number of times a specific number of exposures defaulted out of the 10. In fact, we can do this for each of the 11 possibilities (there is a possibility that 0 out of the 10 exposures default). To do this enter a series of values from 0 to 10, incremented by 1 in B20:L20.
18. In B21 enter the following formula to count the number of times each case occurred:

$$=COUNTIF(\$O\$34:\$O\$5033,B20)$$

Copy and paste this formula over the range B21:L21. Notice that this tells us how many times we saw 0 exposures out of 10 default, 1 exposure out of 10 default, and so on. We can then create a column chart to visualize the data as shown in Figure 3.6.

Interpretation of Model Builder 3.2 and How Correlation Affects a Simulation

Now that the actual construction of this Model Builder is complete we should take some time to interpret what we have done. Notice that the histogram distribution of results is a normal distribution centered on 4.5. This makes sense since we assumed a low correlation, a normal distribution, and all of our companies have a default probability of 45 percent. We can see the distribution looks like a bell curve with the most common scenarios having 4–5 defaults, but there are scenarios with 0 defaults and with 10 defaults.

Change the correlation coefficient in E4 to 0 percent. Make sure the sheet is calculated by pressing F9 if you have Excel set to manual mode (which is a good idea when creating so many formulas on the sheet!). You should see the histogram distribution remain centered on 4.5, but there are fewer scenarios with 0 or 10 defaults, as shown in Figure 3.7.

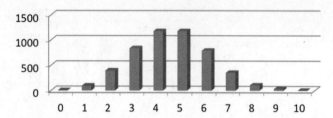

FIGURE 3.7 With a low correlation coefficient and a normal distribution assumption, we can see a very symmetrical normally distributed result.

The interesting effect, though, is when we change the correlation coefficient the other way. Change the correlation coefficient in E4 to 90 percent and make sure the sheet is calculated. The histogram distribution should now change to an extreme barbell distribution with peaks at 0 and 10, as seen in Figure 3.8.

This is because with a high correlation there is a very high probability of doing very well with no defaults or a very high probability of doing very poorly with nearly the entire basket defaulting. This is an effect similar to what we saw in 2007 when the correlation among mortgage-backed securities was revised to a much higher percentage. Rather than having a diverse array of default probabilities the underlying mortgage securities were extremely correlated and many pools of loans started to go into delinquency and default at the same time.

Another interesting characteristic that should be noted about the simulation is that the individual asset default rates among all iterations are close to the assumed default probability, even though the correlation among the assets could be very high. This can be checked by summing up a row of defaults for a single asset and dividing that sum by the total number of iterations. For example, the sum of C34:C5033 divided by 5000 should be approximately 45 percent (i.e., the original default probability that was assumed).

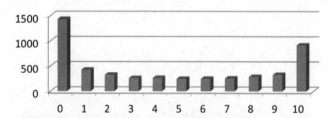

FIGURE 3.8 A high correlation coefficient greatly affects the outcome of a simulation, even if the distribution was originally normal.

PRODUCING SETS OF CORRELATED NORMAL RANDOM NUMBERS USING MATRIX MATHEMATICS

The previous example allowed us to see the effects of a single type of correlation between entities and to understand the effects on simulation results that correlation exerts. However, the example was limited in scope because the correlation coefficient was provided, and there was only a single correlation coefficient assumed. When financial simulations become more developed, they may require more robust methods of generating correlated normal random numbers.

Using matrix mathematics is an efficient means for creating multiple correlated normal random numbers. In the next Model Builder, we will examine historical data on fictitious companies, perform calculations to understand how those companies are correlated, and then set up a system for generating correlated random numbers for eventual use in a broader financial simulation.

MODEL BUILDER 3.3: Advanced Correlation Concepts through the Lens of Corporate Performance

1. Create a new workbook and save it as MB_3.3_User.xls.
2. For this Model Builder we will need a large set of raw data. Open MB_3.3_Complete.xls from the website, copy the range B3:G505, and paste the copied range in your workbook's first sheet in the same range (B3:G505). We need only one sheet for this Model Builder, so you can delete the other sheets and name the sheet you are working in "MB 3.3" to tie with the complete version.
3. The values that we copied over could represent the observable asset values in a company over time. The first real calculation we should do to understand the correlation is to see how each entity's asset value moves each period. To do this, enter the following formula in I7:

$$=C7/C6-1$$

Copy and paste this formula over the range I7:M505. Also, for labeling purposes copy over the names of the entities in I3:M3.
4. We now need to set up a system for analyzing the correlation of each entity's asset value changes to one another. This can be done on the sheet or in code. Since it is not too difficult to implement on the sheet using formulas we will use such a method. The first part of this is administrative. Enter 1 to 5 going down the sheet, increasing by 1 in O7:O11. Enter the same series of 1 to 5 going across the sheet, increasing by 1 in Q3:U3. Next to the numbers in O7:O11, enter the names of each entity in P7:P11. For example, P7 should contain TrustedFinCo1, P8 should contain TrustedFinCo2, etc. Similarly in Q6:U6 enter the same names (e.g. Q6 should contain TrustedFinCo1, R6 should contain TrustedFinCo2, etc.).
5. We will now use the CORREL function to calculate the correlations. Recall that the mathematics behind the CORREL function were detailed in Model Builder 3.1. The implementation of the CORREL function in this case is a little bit challenging because we have to compute correlations for every combination of entities. This can be done using the OFFSET function within the

	O	P	Q	R	S	T	U
3			1	2	3	4	5
4							
5							
6			Trusted FinCo 1	Trusted FinCo 2	Trusted FinCo 3	Trusted FinCo 4	Trusted FinCo 5
7	1	Trusted FinCo 1	1.0000	0.1073	0.0331	0.0831	0.0494
8	2	Trusted FinCo 2	0.1073	1.0000	0.0554	0.0753	0.0495
9	3	Trusted FinCo 3	0.0331	0.0554	1.0000	0.3705	0.4366
10	4	Trusted FinCo 4	0.0831	0.0753	0.3705	1.0000	0.4530
11	5	Trusted FinCo 5	0.0494	0.0495	0.4366	0.4530	1.0000

FIGURE 3.9   We can advance our correlation knowledge by doing multiple correlations.

CORREL function. The OFFSET function allows us to "move" the range references within the CORREL function as we drag it across. Enter the following function in Q7:

=CORREL(OFFSET($H$7,0,Q$3):OFFSET($H$505,0,Q$3),OFFSET($H$7,0,$O7):

OFFSET($H$505,0,$O7))

Let's examine this formula, since it is complicated. The CORREL function as the outermost function will return the correlation coefficient of two ranges of data. To obtain each range of data we use the OFFSET function. The key to this function is that is allows us to reference fixed locations H7 and H505 as the starting and end points of our data from top to bottom, and then select which range of data we want to use in the calculations, depending on the values in Q3:U3 and O7:O11. Recall that we created a two-dimensional range in step 4 and entered values to reference locations in that range. The OFFSET function uses those values as the formula is dragged. Implement this formula by copying and pasting it over the range Q7:U11. Figure 3.9 shows what the sheet should like so far.

6. After completing the correlation matrix in step 5, take a moment to look at the resulting numbers. You may start to see a pattern. Notice that a diagonal of 1s appears where the CORREL function calculated the correlation coefficient of the entity against itself? Now imagine drawing a line down that diagonal. If one were to do this we would have two triangles: an upper triangle and a lower triangle. What's interesting is that the numbers in the upper triangle mirror those in the lower triangle. For example, the value in Q8 is the same as in R8 and the value in Q9 is the same as in S9. The technical term for what we have created here is a symmetric, positive-definite matrix. Look at Figure 3.10 for further clarity.

7. Once we have our symmetric, positive-definite matrix, we then need to find a matrix where $U^T U = C$, where U^T signifies the transpose of the matrix U. One method of solving such an equation is using Cholesky decomposition. The best way to implement Cholesky decomposition in Excel is by creating a custom function in code. In the same workbook you have been working in go to the Visual Basic editor and insert a new module. Enter the following code to start the function, declare variables, assign values, and dimension a dynamic range:

```
Public Function Cholesky(WorkRange As Range)

Dim WorkArray As Variant
```

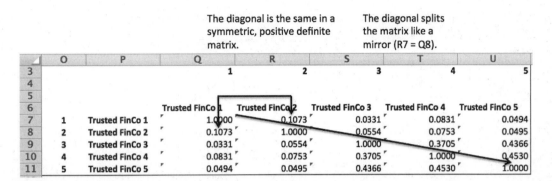

FIGURE 3.10 A symmetric, positive-definite matrix has unique characteristics.

```
Dim AggVar As Double
Dim i As Integer, j As Integer, k As Integer

WorkArray = WorkRange
rCount = WorkRange.Rows.count
cCount = WorkRange.Columns.count

ReDim TransArray(1 To rCount, 1 To cCount) As Double
```

8. The main code for the Cholesky transformation is difficult to explain in a top to bottom order since it is written to work through a matrix with many conditional characteristics. The best way to explain this is to graphically depict a matrix, the location that we are working on, and the code that affects that location. It is recommended that you review the whole code at the end of this chapter or from the MB_3.3_Complete.xls file on the website, since pieces of code will be explained individually.

The easiest place to start in explaining this function is on the matrix in the upper left corner at row 1, column 1. When the function runs, it skips a section of code and doesn't start calculating until it reaches the following section:

```
TransArray(j, j) = WorkArray(j, j)−AggVar

If TransArray(j, j) <=  0 Then
     Exit For
Else
     TransArray(j, j) = Sqr(TransArray(j, j))
End If
```

At this point it looks to the array on the sheet entered as the parameter and only for the diagonals (row 1, column 1 is not only the starting point, but also a diagonal) and subtracts from it an aggregated variable. The aggregated variable does not exist for row 1, column 1, so the transform array (i.e., TransArray(j, j)) is simply the same value as the referenced array from the sheet. If that value is less than or equal to 0 then we move on to the next row; otherwise we take the square root of it. In this specific example the referenced array at row 1, column 1 has a value of 1, meaning the square root is 1.

9. With the diagonal done the code runs until it hits the following section:

```
For i = j + 1 To rCount
   AggVar = 0

   For k = 1 To j-1
       AggVar = AggVar + TransArray(j, k) * TransArray(i, k)
   Next k

TransArray(i, j) = (WorkArray(i, j)-AggVar) / TransArray(j, j)
Next i
```

For row 1, column 1 there will be no aggregate variable, so the focus of the code is on filling out TransArray(i, j). The counter variable i will loop through rows 2 to 5 (i.e., effectively a vertical fill of column 1, below the diagonal point we calculated in step 8. Each of these points takes the value in the sheet array and divides it by the transform array's diagonal for the column under consideration.

10. The outermost j loop then continues, which spatially can be thought of as moving to row 2. This time through the code though there are a few differences than when we moved through the first j loop. The initial difference that we encounter is a part of code that we skipped over earlier:

```
For j = 1 To rCount
   AggVar = 0
   For k = 1 To j-1
      AggVar = AggVar + TransArray(j, k) ^ 2
   Next k
```

Here the k loop will be active and the aggregate variable will take the value of the squared sum of all the points to the left of the diagonal for the row the j loop is working on. See Figure 3.11 for a visual depiction. Looking back at step 8, we can see that when we calculate the diagonal value it is the value from the referenced sheet array, less the sum of the squared values that are to the left of the diagonal of concern. Keep in mind that the final value for the diagonal is the square root of that calculated value, unless it is less than or equal to 0.

	W	X	Y	Z	AA
3					
4					
5					
6	Trusted FinCo 1	Trusted FinCo 2	Trusted FinCo 3	Trusted FinCo 4	Trusted FinCo 5
7	1.0000	0.0000	0.0000	0.0000	0.0000
8	0.1073	0.9942	0.0000	0.0000	0.0000
9	0.0331	0.0522	0.9981	0.0000	0.0000
10	0.0831	0.0668	0.3649	0.9249	0.0000
11	0.0494	0.0444	0.4335	0.3111	0.8431

FIGURE 3.11 The Cholesky function transforms the symmetric, positive-definite matrix.

11. Another part that is different for the second j loop is when we move down from the diagonal (as in step 9). As you can see in the code referenced at the beginning of step 9, we have an aggregate variable again. As with the first aggregate variable we encountered it calculates values from points to the left of the diagonal of concern; however, this time it takes the value on the transform array immediately to the left of the value being calculated and multiplies that value on the left by the value above the value to the left. This process will be done for every column to the left of the diagonal and for every row below the diagonal.

12. The process continues for each diagonal, looping through steps 8 through 11 until the bottom half of the triangle is complete. Once this is done the final piece of code returns the array to the sheet.

```
Cholesky = TransArray
End Function
```

13. The final code for Cholesky, in the proper order, should read:

```
Public Function Cholesky(WorkRange As Range)
Dim WorkArray As Variant
Dim AggVar As Double
Dim i As Integer, j As Integer, k As Integer

WorkArray = WorkRange
rCount = WorkRange.Rows.count
cCount = WorkRange.Columns.count

ReDim TransArray(1 To rCount, 1 To cCount) As Double

For j = 1 To rCount

    AggVar = 0

    For k = 1 To j-1
        AggVar = AggVar + TransArray(j, k) ^ 2
    Next k

    TransArray(j, j) = WorkArray(j, j)-AggVar

    If TransArray(j, j) <= 0 Then
        Exit For
    Else
        TransArray(j, j) = Sqr(TransArray(j, j))
    End If

    For i = j + 1 To rCount
        AggVar = 0

        For k = 1 To j-1
            AggVar = AggVar + TransArray(j, k) * TransArray(i, k)
        Next k
```

```
        TransArray(i, j) = (WorkArray(i, j)—AggVar)
               / TransArray(j, j)
    Next i
Next j

Cholesky = TransArray
End Function
```

14. Note that this custom function is built with an array in mind, and when entered on the sheet, Excel must know that this is an array function. Excel identifies functions as array functions when a user presses Control-Shift-Enter after the formula involving the function is complete. Select W7:AA11, enter the formula "= Cholesky(Q7:U11)", and press Control-Shift-Enter. The sheet should look like Figure 3.11 so far.

15. Even with all of this work we still have more to do. So far we can think of ourselves has having worked on the "correlated" part of creating correlated normal random variables. We should now create the "normal random variables" part. This is much easier given what was learned in Chapter 2. Enter the following formula in AC7:

$$=NORMSINV(RAND())$$

   Copy and paste this to AC7:AG11.

16. The final step is to multiply the entire matrix of normal random variables created in step 15 by the transposed matrix derived from the Cholesky function. This is simplified by using the MMULT and TRANSPOSE functions native to Excel and shown with the formula that should be entered in AI7:AM11:

$$=MMULT(AC7:AG11,TRANSPOSE(W7:AA11))$$

   Note that this is also an array formula and must be entered with Control-Shift-Enter, exactly as the custom Cholesky function must be used. The last section for this Model Builder should look like Figure 3.12.

	AI	AJ	AK	AL	AM
3					
4					
5					
6	**Trusted FinCo 1**	**Trusted FinCo 2**	**Trusted FinCo 3**	**Trusted FinCo 4**	**Trusted FinCo 5**
7	1.6634	0.8548	0.7577	-0.3783	-0.6169
8	-1.0153	0.0956	0.8645	2.0686	0.5792
9	1.3101	0.3282	-1.2684	-0.5040	-1.9588
10	-0.7259	-1.0012	-0.3033	0.8237	2.2486
11	-0.8327	1.1786	0.0724	-0.5135	-1.0223

FIGURE 3.12 Correlated normal random numbers created from asset values and Cholesky decomposition.

GOING FORWARD USING OUR TOOLS

We have built up our tool set for simulation by covering random number generation, distributions, and correlation. While not every aspect of simulation will use these tools, they will be useful for many simulation applications. The next few chapters will take a shift and start focusing on specific financial simulation topics, drawing upon our tool set as necessary.

CHAPTER 4

Option Pricing

With a set of basic skills developed, we can now move on to practical application. The first financial realm that we will apply simulation techniques to is option pricing. As we work our way through option pricing, you will see that simulation techniques can take on many forms and be intertwined with multiple financial disciplines. For instance, in the derivatives or options industry, one routinely encounters discussions about bonds, which then leads to interest rates. One may wonder why, if the purpose of a stock option is to purchase stocks, that one would need to know anything about the bond market? The quick answer to this question is that to price an option, the price must in some way be *enforced* by a market driven asset that represents the cost of borrowing as viewed by the entire financial industry. That asset is a bond, and it is the anchor all the derivative and option pricing models adhere to. We will discuss this concept in a little more detail further on, but to begin with we will start off with the most basic pricing model, the binomial tree. To demonstrate why an *enforcer* is necessary, we will use the binomial tree to model our most basic asset, the stock.

A note: This text is focused on practical application and will not formally explicate binomial trees. It also assumes that the reader is familiar with options and bonds as financial instruments. Binomial trees will be discussed only in a general sense to present ideas and concepts necessary to understand how to implement the Hull-White Trinomial tree later on. If the reader is interested in learning more about the theory of binomial trees, there are many good texts that cover this topic in more detail.

BINOMIAL TREES

The most basic method of presenting stock price movement is a binomial tree. It is very similar to the Brownian motion process we discussed in Chapter 3 except the step size can be of an arbitrary magnitude and the probability of an up or down movement does not necessarily have to be equal.

Figure 4.1 represents a basic recombinant binomial tree, a tree where two nodes can transition to the same node, with an initial starting stock price of

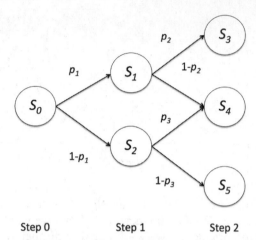

FIGURE 4.1 Basic recombinant binomial tree process where at each node the price can transition to two possible states. This is a recombinant tree because two nodes can transition to the same node in the next step.

S_0 that transitions after step 1 to either price S_1 with probability p_1 or S_2 with probability $1 - p_1$. Furthermore, you can see that from step 1, the price can take a total of 3 possible values at step 2. For the sake of simplicity let us start by examining the starting branch represented by S_0, S_1, and S_2. Given this diagram, what would be the expected or average price of the stock? From statistics, we know the answer to be the value if the event occurs times the probability of occurrence plus the value if the event does not occur times the probability of the event not occurring (equation 4.1):

$$E[S] = p_1 S_1 + (1 - p_1)S_2 \qquad (4.1)$$

If we were to sell an option, the most natural price would be $E[S] - k$, where k is the strike price, since any price set lower would mean we would lose money, and any price that is set higher we would not be able to find a buyer. This guarantees that on the *average* everyone breaks even.

This may seem extremely simple but is this the whole story? The answer is no because we do not know what S_1, S_2, and p_1 are as they can be defined quite arbitrarily. However, there must be certain relationships among the prices of the different derivatives: The particular identity governing this process is known as "put-call parity." Imagine for the moment that a seller of a call option makes a "guess" about the future prices, such that the option is priced in a manner where the return on the option plus the return on a risk-free bond is greater than the return of a stock plus a put option (i.e., priced too low). In this scenario, an investor can then sell the stock and put option to raise funds for the purchase of the calls and the bonds to earn a return without taking any risk, a process known as arbitrage. As we mentioned before, in order to facilitate an arbitrage-free market, there must be a mechanism by which we can anchor the option price that is common to all parties involved. It should be no surprise at this point that the anchoring mechanism is the bond.

Pricing Options

Exactly how are bonds used to fix the option price? Instead of pricing an option by using a portfolio consisting of just stocks, we can construct a portfolio consisting of *both* stocks and risk-free bonds with the same maturity as the option. The value of the call option is then the expected value of the portfolio minus the strike price. Therefore the value of the derivative should be exactly fixed to such a trading strategy. If a seller of an option decides to sell an option at a price that is less than the expected value of the portfolio (different from the expected value of just the stock as mentioned in the last section), then anyone can buy the option and trade based on the portfolio of stocks and bonds and keep the profit. In essence any market player who does not follow this rule will lose!

A question that arises from this phenomenon is, how does the incorporation of the bond affect the way in which we construct our binomial tree? Without going into too much mathematical detail or going through a step-by-step algebraic proof, we can conceptually say that by *knowing* that our portfolio of stocks and bonds is capable of completely *defining* our pricing point, we can see from equation 4.1 this also equates to being able to determine a fixed value for p_1, the probability of the asset price reaching S_1. Without the bond, as we mentioned before, p_1 can be *anything*. Therefore by introducing the bond into our construction strategy we define the probability of transitions throughout our tree, which in essence will allow us to price any option given what we know of the bond market.

As it turns out, after all the algebra is done, we get a portfolio value of (equation 4.2):

$$V = e^{r\Delta t}[q f_1 + (1 - q) f_2] \qquad (4.2)$$

Notice the similarity between this equation and equation 4.1. The probability here is represented by q, which is used to denote the change in p caused by introducing the bond into our portfolio. Also note that f is the value of the portfolio at each of the branching nodes rather than the asset price.

You may notice that there is nothing in the equations above that are unique to equities: Binomial trees can be used to price derivates and forecasting prices of all sorts of assets and rates. With that idea in mind, it should not surprise you that when discussing the Hull-White model, the tree is used to represent the rate movement rather than the stock movement and the valuation is discussed in terms of the bond price rather than the stock price. Of course this is not to say interest rate models are the only means by which options can be priced. Black-Scholes, for example, deals directly with the stochastic movement of the stock price. The construction strategy in the case of Black-Scholes is directly encapsulated in the methodology by which the stochastic differential equation (SDE) is solved.

Example of Pricing Options Using a Binomial Tree

As a quick example of the process of determining the price of an option, let us consider the branch shown in Figure 4.2.

Please note that for the sake of simplicity the probabilities are made up and we will pretend these are the *true* movements so that we needn't worry about using bonds to protect ourselves against arbitrage. What is important here is the methodology of backward inducing the price from the end nodes. According to Figure 4.3, the stock starts at a price of $2 and can transition to $4 with a probability of 1/3 or down to $1 with probability of 2/3. What would the price of option be if the strike price is $3?

If the stock ends up at $4, we win $1 in profit. If on the other hand, the stock goes down to $1, our option has lost all its value and it worth $0. The expected price is then $V = 0*(2/3) + 1*(1/3) = \$0.33$. This result may seem trite, but the backward induction method shown here will be used heavily when discussing the Hull-White Trinomial tree.

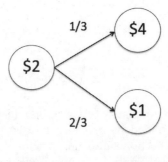

Step 0   Step 1

FIGURE 4.2   Example branch of a stock after one tick.

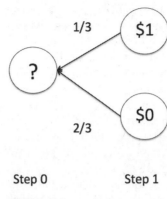

<figure>
1/3 — $1

? ←

2/3 — $0

Step 0   Step 1
</figure>

FIGURE 4.3 Value of our portfolio with strike price of $3.

HULL-WHITE INTEREST RATE MODEL

In the previous chapters we introduced many concepts related to stochastic analysis and in the previous sections we introduced how tree processes can be used to model financial derivatives. In the remainder of this chapter we will use those concepts to understand and implement the Hull-White interest rate model that is used to price bonds and derivatives. A number of methods can be used to perform this analysis. For example, the rating agency Moody's prefers a purely stochastic method by which the forward rate is explicitly determined by fitting the zero coupon yield curve with Nelson-Siegel parameters. For our purposes, however, we will expand on our previous discussion of the binomial tree method by using the trinomial tree strategy that was first proposed by John Hull and Alan White.

At first glance, you might be thinking, "Hey, sequentially constructing branches of a tree is not a simulation! Where is the randomness?" All this talk about random processes might have led you to believe that simulation is relevant only in a stochastic world. It is perfectly reasonable to associate simulation only with a method of getting information about an event that happens by chance. After all, if you can directly calculate an event, why would you need to simulate it? The answer to that question is rooted in the complexity of the problem. Sometimes a problem, even though it is solvable, is far too complex to actually solve! Let's take gravity as a physical example to underpin this concept. I am sure every reader understands gravity in one form or another. A simplified definition states that two massive bodies are attracted to each other with a force that is proportional to the product of their masses and the inverse square of their distance (equation 4.3):

$$F_g = \frac{Gm_1m_2}{r^2} \tag{4.3}$$

Now don't be too concerned about what G is or get flashbacks to the force diagrams you had to suffer through while taking that introductory physics course in college. Just understand that this is a simple equation. If you have only two bodies to deal with, and one of them is so large it barely moves at all (the Earth), then you can precisely compute the exact motion of the second object, say a ball. Now imagine instead of dealing with the Earth and a ball, you have two balls or two earths. At this point you cannot assume one object will be stationary. As the first ball moves toward the second ball, the second ball will also move toward the first! At any given moment they are both moving, and how they move is completely interconnected. As you can see, the system has grown immensely complicated, and solving for their trajectories is not so simple any more. Now what happens if you add a third ball? At this point, the problem is so complex the only way to solve it is by simulations. In this case, unlike financial interest models, all actions are deterministic and not governed by chance. The simulation is performed by incrementally stepping through a small interval when during each interval the forces between the three balls are computed and each ball is then moved as a response to these forces within the given interval. The smaller the interval used in this simulation, the more accurately the balls can be tracked.

You will notice that this analogy is similar to the tree pricing method. Prices can be determined more accurately if the time step between the nodes of the tree becomes finer and finer (i.e., for any given maturity date, the price will be more accurate as you increase the number of nodes needed to get "there" from the present.) Furthermore, this loss in accuracy is a direct result of the fact that in reality we are dealing with a differential equation.

Analytical Solution to the Hull-White Model

Earlier when we discussed possible stochastic models we mentioned there were a few drawbacks. To recap, an equation (equation 4.4) of this form

$$dr = \sigma dW + \mu dt \tag{4.4}$$

has a few notable deficiencies. The two most obvious ones are the facts that r, the interest rate, is unbounded and given enough time it can become infinite. The second one is that it is also possible for the rate to become negative. While the model itself is rather simple, the simplicity comes at the cost of possibly producing incorrect or inaccurate results.

The Vasicek Model fixes this issue by introducing a constant mean reversion term into the drift component of the stochastic equation represented in equation 4.4. This has the effect of keeping the rate fluctuating about a mean value instead of exploding into infinity (equation 4.5):

$$dr = \sigma dW + a(\theta - r)dt \tag{4.5}$$

As you can see here, if r becomes greater than θ, then the drift term will become negative and draw the rate back down during the next cycle. John Hull and Alan White extended this model by solving for the case with a time dependent reversion term (equation 4.6).

$$dr = \sigma\, dW + a(\theta(t) - r)dt \tag{4.6}$$

We mentioned before in this book that we will not discuss in detail how these equations are solved. What is important here is understanding what a solution *means* and how to implement it.

If we have a discount bond that matures at time T, then the price of the bond at time t can be represented by equation 4.7:

$$P(t, T) = A(t, T)e^{-B(t,T)r} \tag{4.7}$$

If we model the rate in equation 4.7 by using the form given in equation 4.6, $A(t,T)$ and $B(t,T)$ can be solved analytically and are defined in equations 4.8 and 4.9:

$$A(t, T) = \frac{P(0, T)}{P(0, t)} \exp[B(t, T)F(0, t) - \sigma^2 B^2(t, T)(1 - e^{-2at})/4a] \tag{4.8}$$

$$B(t, T) = \frac{1 - e^{-a(T-t)}}{a} \tag{4.9}$$

Equations 4.8 and 4.9 look very scary, but their bark is worse than their bite. The only complication here is determining $F(0,t)$, the instantaneous forward rate at time t when observed at time $t = 0$ and formally defined as (equation 4.10):

$$F(0, t) = -\frac{\partial \ln[P(0, t)]}{\partial t} \tag{4.10}$$

In practice the data set is usually composed of the yield curve observed from the bond market. Without an explicit functional form for the yield, it would be impossible to take the derivative in equation 4.10. We can, however, approximate derivatives as an incremental change of the variable, such as $dt \cong \Delta t$. From equation 4.10 we can see that $P(0,t)$ is the price of the bond paid per unit of the currency at origination and maturing at t. In essence, this is just the basic discount bond equation (equation 4.11),

$$P(0, t) = P(t) = e^{-rt} \tag{4.11}$$

Given that the natural log of equation 4.11 is $[-rt]$, we can rewrite equation 4.10 as the shown in equation 4.12:

$$F(0, t) = \frac{r(t - \Delta t)(t + \Delta t) - r(t)t}{\Delta t} \tag{4.12}$$

Now equation 4.10 has been reduced to something fairly simple. However, when using this formula, please be aware that $r(t + \Delta t)(t + \Delta t)$ is the rate at time $(t + \Delta t)$ multiplied by $(t + \Delta t)$.

MODEL BUILDER 4.1: Hull-White Analytical Solution

In the first Model Builder for this chapter, we will implement the basic Hull-White analytical solution to determine a bond price. This Model Builder is more of a stand-alone calculation exercise and is mainly done to help readers understand the complex calculations involved in implementing Hull-White. To assist with this Model Builder, there is a completed version (filename: MB4_Complete.xls) on the website.

1. Open a new Excel workbook and name it MB4_User.xls.
2. The current yield curve is the initial information required for the Hull-White analytical solution. We should collect yields from different terms. To prepare for this enter the following labels in the corresponding cells:

A6: "Maturity (yrs)"	A8: 3
B6: "Yield"	A9: 4
A7: 2	A10: 9

3. To adhere to the example model enter the following interest rates:

B7: 5.79733%	B9: 6.73464%
B8: 6.30595%	B10: 7.39790%

4. Part of this Model Builder assumes specific assumptions regarding *a* (the drift rate), sigma (the standard deviation of the Weiner process, also called the volatility), an arbitrary rate in year 3, and the task at hand of pricing the bond at year 3, assuming a 9-year maturity. To set up this specific example, enter the following labels and assumptions in the corresponding cells:

A12: "a"	B12: .1
A13: "sigma"	B13: .01
A14: "r(t)"	B14: .113206
A15: "T"	B15: 9
A16: "t"	B16: 3

5. The simplest place to start is with our bond discounting formula, where we raise *e* to the power of the product of the rate from the yield curve at maturity and the time period to maturity. To complete this enter "=EXP(-B10*B15)" in B17.
6. Similarly we will create the same formula, but this time using the rate from the yield curve for the period in which we want to price the bond. Enter "=EXP(-B8*B16)" in B18.
7. Next we should calculate the average daily difference between the rate from the year we are pricing and the last year by entering "=(B8-B7)/365" in B19. The result will be used to compute $r(t + \Delta t)$ in the next step where Δt is taken to be 1 day.

8. The next step is to calculate the instantaneous forward rate, given by equation 4.12, for the period we are pricing. To do this enter the following formula in B20:

$$=(B8)*(3*365)-(B7+364*B19)*(2*365+364)$$

　　　Note that the hard-coded numbers could be pulled out and referenced in cells, but since this is a stand-alone example we are entering them directly in the formula. Further note that since we are evaluating at 3 years, we took $r(t + \Delta t)$ to be 3 years (3*365) and $r(t)$ to be 3 years minus one day.

9. Ultimately we are seeking $A(t,T)$ to get the price of the bond. In order to do this, as the equations show, we need to solve for $B(t,T)$ first. This can be done by entering the following formula in B21:

$$=(1-EXP(-B12*(B15-B16)))/B13$$

10. With $B(t,T)$ solved we can calculate $A(t,T)$ in B22 by entering:

$$=(B17/B18)*EXP(B21*B20-(B13*B21)*(B13*B21)*(1-EXP(-2*B12*B16))/(4*B12))$$

11. Finally we are set up to get the price of the bond in year 3 by entering the following formula in B24:

$$=B22*EXP(-B21*B14)$$

HULL-WHITE TRINOMIAL TREE

While the Hull-White interest rate model has a nice analytical solution in the form of equation 4.7, we still need an arbitrage-free method of pricing an option. Equation 4.7 can provide us with a price, but that requires knowledge about the instantaneous rate at maturity, something that we could never know a priori. The best that could be done in an arbitrage-free market is to guess at the *most probable* rate, given the current observation of the yield curve. To accomplish this, Hull and White developed a trinomial tree method to track the migration of the interest rate up to maturity and from there work backward to compute the expected price of the option. A trinomial tree is much like the binomial tree we discussed earlier with the exception that there is now a third option where there exists a possibility that the rate remains the same at the next time step.

Building a Hull-White tree involves two primary stages. The first is to determine the optimal step size and structure of the tree depending on the desired time interval. The second is to realign the mean rate throughout the tree to match the term structure observed from the bond market. To understand why step 2 is necessary we must first understand how step one is accomplished. The first step involves simplifying equation 4.6 into a form that is easier to solve. By setting the drift term, θ, and the initial rate to zero, we can rewrite equation 4.6 with a new variable, r^*, as equation 4.13

$$dr^* = \sigma dW - ar^* dt \qquad (4.13)$$

The idea is to build up a tree corresponding to this simpler equation rather than the more complex equation represented by equation 4.6. Step 2 is then required because we need to add the reversion term back into the tree by using the yield curve as a proxy. This may sound very complicated, and indeed this tree building process is very computationally intensive, but by going through this step by step, we hope to make this process as painless as possible.

MODEL BUILDER 4.2: Basic Structure of the Hull-White Tree

There is no doubt that implementing a Hull-White can be complicated. This Model Builder will build on the calculations we learned in Model Builder 4.1 by simultaneously going though the equations needed to construct the tree and instructing readers on its implementation in a step-by-step fashion.

1. Insert a new sheet in your version of MB4_User.xls and name the sheet MB4.2. The first entry step in this Model Builder is to set up the sheet for the tree calculations. As with our last Model Builder, we will require a yield curve. For this example, enter the following interest rates and labels in the respective cells:

A3: "Yield Curve"   F5: 6.73347%
A4: "Years"   G4: 5
A5: "Rate"   G5: 6.94816%
B4: 0   H4: 6
B5: 5.01772%   H5: 7.08807%
C4: 1   I4: 7
C5: 5.09276%   I5: 7.27527%
D4: 2   J4: 8
D5: 5.79540%   J5: 7.30852%
E4: 3   K4: 9
E5: 6.30456%   K5: 7.39790
F4: 4

2. Additionally, we require more assumptions for our example. Enter the following assumptions with labels in the corresponding cells:

A9: "Δt [yr]"	B12: 3
B9: 1	A13: "T [yr]"
A10: "a [1/yr]"	B13: 9
B10: .1	A14: StrikePrice
A11: "σ [%]"	B14: 63
B11: 1.0%	A15: BondRtn
A12: "t [yr]"	B15: 100

3. Once we have entered the assumptions, we can begin with the nodes of the tree, where each node will contain its respective value of the risk-free rate known as the nodal rate. The first two terms that determine the overall structure of the tree are the expected value (equation 4.14) and the variance of change of the nodal rates (equation 4.15), r^*,

$$E[dr^*] = Mr^* = (e^{-a\Delta t} - 1)r^* \qquad (4.14)$$

$$Var[dr^*] = V = \sigma^2(1 - e^{-2a\Delta t})/2a \qquad (4.15)$$

To implement equations 4.14 and 4.15 enter the following formulas in the corresponding cells:

E9: =EXP(-$B$10*$B$9)-1
E10: =$B$11*$B$11*(1-EXP(-2*$B$10*$B$9))/(2*$B$10)

Also, enter the labels "M" in D9 and "V" in D10.

4. As we mentioned before, at each node of the tree, the rate can move in three directions: up, middle (stays the same), and down. The amplitude of the change is the same whether the transition is up or down and is given by equation 4.16:

$$\Delta r^* = \sqrt{3V} \qquad (4.16)$$

Equation 4.16 can be replicated in E11 by entering "=SQRT(3*$E$10)". There is nothing mathematically magical about this equation. Hull and White claim through numerical procedures that this just happens to be a good value to minimize errors. Make sure to label D11 with "Δr [%]".

5. A few more assumptions are required, but it would be best to explain these through calculation. Earlier we had seen that "moving" through a tree is based on probabilities. The probabilities of transitioning from each node are chosen to match the mean and variance defined in equations 4.14 and 4.15 and are given by equations 4.17 through 4.19:

$$p_u = \frac{1}{6} + \frac{j^2 M^2 + jM}{2} \qquad (4.17)$$

$$p_m = \frac{2}{3} - j^2 M^2 \qquad (4.18)$$

$$p_d = \frac{1}{6} + \frac{j^2 M^2 - jM}{2} \qquad (4.19)$$

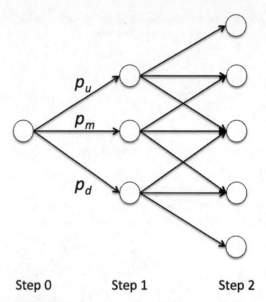

Step 0   Step 1   Step 2

FIGURE 4.4 Basic structure of the tree showing the up, middle, and down transition states.

Here j represents the number of Δr increments the node is away from the mean rate at any given time step i. See Figure 4.4 for a representation of how the trinomial tree is structured.

We can implement this in the Model Builder by creating a section for the probabilities. Keep in mind that this implementation is practical and usable, but difficult to scale up. We will include an example of how to create a more scalable Hull-White solution using VBA on the website with a discussion about it at the end of this chapter. For now enter the following labels:

A20: "Probabilities"	F21: "Pd"
B21: "j"	B22: 2
C21: "jΔr"	B23: 1
D21: "Pu"	B24: 0
E21: "Pm"	B25: -1
	B26: -2

Start the calculation of jΔr for each time step in C22 by entering "=B22*\$E\$11". Copy and paste this over the range C22:C26.

Next, to complete this step in the Model Builder, we will enter formulas to create the probabilities. As mentioned earlier, since the primary purpose of this is to demonstrate an Excel sheet example, while a more efficient VBA example exists in the completed version on the website, there will be some hard-coding in these formulas. We will begin with the initial and first time steps. Enter the following formulas in the corresponding cells:

D24: =(1/6)+(POWER(\$B24*\$E\$9;2)+\$B24*\$E\$9)/2
E24: =(2/3)-POWER(\$B24*\$E\$9;2)

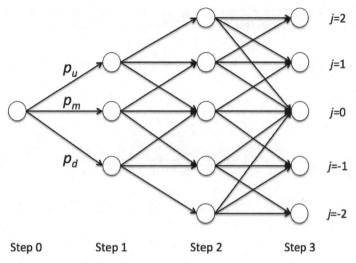

FIGURE 4.5 Trinomial tree with edge effects.

F24: =(1/6)+(POWER($B24*$E$9;2)-$B24*$E$9)/2
D23: =(1/6)+(POWER($B23*$E$9;2)+$B23*$E$9)/2
E23: =(2/3)-POWER($B23*$E$9;2)
F23: =(1/6)+(POWER($B23*$E$9;2)-$B23*$E$9)/2

6. Instead of inserting a similar formula in all of the remaining time steps we have an additional step in order to account for the mean reversion effect we discussed in the last section. This can be done by modifying the edges of the tree such that the transitions at these edge nodes are bounded. This effect can be seen in Figure 4.5.

   You can see from Figure 4.5 that at a certain j_{min} and j_{max}, the tree stops growing vertically. Instead there is downward pressure, from the upper edge, and an upward pressure, from the lower edge, that forces the nodal rates to migrate back toward the center. The values of j_{min} and j_{max} are determined by observing that the branching probabilities remain positive (equations 4.20 and 4.21) only if

$$-\frac{0.816}{M} \leq j_{max} \leq \frac{0.184}{M} \tag{4.20}$$

and

$$\frac{0.184}{M} \leq j_{min} \leq \frac{0.816}{M} \tag{4.21}$$

   Hull and White has found empirically and through practice that it is best to set $j_{max} = -j_{min}$ with j_{max} equaling the value of the smallest integer greater than -0.184/M. For this reason you will see the equation =CEILING(-0.184/$E$9;1) in E12, however it is there as a reference point since it is inflexible to integrate into a purely Excel sheet implementation. The VBA version provided in MB4_Complete.xls on the website makes use of this equation.

A side effect of introducing the edge nodes is that it changes their transition probabilities (equations 4.22, 4.23, and 4.24). At the top edge of the tree the branching probabilities become

$$p_u = \frac{7}{6} + \frac{j^2 M^2 + 3jM}{2} \tag{4.22}$$

$$p_m = -\frac{1}{3} - j^2 M^2 - 2jM \tag{4.23}$$

$$p_d = \frac{1}{6} + \frac{j^2 M^2 + jM}{2} \tag{4.24}$$

And similarly (equations 4.25, 4.26, and 4.27) the bottom edge of the tree becomes

$$p_u = \frac{1}{6} + \frac{j^2 M^2 - jM}{2} \tag{4.25}$$

$$p_m = -\frac{1}{3} - j^2 M^2 + 2jM \tag{4.26}$$

$$p_d = \frac{7}{6} + \frac{j^2 M^2 - 3jM}{2} \tag{4.27}$$

We will implement this into the Model Builder by inserting the following equations in the corresponding cells:

D22: =(7/6)+(POWER($B22*$E$9;2)+3*$B22*$E$9)/2
E22: =(-1/3)-(POWER($B22*$E$9;2)+2*$B22*$E$9)
F22: =(1/6)+(POWER($B22*$E$9;2)+$ B22*$E$9)/2
D26: =(1/6)+(POWER($B26*$E$9;2)-$B26*$E$9)/2
E26: =(-1/3)-(POWER($B26*$E$9;2)-2*$B26*$E$9)
F26: =(7/6)+(POWER($B26*$E$9;2)-3*$B26*$E$9)/2

7. At this point we should note that the nodal rates that migrate throughout the tree are NOT the instantaneous short rate used in equation 4.7. The difference is that the nodal rate is equivalent to the yield between the Δt period steps. The instantaneous, or short, rate on the other hand is the cost of borrowing at time t with an instantaneous return Δt later. The relationship is as follows (equation 4.28):

$$e^{-R\Delta t} = A(t, t + \Delta t)e^{-B(t, t+\Delta t)r} \tag{4.28}$$

Since we know the nodal rate R from our tree, we can solve for r to get the rate needed to price the option (equation 4.29):

$$r = \frac{R\Delta t + \ln[A(t, t + \Delta t)]}{B(t, t + \Delta t)} \tag{4.29}$$

We will pause at this moment in the Model Builder to learn more about using forward induction to assist in correctly pricing our option, and we will then continue with Model Builder 4.2 at the end of the next section.

TERM STRUCTURE RECOVERY USING FORWARD INDUCTION

In the last section we constructed a tree for r^*. This however is not the tree that we want for pricing our option. In this section we will discuss the methodology used to convert the tree for r^* to the tree for r. From equation 4.13 we see that r^* is just r but with an offset α defined by equation 4.30:

$$\alpha(t) = r(t) - r^*(t) \tag{4.30}$$

The goal is to determine α at each node such that the tree, for r, produces expected prices that match the yield curve. An analytical solution to α exists—it was developed by Kijima and Nagayama—but using it in this scenario will result in a loss of accuracy since the tree is a discrete presentation of a continuous stochastic differential equation. Instead Hull and White developed a step-by-step method using forward induction to adjust the r^* tree such that the final tree exactly matches the yield curve. The reason for the forward induction will become clear once we discuss the methodology in detail, but for now it would be helpful to state that the expected rate at time step i is determined in part by the yield at time $i+1$. Therefore if the yield curve, for example, is valid up to time step 10, then we can only price an option up to time step 9.

Let us first define a few terms. As we have mentioned before, let i be the index for the time step away from the origin and j be the branch increment away from the mean. The combination of them together, (i, j), represents a unique node ID. Now let us define Q as the present value of a \$1 bond. If we incorporate the (i, j) indexing scheme, we can define the present value at each node to be $Q_{i,j}$.

As a reminder, the present value of a bond with a \$1 payoff maturing within a unit with rate r, is given by equation 4.31.

$$Q = e^{-r\Delta t} \tag{4.31}$$

Our previous discussion on binomial trees stated that movement throughout the tree is a probabilistic process. A trinomial tree is fundamentally no different, so when we talk about the "present" value at a node, what we really are talking about is the "expected" or "average" value of the bond should it arrive at node (i, j). The simplest case is represented in Figure 4.6, where there is only one path to any given node at step 1.

The fact that we are talking about averages necessitate that we modify equation 4.31 to reflect a more realistic expectation of the price. Statistically speaking

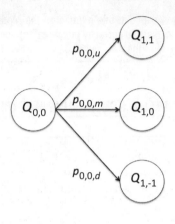

Step 0   Step 1

FIGURE 4.6 Trinomial
showing the present value, $Q_{i,j}$

if there is a process that has set of possible values $[v_1, \ldots, v_j]$ that occurs with
probabilities $[p_1, \ldots, p_j]$, then the expected average (equation 4.32) will be

$$E = \sum_{i=0}^{j} v_i \, p_i \tag{4.32}$$

At this point you may notice that equation 4.32 is just a generalization of
equation 4.1. For the simple case represented in Figure 4.6 we can evaluate, say
$Q_{1,1}$, to be (equation 4.33)

$$Q_{1,1} = p_{0,0,u} e^{-r_0 \Delta t} \tag{4.33}$$

The step is simple because there is only one path to any given node in step
1. Furthermore the first node at $i = 0$ is always \$1 because the nodal rate at the
origin is defined to be zero (equation 4.13). However, what happens during the
second step when there are multiple paths to a given node?

How would one compute the value of $Q_{2,0}$? This is where the formalism of
equation 4.32 becomes important. There is however one more twist in the story.
In this case we do not start from \$1 as we did when computing values for step 1.
Each of the nodes at step 1 have their own values, $Q_{i,j}$, which are different from
\$1. The values at step 2 have to be adjusted accordingly to account for this offset
(equation 4.34).

$$Q_{2,0} = p_{1,-1,u} Q_{1,-1} e^{-r_{1,-1} \Delta t} + p_{1,0,m} Q_{1,0} e^{-r_{1,0} \Delta t} + p_{1,1,d} Q_{1,1} e^{-r_{1,1} \Delta t} \tag{4.34}$$

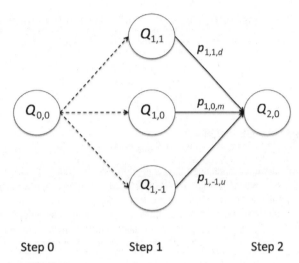

Step 0   Step 1   Step 2

FIGURE 4.7 After the first step, there exist nodes that can be reached by multiple paths. For example, node (2,0) can be reached via (1,1), (1,0), and (1,-1).

At first glance it seems we have just figured out how to compute the value of the option at each node. This is misleading because the $r's$ we used in equations 4.33 and 4.34 are the nodal rates, r^*, plus alpha, which we have yet to determine. Therefore before we can compute $Q_{i,j}$ we must first compute α_{i-1} using forward induction. Given that $Q_{i,j}$ is the value at a node with nodal rate $r_{i,j}^*$, we can ask the question, how much would $r_{i,j}^*$ have to be shifted to recover the price of an option that matures at $i + 1$?

For the sake of simplicity let's examine the first node at $i = 0$. The nodal rate is 0 because that is how the tree was initially defined. The price at $i + 1$ can be observed from the yield curve to be $P(0, 1)$ and can be computed as follows (equation 4.35):

$$P(0, 1) = Q_{0,0}e^{-(\alpha_0 + j\Delta r)\Delta t} = Q_{0,0}e^{-\alpha_0 \Delta t} \qquad (4.35)$$

Equation 4.35 should strike the reader as the basic bond equation for a bond, or option, that matures at time Δt. Therefore, α_0 is the yield rate for that maturity as observed from the yield curve. We can generalize equation 4.35 to nodes further along the tree by using the same idea that we exercised to get us from equation 4.33 to equation 4.34.

$$P(0, i + 1) = \sum_{j=-n}^{n} Q_{i,j}e^{-(\alpha_i + j\Delta r)\Delta t} \qquad (4.36)$$

Solving for α, we get the final equation (equation 4.37):

$$\alpha_i = \frac{\ln\left[\sum_{j=-n}^{n} Q_{i,j}\exp(-j\Delta r\,\Delta t)\right] - \ln\left[P(0,i+1)\right]}{\Delta t} \tag{4.37}$$

CONTINUATION OF MODEL BUILDER 4.2

8. As we have just seen the calculations can be complicated. To finish off this Model Builder, we will break the remaining process down into three separate sections: calculating the nodal rates, calculating $Q(i,j)$, and then calculating $Q(i,j)*\exp(-j\Delta r\Delta t)$. We cannot simply do one section and then move on to the other, since there are many dependencies between these sections. Instead, we will progress by explaining this by moving through the time steps. First we should set up the labeling by entering the following text in the corresponding cells:

> A28: "Nodal Rates, R(I,j)—Computed Using Forward Induction"
> B29: "Steps"
> C29, C37, C46: 0
> D29, D37, D46: 1
> E29, E37, E46: 2
> F29, F37, F46: 3
> A36: "Q(i,j)"
> A45: "Q(i,j)*exp(- jΔrΔt)"
> B52: "ln(P(0,T))"
> B53: "α"

9. We can now start with the 0 time step. Enter into the following cells the corresponding data and formulas:

> C40: 1   C52: 1
> C49: 1

10. Before we can finish time step 0, we need to move on to time step 1. Enter the following equation in D52:

> =-C$5*C$4

While we are there we can finish this row off by copying and pasting this formula over the range D52:G52.

11. We can now finish off time step 0 with two more equations. Enter the following equations in the corresponding cells:

> C53: =LN(SUM(C47: C51))-D52
> C32: =C$53

12. We can now move on to time step 1, where it is easiest to calculate $Q(i,j)$. Do this by entering the following formula in D39:

$$=D24*EXP(-C32)$$

Copy and paste this formula over D39:D41.

13. Next we can finish $Q(i,j)*\exp(-j\Delta r\Delta t)$ for time step 1 by entering the following formula in D48:

$$=\$D39*EXP(-\$B\$23*\$B\$9*\$E\$11)$$

Copy and paste this formula over the range D48:D50.

14. At this point we can get the time step 1 formula for D53 by copying C53 and pasting it in D53. We should copy that formula over the range C53:F53 while we are at this row.

15. Now move back up to the nodal rate section and enter the following formulas in the corresponding cells:

D31: $=\$D\$32+\$B\$23*\$E\$11$
D32: $=\$D\$53$
D33: $=\$D\$32+\$B\$25*\$E\$11$

16. We can progress through the process we did for step 0, but be careful of the formulas that are required since many of them change:

D39: $=D24*EXP(-C32)$
D40: $=E24*EXP(-C32)$
D41: $=F24*EXP(-C32)$

17. The next section for time step 0, $Q(i,j)*\exp(-j\Delta r\Delta t)$, can now be entered:

D48: $=\$D39*EXP(-\$B\$23*\$B\$9*\$E\$11)$

Copy and paste the formula in D48 over the range D48:D50.

18. A similar pattern for each section begins to emerge as we progress through each time step. Rather than repeat many similar formulas in the text, the reader should be able to replicate the process for future time steps with the following guidance:

   a. The "center" nodal rates (i.e., row 32) are always set equal to α. The other nodal rates are always multiplied by their respective probabilities and Δr [%].

   b. The formula in $Q(i,j)$ changes depending on its time step and position on the tree. A listing of the remaining formulas and their corresponding cells is provided here. Also check MB4_Complete.xls on the website if you are confused in any way.

E38: $=D39*D23*EXP(-D31)$

E39: $=D39*E23*EXP(-D31)+D40*D24*EXP(-D32)$

E40: $=D39*F23*EXP(-D31)+E24*D40*EXP(-D32)+D25*D41*EXP(-D33)$

E41: =F24*D40*EXP(-D32)+E25*D41*EXP(-D33)

E42: =F25*D41*EXP(-D33)

F38: =D22*E38*EXP(-E30)+D23*E39*EXP(-E31)

F39: =E22*E38*EXP(-E30)+E23*E39*EXP(-E31)+D24*E40*EXP(-E32)

F40: =F23*E39*EXP(-E31)+E24*E40*EXP(-E32)

       +D25*E41*EXP(-E33)+F22*E38*EXP(-E30)+D26*E42*EXP(-E34)

F41: =F24*E40*EXP(-E32)+E25*E41*EXP(-E33)+E26*E42*EXP(-E34)

F42: =F25*E41*EXP(-E33)-F26*E42*EXP(-E34)

19. Be careful when replicating the cells for $Q(i,j)*\exp(-j\Delta r\Delta t)$. These should be done individually rather than copy and paste.

20. Finally we are now able to calculate the bond prices. First label the last sections:

A56: "Bond Price"	E57: 2
B57: "R(3,j)"	F57: 1
C57: "r(3)"	G57: 0
D57: 3	

21. In B58 enter the reference =F30 to bring down the 3 time step's nodal rate. Copy and paste this formula over the range B58:B62.

22. We then need to transform the nodal rate using the following formula in C58:

$$=(B58*\$B\$9+LN(\$E\$15))/\$E\$14$$

This formula can be copied and pasted over the range C58:C62.

23. Instead of starting at $t = 0$, we will start at $t = 3$ to get to the bond price. Enter the following formula in D58:

$$=MAX(\$B\$14-\$B\$15*\$E\$17*EXP(-\$E\$16*C58); 0)$$

Notice the MAX function is in place to prevent negative values. Copy and paste this formula over the range D58:D62.

24. Time step 2 does not require the MAX function. Instead enter the following formula in E58:

$$=(D22*D58+E22*D59+F22*D60)*EXP(-E30)$$

Copy and paste this formula over the range E58:E62.

25. Next, we move on to time step 1 by entering the following formula in F59:

$$F59: =(D23*E58+E23*E59+F23*E60)*EXP(-D31)$$

This formula should be copied and pasted over the range F59:F61.

26. Finally we enter the following formula in G60 to get the $t = 0$ bond price:

$$=(D24*F59+E24*F60+F24*F61)*EXP(-C32)$$

Hull-White Trinomial Tree Using VBA

With all the work that we just did you might be wondering, "Aren't we done?" Well, as alluded to during parts of this chapter, the implementation in MB4.2 is inefficient due to the inflexible characteristics of working solely on an Excel sheet. While there may be many ways to make the Excel sheet more efficient, ultimately a code-based solution is far preferable, which is why a complete version of the VBA based solution is provided in the MB4_Complete.xls file on the website.

BLACK-SCHOLES OPTION PRICING METHOD

The Black-Scholes method is another common way of pricing options. However, instead of using an interest rate based model, Fischer Black and Myron Scholes modeled the stock price directly and assumed that its price can be adequately described as a geometric Brownian motion (equation 4.38).

$$dS = \sigma S \, dW + \mu S \, dt \tag{4.38}$$

Equation 4.38 by itself, along with the basic solution to S, has no sense of arbitrage or what a "fair" price is. We will not go into the details here, but the pricing equations we will mention a little later depend on the assumptions made on how an option *should* be priced, and those assumptions necessarily take arbitrage into account. Another thing to note here is that a geometric Brownian motion process is very different from a regular Brownian motion, which is shown in equation 4.4. Equation 4.38 can be rewritten to into equation 4.39:

$$\frac{dS}{S} = \sigma \, dW + \mu \, dt \tag{4.39}$$

If you recall from calculus that the integral of $1/x$ is the natural log of x, $\ln(x)$, then you can see that the natural log of S is normally distributed (since the right side of the equation is normally distributed). In summary regular Brownian motion produces normally distributed numbers while geometric Brownian motion produces *lognormally* distributed numbers. We will discuss this effect in more detail in the next chapter when we use the Merton-KMV model to predict corporate default probabilities.

The Black-Scholes method when applied to pricing European call and put options, C and P, respectively, yields the following results (equations 4.40 through 4.43),

$$C = SN(d_1) - Ke^{-r(T-t)}N(d_2) \qquad (4.40)$$

$$P = C - S - Ke^{-r(T-t)} \qquad (4.41)$$

$$d_1 = \frac{\ln(S/K) + (r + \sigma_S^2/2)(T-t)}{\sigma_S\sqrt{T-t}} \qquad (4.42)$$

$$d_2 = d_1 - \sigma_S\sqrt{T-t} \qquad (4.43)$$

where K is the strike price, r is the risk free rate, T is the time to maturity, t is the time at valuation, σ is the volatility of the underlying asset, S, and $N(d)$ denotes the value of the cumulative standard normal distribution at position d with mean of zero and variance of one.

The advantage of the Black-Scholes model over the Hull-White model is in its simplicity. All the terms in the Black-Scholes equations are market observable quantities, independent of time, and unlike the Hull-White interest rate model, there is only one constant stochastic variable that the final result is dependent on. It is quite common in financial applications to extract the market-implied volatility of various asset classes from observations of market prices of its put and call options. If the call or put price is known in addition to the asset value under consideration, then we have one equation, either 4.40 or 4.41, and one unknown, the volatility. The system is therefore uniquely solvable. Unfortunately equations 4.40 and 4.41 are rather convoluted and as such, the volatility cannot be analytically extracted and must be solved for in an iterative fashion. The methodology we chose to use here is the Newton-Raphson method for finding the root of a function. There is a brief explanation of this formalism in Appendix B if you are not already familiar this concept.

The Model Builder we will work through next is solving for the volatility for one asset given all its observables for a call option. Since we are solving for the volatility that produces a given call price, we must first determine the derivative of C with respect to the volatility. Fortunately, this quantity is already predetermined and is one of the *greeks,* a table of equations (equations 4.44 through 4.47) describing the derivative of C or P with respect to S, r, σ, and t.

$$delta = \frac{\partial C}{\partial S} = N(d_1) \qquad (4.44)$$

$$vega = \frac{\partial C}{\partial \sigma} = SN'(d_1)\sqrt{T-t} \qquad (4.45)$$

$$theta = \frac{\partial C}{\partial t} = \frac{S N'(d_1)\sigma}{2\sqrt{T-t}} - r K e^{-r(T-t)} N(d_2) \qquad (4.46)$$

$$rho = \frac{\partial C}{\partial r} = K(T-t)N(d_2)e^{r(T-t)} \qquad (4.47)$$

For our current problem, we will use vega since we will be trying to recover the volatility. One particular thing to note is that $N'(d_1)$ is the derivative of the cumulative distribution function. We know from statistics that the derivative of the cumulative distribution function is simply the probability distribution function, which in our case is the Normal function with mean of zero and standard deviation of one.

MODEL BUILDER 4.3: Using Black-Scholes and Newton Raphson to Calculate Volatility

1. In this Model Builder we will use option and stock data to calculate the instruments' volatility. We should start by creating a new workbook and naming it MB4.3_User.xls. On the first sheet we should set up a number of labels in the following cells:

B3: "Inputs: Option & Stock Data"	B8: "Today's Date"
B4: "Variable"	B9: "Option Expiry Date:"
B5: "Stock Price"	B10: "Vega Threshold Guess"
B6: "Strike Price"	B11: "Call Price:"
B7: "Risk-Free Interest Rate"	C4: "Value"

2. The values for each of these inputs could vary depending on the case at hand, but for now enter the following values in the corresponding cells:

C5: 12	C9: 10/16/2010
C6: 4	C10: .4
C7: 5.00%	C11: 9
C8: 7/6/2010	

3. To assist readers who may be wondering how the inputs in step 2 were derived, we listed out common calculation methods on the sheet. While they are not required for any functionality, you may want to enter them now. The following are only text guides in cells for reference:

D4: "Common Calculation Method"	D8: "Current Date"
D5: "Current Value in Market"	D9: "Give in Option Contract"
D6: "Given in Option Contract"	D11: "Current Value in Market, Mid"
D7: "Appropriate T-bill/T-bond rate"	

4. A very simple initial calculation that we must do is to determine the option expiration as a fraction of a year. This can be done by entering the formula, =(C9-C8)/365 in C15. We can

provide labels by entering "Time to Option Expiry" in B15 and "(Expiry Date-Current Date)/(Days in Year)" in D15.

5. There are a number of names we need to create that are very important since they will interact with the VBA code for this section. Create the following names for the corresponding cells:

C5: stockPrice	C11: callPrice
C6: strike	C15: maturity
C7: riskFreeRate	C16: CallPriceSolution
C10: Threshold	C17: ImpVol

6. The calculations involved to get to the implied volatility should be done in VBA. Open the VBE and insert a new module in this project. Rename this module BlackScholeSolution.

7. Creating three separate functions will make calculation in the subroutine easier. Enter the following code to get the standard D1 calculation from the Black-Scholes equation:

```
Function computeD1(ByVal vol As Double) As Double
    computeD1 = (Log(stockPrice / strike) + (riskFreeRate
+ 0.5 * (vol ^ 2)) * maturity) / (vol * Sqr(maturity))
End Function
```

8. The second function is a normal distribution function:

```
Function myNormDistPDF(ByVal x As Double)
    myNormDistPDF = Exp(-x ^ 2 / 2) / Sqr(2 * WorksheetFunction.Pi)
End Function
```

9. The final function is an initial guess at the volatility. As with all iterative procedures, a question of major concern is "Where do I start my guess?" Sometimes there is a logical starting location, which is true if we are iterating to solve for the asset price (Merton), but solving for the volatility is a bit trickier since it really can be *anything*. At this point you might be wondering, "Why is this issue a big deal and why is it so important?" To get a better understanding, let us first consider the function that we are minimizing (equation 4.48):

$$f(\sigma) = C(\sigma) - C_{market} = 0 \qquad\qquad (4.48)$$

If we plot this function, we will get a curve that will look like the curve shown in Figure 4.8. You will notice that the function asymptotically approaches $+/-2$ where the slope in that region, our vega, will be essentially zero. If our starting point happens to lie within this region, our iterative solver will fail to converge since dividing by zero will produce infinity. Therefore, before the start of each solve, we must do an initial scan to make sure we are not starting within this region.

10. We will go through the code to this function in two sections. The first covers the necessary variables and initial values. Enter the following code in the BlackScholeSolution module:

```
Function volatilityInitialGuess() As Double
    Dim threshold As Double
    Dim i As Integer
```

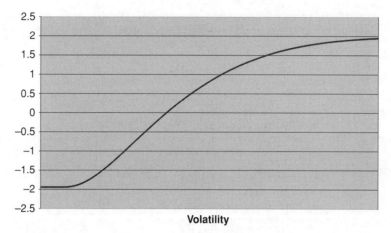

Volatility

FIGURE 4.8 The basic shape of the function in equation 4.46. This curve was generated using fake data and is plotted only to show the general behavior of such a function. The actual values of the volatility and data used are not important. What is important is to note that function asymptotically approaches +/– 2.

```
Dim d1 As Double
Dim vol As Double
Dim vega As Double
Dim vegaConstTerm As Double

' threshold on vega because we want the derivative, ie slope,
  relative to sigma
threshold = Range("Threshold").Value
vol = 0.02
vegaConstTerm = stockPrice * Sqr(maturity)
```

11. The next part loops 500 times to determine the initial volatility guess. Enter the following code after the code where we left off in step 10:

```
For i = 1 To 500
    d1 = computeD1(vol)
    vega = vegaConstTerm * myNormDistPDF(d1)

    If (vega >= threshold) Then
        Exit For
    End If

    vol = vol + 0.02
Next i

    volatilityInitialGuess = vol
End Function
```

12. Now we are ready for the main subroutine. This subroutine will take in values from the sheet, which is stored in VBA variables. The first part of the code focuses on drawing in the information required:

```
Option Explicit

Dim stockPrice, strike As Double
Dim riskFreeRate, maturity As Double
Dim callPrice As Double
Dim vegaConstTerm As Double

Sub BlackScholesSolve()
    'Error Term is known as epsilon in most texts
    Dim errorTerm As Double
    Dim impVol As Double
    Dim d1, d2 As Double
    Dim calcPrice As Double
    Dim vega As Double
    Dim counter As Integer
    Dim vegaConstTerm As Double

    'Take inputs from spreadsheet
    stockPrice = Range("stockPrice").Value
    strike = Range("strike").Value
    riskFreeRate = Range("riskFreeRate").Value
    maturity = Range("maturity").Value
    callPrice = Range("callPrice").Value
```

13. There are a few logical constraints that we should set up and provide information for users of the subroutine. The first of these constraints is the strike price being above the current stock price. If this were the case the strike is already achieved at the current stock price! To avoid this enter the following code after where we left off in step 12:

```
If (strike >= stockPrice) Then
    MsgBox ("Strike cannot be greater than or equal to the stock
    price")
    Exit Sub
End If
```

14. The other constraint is if the call price is less than the stock price minus the strike price. We can avoid this by picking up where we left off in step 13 and entering the following code:

```
If (callPrice < stockPrice—strike) Then
    MsgBox ("Call price cannot be less than stockPrice minus
    strike")
    Exit Sub
End If
```

15. We are now very close to converging on a solution, but first should initialize the values prior to the loop. This is assisted by drawing on the initial volatility guess from step 8 and 9. Enter the following code after the area we left off in step 14:

```
'Initialize variables before start of loop
calcPrice = 0
impVol = volatilityInitialGuess()
errorTerm = 0.0001
counter = 0
vegaConstTerm = stockPrice * Sqr(maturity)
```

16. We can now use Newton-Raphson to solve for the volatility. Enter the following code after the area we left off in step 15:

```
'Use Newton-Raphson Method to Converge on Correct Value
On Error GoTo ErrorHandler
While counter < 100 And Abs(callPrice-calcPrice) > errorTerm
    d1 = (Log(stockPrice / strike) + (riskFreeRate + 0.5 *
(impVol ^ 2)) * maturity) / (impVol * Sqr(maturity))
    d2 = d1-(impVol * Sqr(maturity))
    'N'(d1) = normdist(d1, 0, 1, false) but this is faster
    vega = vegaConstTerm * myNormDistPDF(d1)

    calcPrice = stockPrice * Application.NormSDist(d1)-strike
* Exp(-riskFreeRate * maturity) * Application.NormSDist(d2)

    impVol = impVol-(calcPrice-callPrice) / vega
    counter = counter + 1
Wend
```

17. There are two final steps to complete the process. The first is to export the answer to the sheet. The second is to create an error handler that simply tells the user when an error occurs and the subroutine fails. This will help users troubleshoot any possible problems. Enter the final pieces of code after the code that was created in step 16:

```
'insert values onto spreadsheet
Range("ImpVol") = impVol
Range("CallPriceSolution") = calcPrice
Exit Sub

ErrorHandler:
    MsgBox ("Converge failed. Try another initial guess threshold")
End Sub
```

One final step that we might want to consider, but that is not absolutely necessary, is to create a button to run the subroutine from the sheet.

DISCUSSION ON ERRORS

The Hull-White tree method allows us to price options based on certain assumptions made about the characteristics of our underlying assets. When pricing an entire portfolio of derivatives using this method, it would be beneficial to understand how confident we are of the projected price. To accomplish this, we have to somehow characterize the accuracy of the tree itself. Unfortunately, this is nearly impossible since we have not yet developed a method for predicting the future. We just don't know what the actual price will be. Therefore, from the standpoint of our analysis, the answer we get is the *actual answer* and our error when using this model stems mainly from the number of time steps used in the analysis. Remember, as we increase the number of steps used, we also increase the accuracy of our result. At small-enough intervals, the answers will eventually converge; that is, the difference between finer and finer intervals will become negligible.

In an ideal situation where computational workload is a nonissue, we can run every simulation for every option in our portfolio with thousands of time steps each. However, this is not always practical in reality, as we must limit the number of steps used in order to produce results in a timely fashion. When we limit our simulation in this manner, the price we get will be a certain amount off from the actual price we would have gotten had we not limited our simulation. This difference is our error. Therefore, to characterize the error of our run we would first have to determine the rate of convergence for the particular asset we are analyzing. We can do this by running our simulation, with a given drift, volatility, and yield curve, multiple times with many timing intervals. Once we have this curve, we can choose the appropriate interval size based on the accuracy needed for a particular analysis.

Unfortunately, since the Hull-White tree is a highly nonlinear process, we have no reason to expect that the rate of convergence would be the same for assets having different drifts and volatilities. If we had a portfolio composed of many assets with different drifts and volatilities, we cannot simply assume they would all have the same errors associated with it. In such a scenario, it would be beneficial to produce many convergence curves for different sets of drifts and volatilities. These curves can then be tabulated, and the appropriate curve can then be used for a particular asset in the portfolio. The error associated with the entire portfolio can be calculated by using equation 2.17.

If, on the other hand, we were to use the Black-Scholes model for our analysis, quantifying the error would be far simpler. The uncertainty from solving equations 4.40 and 4.41 are due purely from the uncertainties in the drift and volatility and can be computed analytically by using equation 2.18.

BEYOND PRICE MOVEMENTS

We can clearly see the challenges in option pricing and working with price movements over time. The simulation techniques thus far are powerful tools to help understand and analyze risks. However, there are issues in finance that are larger in scope that simulation can help us with, namely the ultimate default of a company. This we will turn to in Chapter 5.

Corporate Default Simulation

In Chapter 4, we covered the theory and basic applications of forecasting price movements through simulation, which is integral to understanding the value of many financial products. We may use these techniques to help us with equity or debt pricing, but many times we are worried about the worst case. For corporate exposures the worst situation is debt default, which is important in a broad range of markets due to counterparty risk. In many financial transactions, companies that are trading or partnering with one another will run some exposure to loss if their counterparty defaults. Even contractors and other unsecured creditors will be at risk of losing money if a corporate client (or worse, a government client) is unwilling or unable to make their debt payments. Since hedging this risk is sometimes possible, there is often a concentrated effort made to engage in the credit analysis of counterparties.

Compared to modeling equity price movements, building and employing corporate default simulations can be more challenging, particularly given disparities in information. In earlier chapters, we used analyses where equity prices and interest rates (and derivatives related to these) benefited from large, liquid markets, allowing for straightforward information gathering. Daily historical stock information is generally available for all but the most illiquid of stocks, and information on major rates is published in each market's paper of record. However, many fixed income instruments trade with much less liquidity and access to market information may be impossible.

How can we apply simulation and quantitative measures to evaluate characteristics of loans and bonds, and eventually try to measure the risk of default? There are a number of ways that financial modelers have attempted to do so by adapting techniques from the equity and derivative markets. One of the methods that has been most influential on the market is an approach that is ascribed to Robert Merton and is known as the Merton Model.

THE THEORY BEHIND THE MERTON MODEL

The Merton Model was first developed by Robert Merton in 1974 and was the first of what are now called "structural models" of debt and default. Merton worked with Fisher Black and Myron Scholes to develop the Black-Scholes equation for option pricing, and the Merton Model is based on a similar understanding of price movements. The key point in understanding how structural models work is to consider the equity to be a contingent residual claim holder on the value of the assets of the firm. This is a complex idea that we will explain soon in more detail.

First, let us consider how companies default. In general, there are three types of ways that a company can default on its issued debt. One is that a company does not comply with the covenants it has agreed to in the loan documentation. This is sometimes referred to as a "technical default" because often a company will continue to pay its creditors, and the creditors may not take action against the debtor. From a quantitative point of view, while technical defaults may trigger certain legal repercussions or a renegotiation of terms, they are not considered economic defaults, and as a result they are not generally included in default analysis.

The other two general categories of defaults are generally considered "credit events," which can impact all of a company's stakeholders. The first type of credit event is nonpayment, which occurs when a debtor does not pay principal or interest on an assigned date. Occasionally, these defaults are driven by liquidity: whether a company is able to raise cash to make a payment on time. In economies with well-developed financial systems, it is usually simple for a solvent company with capable management to avoid liquidity defaults. However, during financial turmoil such as banking crises, normal lines of liquidity may not be available, and otherwise solvent companies may enter default as a result. These defaults are important and can be extremely difficult to capture in simulation or quantitative forecasting, and the inability to account for these scenarios can be considered one of the shortcomings of classic simulation processes.

Finally, the third category of defaults (and the other category of credit event) is continued insolvency or strategic default. The vast majority of credit events occur when companies decide that they will no longer be able to support their debt or create profits. Companies then file for bankruptcy, restructure, or announce that they will not make payments on their debt. The key factor is that these defaults (and hence the majority of all defaults) are not exactly voluntary, but they are rational decisions based on the economic state of the debtor. In some industries such as banking and insurance, regulatory takeover exists as a fourth category of defaults, but these defaults can be considered similarly: The decision to reorganize, however, is made by regulators instead of the owners or their managers. In both cases, this decision is generally made when the value of the firm's assets is substantially less than the amount that needs to be paid back (i.e., it is unlikely that the firm will be able to make good on its liabilities).

The Model

The Merton Model is primarily focused on the relationship between the value of the firm, the value of the firm's assets, and the face value of the firm's debt. The value of the firm for public companies is generally available by adding the total

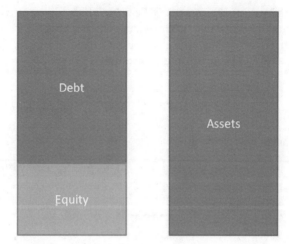

FIGURE 5.1 The simplified structure of a company's balance sheet. Debt holders have first claim on the proceeds of assets, but equity holders retain optionality.

value of the public stock to the total value of the debt (this is sometimes called the enterprise value). However, the true value of the firm's assets is not easily visible to us.

Merton first simplified a company's balance sheet so that it only contained one class of debt and one class of stock. Consider the equity holders in such a situation. They control the assets of the company. One of the opportunities available to the equity holders of a company is the ability to liquidate the company's assets. This means the company closes shop or finds a buyer for the company as a whole. Of course, the decision to sell the company's assets does not mean they do not have to pay back money they have borrowed. Should an equity holder cause this sale, the owners would receive whatever proceeds from the sale remain after the debt holders are paid off. See Figure 5.1.

To restate the equity holders' position: They have the right (but not the responsibility) to receive the excess value of the assets over a defined threshold. Does this sound familiar? It should; the equity is effectively a call option! However, instead of a traditional equity call option, which is an option upon a company's shares, the equity can be considered to be an option on a firm's assets, with a strike price equal to the face value of a company's debt.

Considered this way, the equity value of the firm can be related to the value of the firm's assets, as well as the volatility of the value of these assets, just like the value of an option can be related to the value and the volatility of an equity. The Merton Model starts with this construct in order to determine the volatility of the value of the assets of the firm, which is generally given in texts as σ_v and the actual market value of the assets, which is generally represented as V. The default barrier is represented by B and the period of time is T. So the Merton model can be written as (equation 5.1 through 5.3):

$$E = VN(d_1) - Be^{-rT}N(d_2) \tag{5.1}$$

Where

$$d_1 = \frac{\ln(V/B) + (r + \sigma_V^2/2)T}{\sigma_V\sqrt{T}} \tag{5.2}$$

$$d_2 = d_1 - \sigma_V\sqrt{T} \tag{5.3}$$

With the exception of V and σ_v and potentially μ, the drift term that we will see coming up, all of the key components of the model are visible. Different academics and practitioners have come up with different methods for obtaining the asset value and the volatility of its returns. This chapter offers one version, but more complex, commercially available applications of structural models (the best known of these at the time of writing is Moody's-KMV) include large databases that contain vast amounts of historical data to improve the accuracy of the model's predictions. See Figure 5.2.

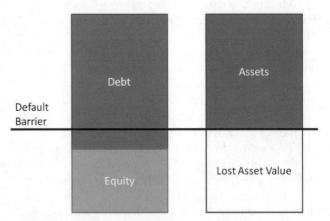

FIGURE 5.2 Conceptually, structural models forecast a firm's default when the value of the firm's assets drops a fixed amount below the debt that needs to be repaid. In this situation the equity holders are sufficiently "under water" that they do not maintain the firm as a going concern.

The output of these models is the probability that a company will default. Since we make the assumption of normalcy when we use the Black-Scholes model, we can state the probability in terms of the number of standard deviations from the mean scenario we see a default. This is referred to as the "distance to default" or DD, and is typically calculated with equation 5.4:

$$DD = \frac{\ln(V/B) + (\mu_V + \sigma_V^2/2)T}{\sigma_V \sqrt{T}} \qquad (5.4)$$

If this is confusing, do not fret. We will walk through these calculations later in the chapter.

SHORT-TERM AND LONG-TERM LIABILITIES: THE BARRIER AND CALIBRATION

One of the key questions with setting up the Merton model, or any structural model, is where the point of default, or "knock-out," occurs. Conceptually, the model is set up on the belief that once the value of the company's assets drops far below the amount of debt that needs to be repaid, the company will default on its debt as continued operation is unlikely to have value to the equity holders. The "barrier" level can be set in any number of ways, but the goal in setting a barrier level is to calibrate the model to the observed market.

In Merton's initial paper, he set the barrier to 100 percent of a company's short-term liabilities (due in a year or less) plus 50 percent of a company's long-term liabilities (due in a year or more). The reasoning behind this was that the management and equity of a company, as holders of an option on the assets of the firm, would tolerate the value of a firm's assets being below the level of liabilities to a certain extent. In these cases where the equity is "out of the money" or "under water," the equity still can have substantial option value, especially in volatile or highly leveraged industries.

Given Merton's influence on the world of quantitative finance, there have been many papers published in peer-reviewed journals discussing the correct calibration of the model to observed defaults. Some of these papers segregate companies by industry and others separate them by the term structure of their debt. The initial assumption that Merton used is usually taken as a reasonable starting point.

Determining Asset Values Using Option Theory

Now that we have the more static components of our model set, we need to determine the two crucial variables, V and σ_v. If you will recall in the original Black-Scholes model we used for equity options, we were able to calculate the

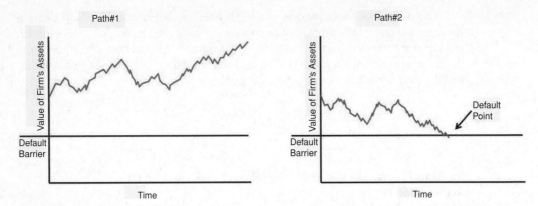

FIGURE 5.3 Potential paths of future firm asset values. In Path #1, asset values V stay above the barrier B; the firm survives. In Path #2 the firm defaults when V falls below B. If we assume the movements in V follow a geometric Brownian motion, we can forecast the probability of default using the distance to default DD.

implied volatility of a stock (σ) based on the price of the option (C for a call), the price of the stock (S), and the strike price (K).

In a structural model, the value of a firm's equity is equivalent to the value of the call, as we are considering the value of the equity to be a call option on the firm's assets. We are also setting the strike price to be the face value of the debt (not the barrier, which does not have an exact equivalent in the Black-Scholes equation). However, the value of the firm's assets and the volatility of these assets are not immediately visible. This presents us with a problem in that we now have two differential equations to solve for two variables that are dependent on each other.

In our application of the Merton Model, we calculate V and σ_ν through an iterative process off of the historical equity volatility of the stock, which we covered in our Black-Scholes example in Chapter 4. This is modeled on the method that Moody's-KMV reports that they use, though we do not have complete clarity as to the exact assumptions that they use in their proprietary models.

Once we have the model set for the company, we can proceed with the simulation. The way we set up the model is with a knock-out barrier option: Once the value of the assets drops below a certain level, the company is considered to have defaulted. This is where the simulation is done. The asset value of the firm is assumed to move with similar volatility to what has previously been calculated, and can be forecast in daily, weekly, monthly, or annual steps. See Figure 5.3.

MODEL BUILDER 5.1: Merton Model

Given the complexity of structural models, we will put together a fairly basic version where we iterate to find many of the key variables, and move toward a model where the variables are calculated using market information.

1. Open a new workbook in Excel and save it as MB5.1_User. A complete version of this Model Builder can be found on the website. We recommend using the proxy data in the complete version to check your methods. Starting in B6, we will enter the inputs from the company's balance sheet that we need to implement the model. In B6, enter the date of the first date that you wish to model where you have the full corporate balance sheet. Generally, this is taken from corporate filings such as a 10-K or 10-Q in the United States. Fill these in for each date at which information is available, in cells B6 for the oldest, then in B7 and B8, and so on.

2. In C6 enter the short-term liabilities, generally defined as debt and other liabilities that are due within one year. We consider all of the other liabilities of the firm to be long term, and enter the long-term liabilities in D6. In E6, we will enter the number of shares outstanding (not the shares authorized, which will be listed in the financials but is not pertinent) at the first date. For all of these fields, we will fill down with data for each period as we did with the dates in column B.

3. Below the accounting information, we will enter the market information we need to implement the model. In B20 we will enter the earliest date that we are using market data, and in C20 the stock price. Make sure that the stock price is adjusted for splits (for more discussion on adjusting stock prices, refer to Chapter 6). In D20 enter the one-year risk-free rate. Fill these values down until the current time is reached.

    Additionally, in column E enter the returns for the benchmark for this stock such as the S&P 500. We may use this to calculate an expected return through the Capital Asset Pricing Model (often abbreviated CAPM).

    Above this, in E17, we will count the number of periods. Enter the formula "=COUNT(B20:B1000)". We will reference this later. See Figure 5.4.

4. For the final set of inputs, enter the barrier threshold, and our default costs numbers. In I4 enter the short-term liabilities component of the barrier level. In the initial Merton model, 100 percent was used, so enter that value in I4. In I5 enter the long term liabilities component of 50 percent, which was the value Merton originally used. There is nothing sacred about these levels: Merton chose them initially because they made intuitive sense. Higher short-term liabilities are more critical to solvency since the company has less time to make the payments.

    Below this, enter a cost of default and impair asset assumption in I6. This does not have an impact on the probability of default; it is solely for calculations around the recovery rate. At default, a company may have expenses that can run into the tens of millions of dollars. In addition, certain assets on the company's balance sheet such as goodwill and brand intangibles may be permanently lost.

5. Now that we have all of the key inputs, calculate the key values for model implementation: the equity valuation, the face amount of liabilities, and the default barrier. In F20 use an index-match or vlookup function in order to get the correct number of shares outstanding for each period. For simplicity, we will assume that the share count stays constant all period, rising at the next report date. In F20 enter:

$$=INDEX(\$E\$6:\$E\$13,MATCH(B20,\$B\$6:\$B\$13,1))$$

With this value we can calculate the market value of the equity in each period in column G: in G20 enter "=F20*C20". Extend these formulas down.

	A	B	C	D	E
1		'Merton' Model - Historical Data for Calculations			
2					
3		Balance Sheet Information			
4					
5		Date	ST Liablities	LT Liablities	Shares Outstanding
6		12/31/2008	9,048,631,332	4,000,000,000	464,811,800
7		3/31/2009	9,048,641,571	4,000,000,000	464,811,800
8		6/30/2009	8,923,874,993	4,000,000,000	464,811,800
9		9/30/2009	9,086,693,637	4,200,000,000	465,311,800
10		12/31/2009	9,173,454,764	4,200,000,000	465,311,800
11		3/31/2010	9,213,532,465	3,900,000,000	465,311,800
12		6/30/2010	9,026,529,344	3,900,000,000	465,311,800
13		9/30/2010	9,007,446,913	3,900,000,000	465,311,800
14					
15					
16					
17		Market Info		Trading Days	489
18					
19		Date	Stock Price	Risk Free Rate (annualized)	Benchmark (only for CAPM Drift)
20		12/31/2008	4.33	2.24%	903.25
21		1/2/2009	4.77	2.42%	931.80
22		1/5/2009	4.71	2.49%	927.45
23		1/6/2009	5.02	2.51%	934.70
24		1/7/2009	5.23	2.49%	906.65
25		1/8/2009	5.04	2.44%	909.73
26		1/9/2009	5.3	2.41%	890.35
27		1/12/2009	4.54	2.31%	870.26
28		1/13/2009	4.39	2.30%	871.79
29		1/14/2009	4.72	2.21%	842.62
30		1/15/2009	4.53	2.20%	843.74
31		1/16/2009	4.74	2.30%	850.12
32		1/20/2009	4.67	2.35%	805.22
33		1/21/2009	4.22	2.53%	840.24
34		1/22/2009	4.38	2.59%	827.50
35		1/23/2009	3.94	2.62%	831.95
36		1/26/2009	4.24	2.64%	836.57
37		1/27/2009	4.38	2.52%	845.71
38		1/28/2009	4.41	2.66%	874.09
39		1/29/2009	4.66	2.82%	845.14
40		1/30/2009	4.33	2.84%	825.88
41		2/2/2009	4.22	2.72%	825.44
42		2/3/2009	4.25	2.84%	838.51
43		2/4/2009	4.18	2.91%	832.23

FIGURE 5.4 Model Builder 5.1 after step 3. This proxy data is available on the website for this text.

6. We will use similar formulas to track the face value of the company's liabilities and the default barrier. In H20 enter the following:

$$=INDEX(\$C\$6{:}\$C\$13,MATCH(B20,\$B\$6{:}\$B\$13,1))$$

$$+INDEX(\$D\$6{:}\$D\$13,MATCH(B20,\$B\$6{:}\$B\$13,1))$$

This adds short-term and long-term liabilities together to get the face value of all liabilities. In I20 calculate the value of the default barrier by including the weightings in I4 and I5 into the equation.

$$=\$I\$4*INDEX(\$C\$6{:}\$C\$13,MATCH(B20,\$B\$6{:}\$B\$13,1))$$

$$+\$I\$5*INDEX(\$D\$6{:}\$D\$13,MATCH(B20,\$B\$6{:}\$B\$13,1))$$

Extend these formulas down.

7. Now we have all of the variables that we need for the calculation of the asset value V and the asset volatility σ_V. Since the calculation of these values through a direct solution to equations 5.2 and 5.3 is extremely difficult, we will start with an initial guess for the asset values and the volatility, then iterate until we converge on a solution. In column J we will start with an initial guess of the asset value that is simply the sum of the liabilities and the market value of the equity. In J20, enter "=G20+H20" and extend down.

8. We are going to write a short macro to help us with our iteration, which will be performed in columns K and M. Start by taking the initial guess of the asset values in column J and finding what asset volatility σ_V is implied by the asset values. Then, plug that asset volatility number into the Black-Scholes equation to get the next iteration of the asset values. We will continue to iterate the two variables until the sum of the squared errors between the two iterations drops well below 1. Open up the VBE window with ALT + F11 and insert a new module. In the module enter the following code:

```
Sub iterateMerton()
    Range("K20:K1000").Value = Range("J20:J1000").Value
    Do While Range("sumSquaredErrors") > 10 ^ -4
        Range("K20:K1000").Value = Range("M20:M1000").Value
    Loop
End Sub
```

Note that we haven't created the range "sumSquaredErrors" yet; we will do this in a few steps. For now, copy the cells in J20:J1000 and paste values in K20:K1000 so we have values for the first step. This isn't necessary but will help you visualize how the spreadsheet will work.

9. In column L we will calculate the daily returns of the assets in order to calculate volatility. We leave L20 empty and in L21 we enter the formula "=LN(K21/K20)". We extend this down and above the column in L18 we enter our calculation for an annualized volatility (assuming 250 trading days in a year) of "=STDEV(L21:L1000)*SQRT(250)". This is our initial calculation of σ_V.

10. Now that we have σ_V we can calculate the next iteration value of asset value V through the Black-Scholes equation. However, the calculation is complex, so we will simplify it a little bit by creating a user defined function to calculate the "d_1" term of the equation. Again, open the VBA Editor window and under the macro we wrote earlier we will define our function.

```
Function BlackScholesD1(assetVal, strikePrice, rfRate, assetVol,
timeMat)
    BlackScholesD1 = (Log(assetVal / strikePrice) + (rfRate + 0.5 *
assetVol ^ 2) * timeMat) / (assetVol * timeMat ^ 0.5)
End Function
```

Now to actually calculate the asset value in each period we will create the current period's asset values in column M. In M20 we will enter the Black-Scholes formula to calculate asset values. Enter the following (and be careful to handle the parentheses correctly):

$$=(G20+H20*EXP(-D20*1)$$

$$*NORMSDIST(BlackScholesD1(K20,I20,D20,\$L\$18,1))-$$

$$\$L\$18)/NORMSDIST(BlackScholesD1(K20,I20,D20,\$L\$18,1))$$

This is a rearrangement of equation 5.1 in order to solve for the asset value *V*.

11. While most of the difficult math is now done, we still need to create all of our reporting and outputs. In order to keep the output reporting clear, we will name some key ranges.

> E17: numDates
> D20: riskFreeRate
> G20: equityValue
> H20: bookLiabilities
> I20: defaultBarrier
> K20: finalAssetValues

12. Now we will calculate the key results from our model. Most of the results are straightforward and do not require further calculation.

> L4: Asset Volatility: "=L18"
> L5: Asset Value: "=OFFSET(finalAssetValues,numDates-1,0)"
> L6: Liability Value: "=OFFSET(bookLiabilities,numDates-(1,0)"
> L7: Sum of Squared Errors: "=SUMXMY2(K20:K1000,M20:M1000)".
>   Be sure to name this range "SumSquaredErrors" so the
>   "iterateMerton()" macro references it.
> L8: Drift: we will come back to the drift calculation in a moment.
>   Leave this blank for now.
> L9: Default Barrier: "=OFFSET(defaultBarrier,numDates-1,0)"
> L10: Distance to Default: "= (LN(L5/L9)+(L8 - (L4^2)/2))/L4".
>   This is equation 5.4.
> L11: One Year Default Probability: "=NORMSDIST(- L10)"
> L12: Current Liabilities: "=(OFFSET(bookLiabilities,numDates-1,0))"
> L13: Estimated Recovery: "=(OFFSET(defaultBarrier,numDates-1,0)-
>   I6)/L12"

13. The final component of the model is in many ways the hardest to grasp: the concept of drift. Drift is the average return over the long term that can be expected on the assets. The concept of a long-term average return is fairly simple, but what value is appropriate to use is contested. Some modelers do not use drift, setting it to 0 percent; others use historical return, the risk-free rate, or a CAPM-type calculation. In the full version of our model, available online, you can see a few ways of handling this concept. Otherwise, to be conservative, setting drift to 0 is a reasonable approximation for shorter-term applications (i.e., 1 year). See Figure 5.5 for a view of the completed Merton Model.

Structural Models for Practitioners: Moody's KMV and Other Providers

As of 2010, in addition to constructing your own model using the previous steps, a number of companies provide structural models for default analysis. Moody's-KMV, which has been previously mentioned, was one of the first commercial outfits to make structural model results publicly available. KMV is an acronym made from the last names of Stephen Kealhofer, John McQuown, and Oldrich Vasicek, who started their company to provide extensions of the Merton Model in 1989 and sold it to Moody's in 2002.

Bloomberg also made a structural model available to its subscribers in 2010. This model is available by using the CRAT command for most public companies. Like Moody's-KMV, Bloomberg calculates a distance to default and then assigns a rating to different default probabilities. While Bloomberg does provide some documentation for its model, it is unclear how much back-testing has been done to check the calibration of the model. Similarly, MSCI, a spinoff of Morgan Stanley, also indicates that it provides a structural model of credit risk. This model is also bundled within other products that have been developed under the Barra brand name. Additionally, a number of small consulting services provide customized credit analysis work under the structural model family of analysis.

TUNING THE MODEL—DATA SETS AND DRIFT

While the traditional Merton Model is fairly robust, certain assumptions in its application have major implications for the results. One key factor is μ, the expected return or "drift" of assets over time. Some practitioners set the drift term to equal zero on the theory that most assets used by an operating company need to be financed, so riskless returns associated with these assets go to note holders and do not impact the optionality of the equity. Other practitioners use the risk-free rate or the inflation rate. To our knowledge, as of 2010 there has not been a comprehensive study or analysis published on the role of drift in credit modeling. However, for longer-term analysis, the drift term can have a major impact on the results.

'Merton' Model - Historical Data for Calculations

Balance Sheet Information

Date	ST Liabilities	LT Liabilities	Shares Outstanding
12/31/2008	9,048,651,332	4,000,000,000	464,811,800
3/31/2009	9,048,641,571	4,000,000,000	464,811,800
6/30/2009	8,923,874,995	4,000,000,000	464,811,800
9/30/2009	9,086,693,637	4,200,000,000	465,311,800
12/31/2009	9,173,454,764	4,200,000,000	465,311,800
3/31/2010	9,213,532,465	4,200,000,000	465,311,800
6/30/2010	9,026,529,344	3,900,000,000	465,311,800
9/30/2010	9,007,446,913	3,900,000,000	465,311,800

% ST Liabilities in Barrier	100%
% LT Liabilities in Barrier	50%
Costs at Default + Impaired Assets	$100,000,000

Drift	Zero
Zero	0.00%
Annual Risk Free Rate	3.24%
Historical Annual Asset Return	133.15%
CAPM Returns (5% mrkt premium)	3.57%

Results	
Firm Asset Vol	14.18%
Firm Asset Value	16,028,091,123
Firm Liability Value	12,907,446,913
Sum of Squared Errors	2.61E-06
Asset Drift (Annual)	0.00%
Barrier	10,957,446,913
Distance to Default	2.610391982
1-year Default Probability	0.45%
Current Liabilities	$12,907,446,913
Estimated Recovery	84%

Iterate to Solve for Asset Values

Market Info

Trading Days	489

Date	Stock Price	Risk Free Rate (annualized)	Benchmark (only for CAPM Drift)	Stock	MV of Equity	Est. Book Liabilities	Est Default Barrier	Naive Asset Value Guess	step i-1	ln(return) 14.18%	step i 14.18%	market returns 0.0659
12/31/2008	4.33	2.24%	903.25	464,811,800	2,012,635,094	13,048,651,332	11,048,651,332	15,061,266,426	15,061,266,426		14,794,798,142.85	
1/2/2009	4.77	2.42%	931.80	464,811,800	2,217,152,286	13,048,651,332	11,048,651,332	15,265,783,618	15,265,783,618	0.011968	14,972,929,391.46	0.031118829
1/5/2009	4.71	2.49%	927.45	464,811,800	2,189,263,578	13,048,651,332	11,048,651,332	15,237,894,910	15,237,894,910	-0.002434	14,936,530,022.20	-0.004679315
1/6/2009	5.02	2.51%	934.70	464,811,800	2,333,355,236	13,048,651,332	11,048,651,332	15,381,986,568	15,381,986,568	0.009285	15,075,854,384.15	0.007786738
1/7/2009	5.23	2.49%	906.65	464,811,800	2,430,965,714	13,048,651,332	11,048,651,332	15,479,597,046	15,479,597,046	0.006529	15,174,611,034.18	-0.030469134
1/8/2009	5.04	2.44%	909.73	464,811,800	2,342,651,472	13,048,651,332	11,048,651,332	15,391,282,804	15,391,282,804	-0.005329	15,093,960,195.14	0.003391364
1/9/2009	5.3	2.41%	890.35	464,811,800	2,463,502,540	13,048,651,332	11,048,651,332	15,512,133,872	15,512,133,872	0.008113	15,216,900,658.75	-0.02153328
1/12/2009	4.54	2.31%	870.26	464,811,800	2,110,245,572	13,048,651,332	11,048,651,332	15,158,876,904	15,158,876,904	-0.022268	14,881,635,338.24	-0.023822826
1/13/2009	4.39	2.30%	871.79	464,811,800	2,040,523,802	13,048,651,332	11,048,651,332	15,089,155,134	15,089,155,134	-0.004632	14,814,329,996.72	0.001756552
1/14/2009	4.72	2.21%	842.62	464,811,800	2,193,911,696	13,048,651,332	11,048,651,332	15,242,543,028	15,242,543,028	0.010904	14,976,344,141.47	-0.034092484
1/15/2009	4.53	2.20%	843.74	464,811,800	2,105,597,454	13,048,651,332	11,048,651,332	15,154,228,786	15,154,228,786	-0.003732	14,891,337,990.45	0.001328505
1/16/2009	4.74	2.30%	850.12	464,811,800	2,203,207,932	13,048,651,332	11,048,651,332	15,251,839,264	15,251,839,264	0.005573	14,974,562,442.48	0.007533126
1/20/2009	4.67	2.35%	805.22	464,811,800	2,170,671,106	13,048,651,332	11,048,651,332	15,219,302,438	15,219,302,438	-0.002569	14,936,141,206.89	-0.054261984
1/21/2009	4.22	2.53%	840.24	464,811,800	1,961,505,796	13,048,651,332	11,048,651,332	15,010,137,128	15,010,137,128	-0.015431	14,707,424,755.21	0.042572033
1/22/2009	4.38	2.59%	827.50	464,811,800	2,035,875,684	13,048,651,332	11,048,651,332	15,084,507,016	15,084,507,016	0.004440	14,772,869,791.39	-0.015278458
1/23/2009	3.94	2.62%	831.95	464,811,800	1,831,358,492	13,048,651,332	11,048,651,332	14,879,989,824	14,879,989,824	-0.013963	14,568,004,836.69	0.005363296
1/26/2009	4.24	2.64%	836.57	464,811,800	1,970,802,032	13,048,651,332	11,048,651,332	15,019,433,364	15,019,433,364	0.009189	14,702,512,559.94	0.005537856
1/27/2009	4.38	2.52%	845.71	464,811,800	2,035,875,684	13,048,651,332	11,048,651,332	15,084,507,016	15,084,507,016	0.005379	14,781,312,703.18	0.010866312
1/28/2009	4.41	2.66%	874.09	464,811,800	2,049,820,038	13,048,651,332	11,048,651,332	15,098,451,370	15,098,451,370	-0.000282	14,777,864,439.00	0.033005834
1/29/2009	4.66	2.82%	845.14	464,811,800	2,166,022,988	13,048,651,332	11,048,651,332	15,214,654,320	15,214,654,320	0.006334	14,871,547,779.53	-0.035681051
1/30/2009	4.33	2.84%	825.88	464,811,800	2,012,635,094	13,048,651,332	11,048,651,332	15,061,266,426	15,061,266,426	-0.010370	14,718,131,583.64	-0.023052281
2/2/2009	4.22	2.73%	825.44	464,811,800	1,961,505,796	13,048,651,332	11,048,651,332	15,010,137,128	15,010,137,128	-0.003378	14,683,166,841.77	-0.000532907
2/3/2009	4.25	2.84%	838.51	464,811,800	1,975,450,150	13,048,651,332	11,048,651,332	15,024,081,482	15,024,081,482	0.000108	14,681,576,408.72	0.01570993
2/4/2009	4.18	2.91%	832.23	464,811,800	1,942,913,324	13,048,651,332	11,048,651,332	14,991,544,656	14,991,544,656	-0.002789	14,640,680,720.14	-0.007517662

FIGURE 5.5 The completed Model Builder 5.5, with potential options for drift laid out in H9:I12. Note that the applied drift rate in L8 is 0.00 percent.

Perhaps more important to the results is how volatility is calculated. There is no widely accepted rule as to how equity volatility should be calculated. Different methods of gathering volatility data can result in substantially different estimations of default risk.

Volatility

In general, volatility will be the most important variable for determining the risk of a company, and as a result most of the work in tuning the model will be done with this variable. Admittedly, to calibrate the model is much more of an art than a science, and different financial engineers will have different opinions on how to best calibrate their model to best determine default probability in the future.

One key factor to consider is that the observed volatility of equity, and therefore the volatility of a company's assets, is correlated with the market as a whole and will move up and down for reasons that are likely not related to the particular company that is being analyzed. Whether to correct for these global changes is a difficult question to answer. On one hand, it hardly seems accurate to incorporate marketwide volatility when looking at a company that does not hold a large number of financial instruments among its assets (an airline, for example). On the other hand, economic downturns do increase the propensity of all companies to default; default rates during recessions can be many multiples of the rates observed during expansion. In general, most modelers do not make distinctions between the volatility associated with the company (idiosyncratic volatility) and volatility experienced by the market as a whole.

Strengths and Weaknesses of Structural Models

The Merton model was the first in a class of models that are called "structural models" because they take into account the structure of a company's balance sheet. Later in this chapter we will consider "reduced form models," which calculate default probability from debt or credit default swap prices.

Structural models are premised on the fact that publicly traded equity is the market that offers the most accurate information about a company's health and riskiness. By accounting for the structure of a company's balance sheet, these models offer a framework for using the information-rich equity markets to measure risk in the debt markets. There is some evidence that structural models pick up on signs of corporate distress substantially before other measures, primarily rating agencies, are able to see them.

Many times, structural models will offer some guidance for debt instruments where the documentation is not easily obtainable and there is minimal trading history available. Structural models can also be expanded to nonpublic companies by creating indexes of similar companies and using their returns as proxy for the firm in question. Some methods for accounting for incomplete data sets are covered in Chapter 7. And importantly, estimating recovery in the case of default is fairly straightforward as there is already a projection of asset values at default that is plugged in.

However, there are a number of weaknesses inherent in structural models, both theoretically and from a practitioner's point of view. In general, all models that are built on the Black-Scholes methodology are explicitly assuming a lognormal distribution of future price movements, an assumption that has been widely (and rightly) criticized for ignoring the importance and frequency of large swings in value. A more in-depth discussion of this issue is available in Chapter 8.

Additional theoretical issues include the oversimplification of company structure and the inability of structural models to account for specific debt covenants or actions that may increase the value of equity but decrease the value of debt (such as dividend recapitalizations or mergers). But the most glaring theoretical deficiency is the fact that Merton's model does not account for cash flow or liquidity. Measures of a company's ability to make payments in the short term are mainstays of traditional credit analysis and can be important guides to whether companies will run into trouble. Many companies that look relatively stable can run into trouble quickly if liquidity is threatened; witness Bear Stearns and AIG during the credit crunch of 2008. While the equity prices were late to reflect the vulnerability of these companies, classic debt analysis highlighted the weaknesses, and as a result debt valuations led equity as the companies collapsed.

From an academic's perspective, a number of key assumptions are required for the structural model to be an accurate representation of the market. Lack of transaction costs, the applicability of stochastic processes under a known distribution, and stationary asset volatility are three primary assumptions with which concerns have been voiced. While all modelers need to be aware of these basic assumptions, we will not cover these issues here.

From a practitioner's perspective, the main barriers to using structural models are their computational complexity and their consistent overpricing of debt, as well as the amount of data that they require. In order to properly calibrate the calculation of a firm's asset value and the volatility associated with it, there needs to be a historical record of not only equity prices, but also of historical liability levels. This data, while possible to obtain, can be difficult to gather and employ. Moody's-KMV has distinguished itself as having a large database, which allows users to quickly employ their structural model effectively.

However, even if an analyst is faithfully recreating a company's historical financial situation, structural models consistently price debt to a higher level than the market does. This either means that the market is accounting for some of the risks that structural models are not accounting for, or there is a liquidity premium built into the market pricing that structural models are not catching. In general, premiums for factors other than credit risk (such as liquidity or regulatory risk) make projecting credit risk from market pricing very difficult.

OTHER METHODS TO DEVELOP DEFAULT PROBABILITIES

While structural models have a rich academic heritage and have been used for a generation by academics, practitioners have often looked to other techniques to assess credit. In general, risk managers are asked to assess a wide variety of assets, including non-public companies and municipal or sovereign bonds. Often, non-simulation-based techniques such as credit scoring are used and then are placed into a simulation framework using external default and correlation assumptions. However, there are also credit analysis techniques that depend on market information and are well suited for simulation.

The most common quantitative credit alternatives to the structural models already discussed are credit scoring and reduced form models. We will discuss credit scoring in the context of how credit scores are used in reduced-form models. Reduced form models are in many respects an extension of structural models, but they require less data in order to construct. However, there are downsides to the simplicity offered by reduced form models.

Robert Jarrow, one of the original developers of reduced form models as they are currently used, had this to say about reduced form models in a 2004 paper:

> *Structural models assume that the modeler has the same information set as the firm's manager—complete knowledge of all the firm's assets and liabilities. In most situations, this knowledge leads to a predictable default time. In contrast, reduced form models assume that the modeler has the same information set as the market—incomplete knowledge of the firm's condition. In most cases, this imperfect knowledge leads to an inaccessible default time. As such, we argue that the key distinction between structural and reduced form models is not whether the default time is predictable or inaccessible, but whether the information set is observed by the market or not. Consequently, for pricing and hedging, reduced form models are the preferred methodology.*

Credit Scoring: Determining Default Probabilities from Ratings

"Rating agencies" include a broad swath of companies that assess the probability that borrowers will pay back money lent to them along with any interest that they have agreed to pay. While there are numerous companies that provide such assessments, nationally recognized statistical rating organizations (NRSROs) are companies registered with the U.S. Securities and Exchange Commission. As of the end of 2010, there were approximately 10 such companies, with another two companies known to be actively seeking the designation.

The most prominent rating agencies in the United States are Moody's and Standard & Poor's, with Fitch and DBRS increasing their coverage dramatically over the first decade of the 21st century. While their models and coverage can differ substantially, all agencies at their core attempt to analyze the wide range of risks that may cause a borrower not to make good on its debts and summarize these risks with a credit score or rating. These ratings are implicitly or explicitly tied to a default or loss probability.

For example, Moody's publishes its idealized loss and default rates on a regular basis. The 2009 version of this paper includes Table 5.1.

We can see here that when Moody's assigns a rating of Baa to a security (the lowest of the "investment grade" ratings), Moody's is projecting a loss rate of

TABLE 5.1 Average Cumulative Issuer-Weighted Global Default Rates by Alphanumeric Rating, 1983–2008

Rating	Year 1	Year 2	Year 3	Year 4	Year 5	Year 6	Year 7	Year 8	Year 9	Year 10
Aaa	0.000	0.016	0.016	0.049	0.088	0.136	0.188	0.193	0.193	0.193
Aa1	0.000	0.000	0.000	0.094	0.141	0.159	0.159	0.159	0.159	0.159
Aa2	0.000	0.010	0.042	0.104	0.201	0.245	0.294	0.350	0.412	0.483
Aa3	0.038	0.118	0.174	0.246	0.319	0.370	0.402	0.417	0.420	0.468
A1	0.018	0.154	0.366	0.544	0.692	0.793	0.868	0.935	0.997	1.076
A2	0.026	0.092	0.244	0.445	0.639	0.891	1.230	1.615	1.955	2.209
A3	0.032	0.151	0.318	0.463	0.714	0.997	1.203	1.432	1.660	1.799
Baa1	0.135	0.357	0.622	0.867	1.091	1.289	1.547	1.730	1.859	2.088
Baa2	0.139	0.426	0.796	1.367	1.850	2.317	2.756	3.178	3.666	4.292
Baa3	0.291	0.816	1.459	2.129	2.926	3.741	4.463	5.189	5.859	6.520
Ba1	0.682	1.862	3.363	4.857	6.280	7.789	8.889	9.649	10.346	11.120
Ba2	0.728	2.066	3.760	5.608	7.230	8.425	9.661	11.006	12.330	13.365
Ba3	1.791	4.954	8.873	12.932	16.209	19.227	22.017	24.755	27.188	29.601
B1	2.450	6.800	11.358	15.361	19.513	23.576	27.853	31.305	34.187	36.717
B2	3.827	9.116	14.386	19.204	23.232	27.013	30.514	33.495	36.607	39.110
B3	7.666	15.138	22.336	28.744	34.261	39.643	44.081	48.016	50.948	53.684
Caa1	9.150	18.763	28.028	35.629	42.389	46.914	49.140	51.686	57.028	62.344
Caa2[2]	16.388	25.807	32.990	38.799	41.983	45.823	48.900	51.959	55.997	61.737
Caa3	24.806	36.604	43.417	49.310	55.959	57.672	60.527	64.744	70.661	82.018
Ca-C	32.949	44.297	53.255	58.406	63.932	66.489	70.337	74.990	74.990	74.990
Investment-Grade	0.072	0.229	0.436	0.673	0.917	1.154	1.381	1.599	1.803	2.008
Speculative-Grade	4.351	8.917	13.373	17.316	20.686	23.696	26.388	28.687	30.708	32.516
All Rated	1.565	3.192	4.726	6.037	7.118	8.037	8.824	9.482	10.045	10.544

Source: Moody's, accessed at http://v2.moodys.com/cust/content/content.ashx?source=StaticContent/Free%20Pages/Credit%20Policy%20Research/documents/current/2007400000578875.pdf

2.129 percent over a four-year horizon. However, this does not mean that we will experience that number of defaults. Since we will recover some of our initial investment, our loss will usually be smaller than the positions defaulting. Stated in another way, our default rate will be greater than our loss rate. Assuming a 50 percent recovery (an assumption we will speak more about later) we obtain a default probability of 4.258 percent over this four year horizon. Additionally, Moody's and other NRSROs produce full transition matrices, which show the historical upgrade/downgrade experience of credits assigned a certain rating.

These explicit probabilities offer a simple, straightforward way to include default assumptions in any model. A modeler needs to be careful to distinguish between whether the table specifies default probabilities or loss probabilities. Moody's traditionally produces tables that look at expected loss, while Standard and Poor's and Fitch both produce tables of default probability.

The primary advantage of using rating agency information is the ease and accessibility of determining ratings for issuers. The major agencies have proven themselves to be fairly strong at assessing corporate credit risk, and their ratings do convey useful information about a company's ability to repay its debts. However, ratings are not perfect. Ratings for new or structured products historically have been prone to severely inaccurate assessments. Examples include constant proportion debt obligations (CPDOs) in 2006 and many residential mortgage products before 2008. Additionally, agencies do not have the capacity to constantly monitor and update their ratings in "real time"; their assessments often lag behind the market.

DETERMINING LOSS PROBABILITIES FROM BOND PRICES OR CREDIT DEFAULT SWAPS

Another frequent method of calculating default probability is by using market information. Two general markets can be used for these calculations: the credit default swap (CDS market) and the bond market. There is a third potential market, the bank loan market, but this market is generally considered to be less liquid and more difficult to obtain information on.

A credit default swap is a derivative contract based on whether or not a specified company will experience a credit event during a specified period. One party to the contract (a protection buyer) is paid if and only if the specified company experiences a credit event. In return for this contingent payment, the party agrees to make payments to the other party (a protection seller).

Entering into a CDS contract is often compared to buying or selling insurance on a corporate bond. If Brenda owns $1 million of IBM bonds and is worried about a default over the next five years, she may buy $1 million of protection through a CDS with Sam. In this case, Brenda will agree to pay Sam $50,000

FIGURE 5.6 A schematic of the relationship between a credit default swap buyer and seller.

(5 percent of $1 million) per year. In return, if IBM undergoes a credit event, Sam agrees to cover Brenda for any losses (the difference between $1 million and the recovery on the bond). When Brenda buys the protection on the bonds, she is effectively insuring the bond against any credit events. See Figure 5.6.

This is generally how a CDS works, though there are a number of details that change from contract to contract. The definition of a credit event generally includes the company declaring bankruptcy, entering into receivership, and being unable to make contractual payments on its bonds. Other events, such as debt restructuring, however, are included in the definition of a credit event in some markets but not others. Timing of protection payments, delivery options, and collateral posting all change from contract to contract, and though substantial progress has been made in standardizing CDS contracts, there needs to be some level of awareness of terms in order to gain useful information from the market. All of these factors need to be known before we can begin to extract the probability that a company will default from its CDS pricing, as we will in Model Builder 5.2. One note before we go further: A CDS market exists for asset-backed securities (ABS), including mortgage-backed securities, which work substantially differently from the CDS described here. We do not recommend using the upcoming methods for ABS issuers.

For entities with liquid CDS markets, the CDS price has become the instrument of choice for calculating "risk-neutral" default probabilities. A risk-neutral default probability is one in which the expected payout to the protection buyer matches the expected payout to the protection seller. The probability of default is generally calculated either as an annual probability of default or as a more complex term structure, where the probability of default for a number of years can be calculated from CDS contracts of different tenors. We will cover the case of a company where we have a single term of CDS, which is more widely applicable but which provides slightly less information about the relative timing of credit events. We will exclude the impact of accrued CDS interest for simplicity. If the company does not default during the term of the CDS, the protection seller will receive the sum of all protection payments S to the seller discounted to present value by d. So the PV of payments to the seller are represented in equation 5.5 as:

$$PV_{seller} = \sum_{i=1}^{T} d_i S_i \tag{5.5}$$

Meanwhile, in the case of a default at any time X (equation 5.6), the protection buyer will earn the total notional amount of the CDS minus the recovery rate R, minus any payments that have already been made to the protection seller before time x (so payments through period $x - 1$).

$$PV_{buyer} = d_x(1 - R) - \sum_{j=1}^{x-1} d_j S_j \tag{5.6}$$

For a risk-neutral probability, the payoffs in these two scenarios need to be equal once weighted by the probability of default (PD). The only complication to this is that the default of the company can happen in any period. To account for this, we will also assume a constant probability of default for each period out to the term of the CDS. This leaves us with equation 5.7:

$$(1 - CPD) \times \sum_{i=1}^{T} d_i S_i = PD \times \sum_{i=1}^{T} \left\{ d_i(1 - R) - \sum_{j=1}^{i-1} d_j S_j \right\} \tag{5.7}$$

Where CPD is equal to the cumulative probability of default. In equation 5.7, the left side of the equation represents the probability of no defaults until time T (measured in periods) multiplied by payments to the protection seller in the case that there is no default. The right side is periodic probability of default times the net payments that would go to the protection buyer in the case of a default. We can rearrange and simplify this to the following (equation 5.8):

$$\frac{PD}{(1 - CPD)} = \frac{\sum_{i=1}^{T} d_i S_i}{\sum_{i=1}^{T} \left\{ d_i(1 - R) - \sum_{j=1}^{i-1} d_j S_j \right\}} \tag{5.8}$$

Once we analytically solve the right side of the equation, simple algebra allows us to solve for the periodic probability of default. We will implement this in the upcoming model builder.

MODEL BUILDER 5.2: Reduced form Models

1. Open a new workbook in Excel and save it as MB5.2_User. In C5:C10, enter the key market and contract information that pertains to the contract. Par value, frequency, spread, and tenor should all be immediately known. For some deeply troubled credits, premiums may be paid upfront as well as on an ongoing basis. For our recovery rate assumption we will use a market standard rate of 40 percent. We have entered proxy data for all of these fields in the complete version available on the website and CD.

2. Enter columns for the number of months, the risk-free rate, and the discount factor. We have built all of these previously, so we will not rehash how to put them together here.

3. In columns F and G, enter the fixed payment leg of the transaction. These are the payments that go from the protection buyer to the protection seller. In period 0, the upfront payment is made. In subsequent payment periods, we can model the payments in column F, from row 16 down using the formula:

$$=IF(MOD(C16,12/\$C\$8)=0,(1/\$C\$8)*\$C\$5*\$C\$7/10000,0)$$

The "MOD()" command returns a remainder after a number is divided by a divisor. The function returns a zero whenever the number is divisible by the divisor. In this case, we are using the function to ensure that payments are only made during the appropriate months. For example, if payments are quarterly, then the divisor is $12/4 = 3$. So in months, 3, 6, 9, 12, and so on, the payments will be made. On other dates we will enter a zero.

In F15 we will enter the value for the special case of the first period: simply the upfront payment (if any) that would be made. Since the upfront payment as a percentage of the notional is an input into the model we simply take that and multiply by the notional, "=C6*C5/10000".

4. Column G is the present value (PV) of these payments, which is obtained by multiplying the discount factor in column E by the payment in column F. Make sure to sum the present values in G13.

5. Next we will model the contingent payment leg (the payments to the protection buyer) of the transaction. Since a credit event can happen at any time, we will look at what the payments would be in the case of a default in any period. So in column I we are showing the contingent default payment in every single period. This is simply the notional value of the CDS multiplied by one minus the recovery rate: "=IF(C16="","",\$C\$5*(1-\$C\$9))".

6. In column J we take the PV of this contingent leg, similar to the calculations in column G. In Column K we take the net PV of the contingent leg, which subtracts out the present value of all protection payments that the fixed rate payer (who is the contingent pay receiver) has already paid in protection, which are in column G. In K16 we calculate this by entering the equation "=IF(C16="","",J16-SUM(\$G\$15:G15))". We extend this down, and in K13 we take the sum of all the net contingent payments. This is the PV of the trade from the buyer's side as set out in the right side of equation 5.7 (without the probability of default term).

7. Now we have the expected payment to the protection seller if there is no credit event, and the sum of expected payments to the protection buyer if there is a credit event in each period. In a risk-neutral default probability, the total expected payouts of the two sides should match. Use this fact to calculate the probability of a credit event occurring in J4: We rearrange equation 5.8, "=1/((1/(G13/K13))+(12*C10))", to get the probability of default in each period. To get the cumulative and annual probabilities of default in J5 and J6, just multiply the periodic PD by the number of periods in the CDS or the number of periods in a year, respectively. See Figure 5.7.

Probability of Default from CDS Spreads

Inputs: CDS Market Data

Variable	Value	Common Calculation Method
Par (Dollars)	$1,000	Market Value
Upfront Payment (bps):	0	Market Value
Spread (bps):	500	Market Value
Payment Frequency (x/year):	4	In contract, generally quarterly
Recovery:	40%	Assumption
Tenor (years):	5	In contract

Periodic PD	0.57%
Cumulative Probability of Defau	34.29%
Annual Default Probability	6.86%

Fixed Leg — Value- No Credit Event (numerator): 226

Contingent Leg (Assumes Constant Default Probability) — Value- Credit Event (denominator): 25.978

Month	Risk Free Rate	Discount Factor	Fixed Leg Payment	Fixed Leg PV	Contingent Leg Payment	PV of Contingent Leg	Net PV of Contingent Leg
0		1.000					
1	4.00%	0.997	-	-	600	598.0421656	598.04
2	4.00%	0.993	-	-	600	596.0907197	596.09
3	4.00%	0.990	12.50	12.38	600	594.1456414	594.15
4	4.00%	0.987	-	-	600	592.2069101	579.83
5	4.00%	0.984	-	-	600	590.274505	577.90
6	4.00%	0.981	12.50	12.26	600	588.3484054	575.97
7	4.00%	0.977	-	-	600	586.4285908	561.79
8	4.00%	0.974	-	-	600	584.5150407	559.88
9	4.00%	0.971	12.50	12.14	600	582.6077345	557.97
10	4.00%	0.968	-	-	600	580.7066521	543.93
11	4.00%	0.965	-	-	600	578.811773	542.04
12	4.00%	0.962	12.50	12.02	600	576.9230769	540.15

FIGURE 5.7 Completed Model Builder 5.2.

BOND TERM STRUCTURE AND BOOTSTRAPPING

For more frequently traded CDS where multiple tenors are available, "bootstrapping" is done to calculate the implied default probability for each individual year. This process can be completed using bond prices as well. Bonds, however, have additional layers of complexity, due to their variety. Fixed/floating differences, optionality, different covenants, and different payment schedules all make modeling bonds more difficult than CDS. However, for this analysis we will consider only the risk of default in our calculations.

Bootstrapping, at least as it is used in quantitative finance, is the term for creating a term-structure from a set of traded securities or derivates. While we can obtain reasonable default probability estimates from markets with only a single tenor security trading, we want to take advantage of the additional information that is available when a number of securities or derivates are in the market. The concept requires us to start with the shortest-term debt we have liquid prices for. With this first security (let's assume it's a one-year bond), we find the default probability as we did with the CDS (the only difference being that we need to subtract out the risk-free rate).

After we have the probabilities of default determined for the first security, we move on to the next security (let's assume it's a three-year bond). We could determine default probabilities in the same fashion; however, we already have specific data for the first year. So instead of finding an average default probability, we will find a cumulative default probability through three years, then subtract out the year 1 default probabilities to understand the default probabilities for years 2 and 3.

In order to understand this, we will build a probability of default model from a company's bond term structure. We treat this slightly differently from our CDS pricing exercise in Model Builder 5.2. Here we need to find what part of the bond's pricing is due to credit pricing versus what part is due to interest rate movements. In order to do this, we will first figure out from the forward interest rate curve what the price would be for a proxy bond PB with the same interest rate and payments as this bond B, but pricing at the treasury rate. Starting with this, the price of the bond is equal to PB times the survival probability plus any payments in a default scenario time the probability of default (equation 5.9).

$$P = \sum_{i=1}^{T} \left\{ PD \times \left(d_i(R) + \sum_{j=1}^{i-1} d_j S_j \right) \right\} + (1 - T \times PD) \times PB \qquad (5.9)$$

We can rearrange equation 5.9 to solve for the periodic probability of default for the first bond by assuming that the probability is constant (equation 5.10).

$$PD = \frac{PB - P}{PB \times T - \sum_{i=1}^{T} \left\{ \left(d_i(R) + \sum_{j=1}^{i-1} d_j S_j \right) \right\}} \qquad (5.10)$$

Then, once we have the probability of default for this bond, we can refine our estimated probabilities of default for future periods by determining what default probability would account for the difference in price between bonds from the same issuer.

MODEL BUILDER 5.3: Reduced form Models with Multiple Tenor Bonds

1. Open a new workbook in Excel and save it as MB5.3_User. Before we start, this model will require functions that are built into the Analysis Toolpak Add-In for Excel, so make sure this is installed before you begin. In B5:D7 we insert basic market information about the bonds. Some bonds trade on a quoted dollar-price, while other bonds trade on yield. We will calculate yield from dollar price in column E; if the bond is quoted in yield, the dollar price can be calculated in a fairly straightforward manner using the "PRICE()" function. The bonds MUST be inserted in order of maturity, with the shortest bonds first. Number the bonds in column A, with a 1 in A5, a 2 in A6, and so on.

   Before we complete the yield calculations, we need to include a few key parameters, including the bond's coupon frequency, an assumed recovery rate, and a settlement date (generally three business days after the bond is purchased, though there are some exceptions). We include these in C13:C15.

2. Next, we will calculate the yield on the bonds. Excel includes a YIELD() function, so we will enter "=YIELD($C$15,B5,D5,C5,100,$C$13,0)" in E5 and drag down to include all bonds that there is information on—in this case, with three bonds, fill E6 and E7.

3. We will also need the interest rate "term structure," the theoretical interest rates on risk-free bonds as they currently stand in the market. It is often commented in academic circles that the most frequently used sources for the risk-free term structure, LIBOR and U.S. Treasury rates, are not truly risk-free, as there is still hedgeable mark-to-market risk. However, using the Treasury curve is a widely used convention, and we will follow it here. Treasury rates are updated daily at www.treasury.gov.

4. Though the term structure is useful, we need to estimate what the interest rate would be on a risk-free bond with the same maturity as the bonds that we are analyzing. The standard practice here is to use "straight-line interpolation," which means that we find the maturities of the nearest Treasuries and we assume the change in yield for risk-free securities with maturity between these two is linear over time. In this worksheet we implement a user defined function to accomplish these calculations. Open the VBA editor by pressing Alt + F11 and create a new module. The code is here:

```
Function interpRates(matDate, spotDates, spotRates)
  'interpolates interest rates from yield curve
    Dim i As Integer, numRates As Integer
    numRates = spotRates.Rows.Count

    If numRates = 1 Then
        interpRates = spotRates(1, 1)
    End If
    If matDate<spotDates(1, 1) Or matDate>spotDates(numRates, 1)
        Then interpRates = "Maturity Outside Series"
```

```
End If

i = 0

Do
i = i + 1

Loop Until spotDates(i, 1) >= matDate

If matDate = spotDates(1, 1) Then
    interpRates = spotRates(1, 1)
Else
    interpRates = (spotRates(i, 1) * (matDate−spotDates(i−1, 1))
        / (spotDates(i, 1)−spotDates(i−1, 1))) + _
        (spotRates(i−1, 1) * (spotDates(i, 1)−matDate) /
        (spotDates(i, 1)−spotDates(i−1, 1)))
End If

End Function
```

This function works by using the Loop Until command to find the correct points in the term structure, then calculates the correct rate based on the distance each point is from the bond's maturity. We apply this for the first bond in F5 using "=INTERPRATES(B5,$C$19:$C$25,$D$19:$D$25)" and then extend the formula down.

5. Now that we have the prices, coupons, and yields of each of the bonds, we are going to estimate what yield the risk-free bond PB for each of these bonds would trade at. In F5 we will use the "interprates()" function we previously created to make this determination. Enter "=interprates(B5,$C$19:$C$25,$D$19:$D$25)" in F5, and extend this formula down to F7.

6. In G5 we will determine the price of the risk-free bond with the "PRICE()" function. This function is set up to automatically calculate the price of a fixed-rate bond given its yield, coupon payments and frequency, and maturity. Enter "=PRICE($C$15,B5,D5,F5,100,$C$13,0)" into G5 and extend this formula down to G7.

7. Now that we have all of the inputs, we will move to the core of the models calculations. In columns J we will enter the date: in J13 set the initial date to the settle date, and in J14 enter the formula "=IF(J13<(MAX($B$5:$B$10)),EDATE(J13,1),"")". This will create periods with one-month intervals, until the final period, and then cells will be blank after that in order to keep the sheet easily readable

In column K we will track which bond is the next to mature. We will start the formula in K14 (one row below where the formulas in column J start). We will enter the following formula:

$$=IF(J13="","",IF(J13<MIN(\$B\$5:\$B\$10),MIN(\$A\$5:\$A\$10),1$$

$$+MATCH(J13,\$B\$5:\$B\$10,1)))$$

This formula is looking at the date in the row above and seeing where that date falls compared to the maturities of the bonds. The reason that we need to look at the row above is that bond maturities may not fall right on a period end date. For example, a bond may mature on the first of the month, but the period may end on the 15th. In that case, we would consider the bond to be outstanding during the next period.

One other unusual part of this formula is the "MATCH()" command. Here we are using this command to find the bond maturity before the date in question (J13) by setting the match type to 1. Then we add 1 to it to look for the next bond.

8. After all this setup, we are almost ready to determine the PV of the recoveries in the case where there is a default. The last thing that we need is to determine the net payment by adding in the interest payments. This is similar to what we did in Model Builder 5.2, only this time we will have a number of payments to track and we don't want to dedicate so much space to the PV calculations. So we will write a user-defined function to do this for us.

We will use some of the Analysis Toolpak worksheet functions in this function, so we need to make sure that this add-in is installed. The functions that require the add-in are "COUPNUM()", which returns the number of coupon payments between a settlement date and a bond's maturity, "COUPNCD()", which returns the next payment date for a bond, and "YEARFRAC()", which returns the fraction of the year between two dates.

We will call our function "PVInterestPayments()", and we will begin by opening the VBA editor and entering the following:

```
Function PVInterestPayments(settleDate, measureDate, couponRate,
        maturity, couponFrq, spotDates, spotRates)
    'sums the PV of Interest Payments between settle Date and a
    measurement date
    Dim coupPayments() As Variant, paymentsPV As Double
    Dim j As Integer, numPayments As Integer, fstPayment As Variant
    numPayments = Application.WorksheetFunction.CoupNum(settleDate,
    maturity, couponFrq)-Application.WorksheetFunction.
    CoupNum(measureDate, maturity, couponFrq)
```

The calculation for numPayments is designed to give us the number of payments that have occurred between the settlement date and each period of possible default (the measureDate). This is how the program knows how many coupon payments to add into the recovery for each period. And we continue with the code:

```
If numPayments = 0 Then
    PVInterestPayments = 0
Else
    fstPayment = Application.WorksheetFunction.CoupNcd(settleDate,
    maturity, couponFrq)
    ReDim coupPayments(1 To numPayments, 4)

 'populate coupon payments table
    For j = 1 To numPayments
        coupPayments(j, 1) - Application.WorksheetFunction.
        EDate(fstPayment, (j-1) * (12 / couponFrq))
        coupPayments(j, 2) = interpRates(coupPayments(j, 1),
        spotDates, spotRates)
        coupPayments(j, 3) = (couponRate / couponFrq) * 100
```

```
        coupPayments(j, 4) = Application.WorksheetFunction.YearFrac
        (settleDate, coupPayments(j, 1))
    Next j
```

The coupPayments () array accounts for each payment of coupon, starting with the first payment, fstPayment. In column 1 we figure out the date of each coupon payment, in column 2 we use the interpRates() function we wrote in step 4 to get the correct discount rate for each payment, in column 3 we calculate the actual nominal payments, and in column 4 we calculate the time period between the settlement and the coupon payment, so we can discount correctly, which we do in the final steps.

```
'calculate and sum PV of payments
   For j = 1 To numPayments
       paymentsPV = paymentsPV + coupPayments(j, 3) / ((1 +
       coupPayments(j, 2)) ^ coupPayments(j, 4))
       Next j

   PVInterestPayments = paymentsPV

   End If
End Function
```

9. Now we can calculate the present value of any recovery payment. In L14 enter the following:

$$=IF(K14>1,"",((100*\$C\$14)/((1+interpRates(J14,\$C\$19:\$C\$25,$$

$$\$D\$19:\$D\$25))^\wedge(DAYS360(\$J\$13,J14)/360)))+PVInterestPayments$$

$$(\$C\$15,MIN(J14,\$B\$5-1),\$D\$5,\$B\$5,\$C\$13,\$C\$19:$$

$$\$C\$25,\$D\$19:\$D\$25))$$

In this formula we are taking the recovery on $100 of bonds and adding the PV of Interest Payments. Notice in the PVInterestPayments we actually need to use a payment date of "MIN(J14,$B$5–1)". We do this because the Analysis Toolpak functions do not recognize that the bond can default on its maturity date. This tweak technically will throw our calculations slightly off, but they speed up implementation substantially.

Once this formula is entered, extend it down. If you have set this up correctly, you should see the recovery value decreasing slowly (due to discounting) with jumps where interest payments are received.

10. Now that we have our first bond's recovery rates, we are ready to determine the probability of default. Up in H5, enter the following formula:

$$=(G5-C5)/((G5*COUNTIF(\$K\$14:\$K\$149,A5)-SUM(\$L\$14:\$L\$149)))$$

Can you see the similarity to equation 5.10? This is our implementation of that equation. We use the "COUNTIF()" function to make sure we are only counting periods that apply to this bond.

11. Now that we have our first bond's default probability, we need to account for it when we look at the next bonds we are using to create default probabilities. In Column M we will track the default probability during the life of bond 1. This is admittedly very simple, but it will become more complex as we move on. In M14 enter "=IF(K14>1,"",$H$5)"

12. In Column N we will begin the same process for Bond 2. In N14 enter the equivalent to L14, only for bond 2.

$$=IF(K14>2,"",((100*\$C\$14)/((1+interpRates(J14,\$C\$19:\$C\$25,$$

$$\$D\$19:\$D\$25))^\wedge (DAYS360(\$J\$13,J14)/360))) + PVInterestPayments$$

$$(\$C\$15,MIN(J14,\$B\$6-1),\$D\$6,\$B\$6,\$C\$13,\$C\$19:\$C\$25,$$

$$\$D\$19:\$D\$25))$$

13. Again, we are ready to calculate the periodic default probability. We could enter a formula in H6 that is similar to the formula in H5 and get an even probability of default. However, we do not want to lose the information we have gained from the shorter bond. So we will subtract out the loss probability that is accounted for by the previous bond and distribute it only on periods where the second bond is the proximate bond to defaults.

$$=(G6-C6-SUMPRODUCT(\$M\$14:\$M\$149,\$N\$14:\$N\$149))/$$

$$((G6*COUNTIF(\$K\$14:\$K\$149,A6))-SUMIF(\$K\$14:\$K\$149,$$

$$A6,\$N\$14:\$N\$149))$$

14. Now that we have the periodic probability of default for the second bond, we will make columns O and P in a similar way to columns M and N. In O15 we will enter "=IF(K14>2,"",INDEX($H$5:$H$8,K14))" and in P15 we will enter

$$= IF(K14>3,"",((100*\$C\$14)/((1+interpRates(J14,\$C\$19:\$C\$25,$$

$$\$D\$19:\$D\$25))^\wedge(DAYS360(\$J\$13,J14)/360)))+PVInterestPayments$$

$$(\$C\$15,MIN(J14,\$B\$7-1),\$D\$7,\$B\$7,\$C\$13,\$C\$19:\$C\$25,$$

$$\$D\$19:\$D\$25)).$$

Extend both of these formulas down.

15. Finally, we are ready to enter the periodic default probability for the periods before bond 3's maturity. In H7 enter the following:

$$= (G7-C7-SUMPRODUCT(\$O\$14:\$O\$149,\$P\$14:\$P\$149))/$$

$$((G7*COUNTIF(\$K\$14:\$K\$149,A7))-SUMIF(\$K\$14:\$K\$149,$$

$$A7,\$P\$14:\$P\$149))$$

This is very similar to the formula in H6. As there are additional bonds to account for, there is the ability to extend this model as needed. See Figure 5.8.

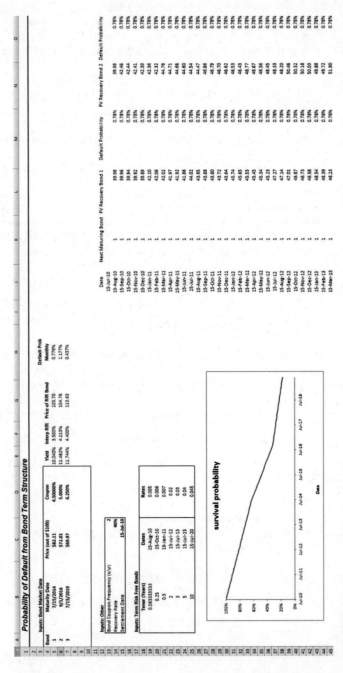

FIGURE 5.8 The completed Model Builder 5.3, with a graph showing survival probability over time. The version with this graph is available on the website and the CD for this text.

RECOVERY ASSUMPTIONS

One major factor that is often glossed over in texts on modeling is where recovery assumptions come from. Recovery assumption can have a tremendous impact on the implied default rate that an analyst may get from the market. An analyst assuming a 60–70 percent recovery may believe that the default likelihood is many times larger than an analyst using a similar model but assuming no recovery.

As defaults and credit events generally end up in court, there is considerable uncertainty as to what an accurate recovery would be if a company defaults. Despite this, practitioners often look to historical defaults in order to get a feel for what an appropriate rate might be. One good source for historical data is provided by www.creditfixings.com, which posts historical CDS credit event auction results. However, due to the wide variance of recoveries (from over 96 percent to less than 1 percent), it is important to understand how similar the debt being modeled is to the debt of the companies that may be used as a comparison.

Generally, four major variables are commonly used in performing a recovery or "loss given default" (LGD) analysis: the seniority of the debt, the industry of the company, the ratio of assets to liabilities, and the state of the overall economy.

The seniority of the debt is generally the most important factor. Whether the bond is senior or subordinate, and how much senior and subordinate debt is outstanding, is crucial to a recovery assumption. Whether the loan is secured or not can be a major determinate as well. One assumption that is commonly used is that senior loans have recoveries of 40 percent while subordinates have recoveries of 15 or 20 percent. Extremely subordinated debt, such as debentures or trust preferred securities, often are assumed to have a recovery of zero. One method to get market opinions of relative recoveries is by looking at whether the company has both senior and subordinate debt, and assuming that they both have the same default probability (this isn't always the case but is often true). The gap in recovery that accounts for the pricing differential can be obtained by using solver or simple algebra. This will only give information on the relative recovery of the two securities and not the absolute recovery rate.

The industry of the company is also important. Generally, banks and other financial companies are assumed to have lower recoveries, since they often are taken over by governments that insure depositors or policy holders to the detriment of the creditors. Large industrial or consumer goods companies with lots of hard assets to support the debt often have higher recoveries.

Knowing a company's industry also gives guidance about a company's ratio of assets to liabilities. Generally, companies in the same industry have similar capital structures, which can give guidance on what recoveries can be expected. Additionally, information from our work with structural models can come in handy here. The general assumption is that the knock-out barrier is hit when the value of the assets reaches the sum of the short-term liabilities and one-half of the long-term liabilities. Setting this (minus some workout expenses) as the total recovery amount is consistent with a structural analysis.

Finally, the state of the economy is recognized as being a very important contributor to the recovery rates. Bonds that default during economic downturns as a whole can be expected to produce lower recoveries than defaults while the economy is performing well. As a result, some modelers include "state variables," which account for the state of the economy and alter the recoveries that can be expected in different economic climates. These state variables can be constructed either as a continuous process or as a discrete "regime-change" variable (i.e., economic expansion/contraction).

Simulation Setup

While in many cases the market's default probability is all that is needed for an analysis, there are still situations when a full model is necessary. Where the decision has been made to use a reduced form model, implementation of the default probability into a model is relatively straightforward and differs mostly based on how recovery rate is modeled and what output is required. The most common reason for creating a simulation is the desire to understand how a portfolio of credits would be expected to perform. Simulation allows us to consider not only the riskiness of the assets in a pool, but also the impact of the correlation between these assets.

Another reason to simulate asset performance is that simulations allow us to relax some assumptions that go into building default probabilities. For example, in a structural model, the assumption that returns on assets follow a normal distribution can be relaxed (e.g., other distributions that match historical price movements or ones with fat tails could be used). While it is not internally consistent, it does allow the analyst some ability to respond to requests for fat-tailed distribution analysis or other types of analysis that are less dependent on normal distribution assumptions.

Accounting for Liquidity

While so far we have assumed that the entirety of the spread over the risk-free bond is due to the risk of loss due to a default, there is ample evidence that bond prices include other factors as well. Markets are not truly efficient, and transaction costs, regulatory requirements, and restrictions on capital movements across borders all impact the relative pricing of bonds, as do a number of other factors. The most important of these factors is liquidity, and as a result researchers into quantitative finance often group all the non-credit-related factors in a bond's pricing under the label of liquidity.

Empirically, spreads have proven to be wide of where the risk-neutral default probability would indicate. To say this in another way, bonds default less often than they should, given where they price. This persistent discrepancy has generally been ascribed to liquidity in the research, specifically to the worry that liquidity for securities may disappear at a time when cash is desperately needed. Such a liquidity crunch has been observed in the market on a number of occasions, in particular during late 2008, when even debt securities issued by high-quality nonfinancial companies such as Pfizer saw precipitous drops in value despite little exposure to the credit events that were occurring.

Since the relationship between price and default rate is different in the two types of models that we have discussed in this chapter, liquidity adjustments will have opposite impacts. In structural models, we use accounting information and historical equity volatility to estimate a default probability (and hence, a price). However, since prices reflect risks above and beyond credit risk, structural models tend to underestimate price, so typically a liquidity adjustment needs to be added to the spread that the model predicts. Reduced form models, on the other hand, start with market pricing and are used to compute default probability from there. Since market spreads are wide of the observed loss rates, our default probabilities will be too high unless we subtract out a liquidity component.

SOVEREIGNS AND MUNICIPALS: NONCORPORATE ISSUERS

Finally, let's discuss modeling default risk from government issuers. While corporate credit modeling is primarily predicated on measuring a borrower's *ability* to pay, the key variable in most government credit analysis is measuring a government's *willingness* to pay back its creditors. Quantitative analysts do not have a particularly enviable record of predicting and modeling sovereign risk. The default by Russia in 1998 was widely considered the catalyst for the collapse of Long Term Capital Management (LTCM), one of the most prominent quantitative hedge funds of that decade. The fund included Myron Scholes and Robert Merton (of Black-Scholes fame) on its board.

The primary distinction that is usually made for these types of issuers is whether the issuer has, or is supported by an actor that has, the power to print the currency that they are borrowing in. Sovereigns that borrow in their national currency (the United States, England, and Japan, for example) are considered very unlikely to actually default, as they have the ability to print money to meet their obligations. Sovereigns that do not have the ability to print the currencies that their debt is denominated in (countries in the Euro area and smaller countries that issue in U.S. dollars such as Grenada or Ecuador) are at much higher risk of default, and in some ways their situation is more akin to a state or city than it is to larger issuers.

While there have been attempts to apply the structural model to sovereign debt, reduced form models are used much more frequently. As with corporate borrows, the likelihood of default and the loss given default both need to be estimated. According to data published by Moody's, over the 25 years between 1983 and 2007, the issuer-weighted recovery rates on defaulted sovereign bonds has averaged 54 percent. However, there has been considerable variability, with observed recoveries ranging from 18 percent to 95 percent of the par value of the bonds. Standard and Poor's publishes recovery ratings that are based roughly on a structural debt concept and the assumption that post-default, the value of the restructured debt will put the country's debt/GDP ratio (and other ratios) in line with solvent peers.

Subnational municipal debt offers similar problems, but with added questions of disclosure. Smaller issuers often fall behind on providing information to investors. As of 2011, there were a number of questions about the solvency of cities and states in the United States, and additional research on the risks to investors in this market is being produced.

FROM ASSETS TO POOLS

In this chapter we covered a number of methods to estimate credit risk from both information about a company's balance sheet and from market data. The models that we have built are complex, but it is important to remember that they are simple representations of much more complex entities. While these will help us to see which companies are likely to be good credits and which companies are riskier, qualitative measures that may not show up in historical numbers, such as changes in management or the development of disruptive technologies, can have major implications on the survival of a company.

It is important to remember this as we move to Chapter 6, where we will take a step further away from the fundamental credit of each company to look at simulating pools of assets. Here we will be taking the outputs from this chapter (the probability of a company defaulting or the probability that asset values drop below a certain threshold) and using it to evaluate portfolios of hundreds or even thousands of investments.

Simulating Pools of Assets

Observing relationships among asset prices and then using these relationships to forecast future prices is at the heart of simulation modeling. Generally, investors hope to do in-depth research and analysis on each investment they make and on the risks associated with the idiosyncrasies of each asset. However, as portfolios grow, such analysis is often impractical or even impossible. Certain asset-backed securities, for example, are made up of tens of thousands of loans, each one in an amount of less than $10,000.

In situations involving too many assets for individual analysis, the typical methods of analysis are to implement a simulation of either price movement or of defaults. Typically, "Monte Carlo" simulations are used for this type of analysis. Although we covered Monte Carlo–style simulations previously in this text, they will be at the center of this chapter, and so a quick background on this important method may be helpful.

Monte Carlo simulations were first developed during World War II as part of the Manhattan Project. They take their name from a famous casino located in Monaco. They were named as such not because they were developed for gambling, but because they reminded their creators of the draws in card games, and so a gaming name was chosen to convey their probabilistic nature.

To this day we use similar terminology. These simulations involve repeated random "draws" from a defined set of possible values, so-called because you can think of the number being selected as being analogous to drawing from a deck of playing cards. As with playing cards, you can calculate your probability of selecting a number, but you do not know what card or value you are going to get until it is actually pulled out (or in the case of simulations, generated). This set of characteristics represents both the greatest strength and greatest weakness for these simulations.

The strength of these simulations is that they allow us to calculate the impact of thousands or even millions of combinations of price movements or defaults. Since we cannot know the price movements of the market before they happen, Monte Carlo simulations allow us to obtain reasonable projections of how likely different price movements are and to estimate portfolio characteristics accordingly. An analyst can design a portfolio based on the anticipated correlation in price movement between different assets to minimize downside risk, just like the way a card player can decide whether to draw a card or not based on the odds of winning a hand.

The major weakness of these simulations is that the *probability* of price movements in the future cannot be known with certainty. A card player can calculate with certainty the probability of drawing the nine of diamonds from a full deck, and this probability will be true at all times, assuming that the deck is full. However, we cannot calculate with certainty the probability that any asset will experience a nine-percent drop in value in a day; we can only estimate that probability based on historical price movements. Furthermore, the probability of a drop in asset value is likely to change over time; there is no guarantee that the future will look like the past, or that prices will behave in the future the way they have in the past. We cover more about the weaknesses of simulation modeling and the "Ludic fallacy" in Chapter 8.

While we need to be aware of these deficiencies, the value of simulating pools of assets can be a valuable tool in the process of portfolio design and risk assessment, as well as being required under certain regulatory regimes. Correlation, which we covered in Chapter 3, is a key variable in simulating pools of assets, but it is not the only variable that we will need to consider.

DIFFERENCES BETWEEN PROJECTING DEFAULTS AND PRICE MOVEMENTS

While there are many applications of Monte Carlo simulations, the two most frequently used are for measuring defaults and price movements. While equivalences can be drawn between values and defaults (such as in the Merton Model), we still need to account for the fact that default is a binary situation, whereas price can theoretically move to infinitely different levels. In order to account for this difference for Asset A in period i, we will start with the random draw variable R. In this construct, the movement of asset price (in a price simulation) will be produced as a function of the randomly drawn variable as in equation 6.1:

$$A_i = f(R_i, \mu) \times A_{i-1} \qquad (6.1)$$

In this, we can see that the change in price of the asset is based on a percentage of the price in the previous period. The function $f(R_i)$ is defined by mapping the randomly drawn number to a price movement. In many cases, a drift term, μ, will be added to this movement. However, for default simulations, we can use a number of methodologies. A very-in-depth simulation might use structural models for each asset, and as a result default is created by asset movements considering the capital structure of each company. However, for reduced form models, the forecasting is much simpler. We have a probability of default for each period D. We will simply draw a uniformly distributed random number R, and if R is less than the probability of default D, we consider the asset to default. In equation 6.2 we will create a proxy variable, P, which will be 0 until an asset defaults, in which case $P = 1$.

$$
\text{No Default}_i \Leftrightarrow R_i > D \Leftrightarrow P = 0
$$
$$
\text{Default}_i \Leftrightarrow R_i \leq D \Leftrightarrow P = 1
$$
$$(6.2)$$

As we learned in Chapter 3, our random draws R are often correlated. So when we create our simulation, we will account for this by splitting our random draw R into a correlated portion and a noncorrelated portion. We built a basic version of a default model in Chapter 3 as well, so we will primarily focus on price models in this chapter.

MODEL BUILDER 6.1: Creating a Price Movement Simulation for a Single Asset

Before we create a simulation for a pool of assets, in Model Builder 6.1 we will do a quick single asset price simulation to refresh the concepts necessary for a price simulation.

1. Create a new workbook and name it MB_6.1_User. While we have provided versions of each Model Builder, we believe that to understand the material it is best for readers to use these as guides off of which they will build their own models. A complete version can be found on the website, with all of the proxy data we will be referencing here. Keep in mind that for the following Model Builders the completed versions are in multiple sheets in one workbook, while for user clarity the instructions indicate creating multiple workbooks. For each workbook, make sure to copy over or insert any user-defined functions that are indicated in the Model Builder; otherwise you may get a calculation error.

2. In C4 enter the initial price for the asset (we will use 100); in C5:C6 enter the annual volatility and the annual drift for the asset. Volatility is generally either determined by historical asset volatility or by forward-looking market measures like option price information. In our example, we will use an estimate of 30 percent annual volatility and 6 percent annual drift.

3. We need to adjust these numbers into periodic (daily) volatility. In C8 we will adjust the volatility by entering "=C5/SQRT(252)". We use 252 because it is commonly considered the number of trading days in the year. In C9 we will take the daily drift, which is simply "=C6/252".

4. In C12:C212 we will create a counter column to track the number of periods and the price movement in each period. Enter the beginning of the natural number sequence (0,1,2 ...) and then select the numbers and drag them down to C212.

5. In D13:D212 we enter "=NORMSINV(RAND())". This gives us a random sampling of a normal distribution. Making the assumption of the normality of returns is an important decision; other ways to construct a simulation will be discussed in the VaR section in this chapter and later in this book.

6. Finally, we will create the prices for each period based on the prior formulas. In E12 enter "=C4" to get the initial price. Below this, in E13, enter "=E12*(1+$C$9+($C$8*D13))", which incorporates the previous price, the volatility, the drift, and the draw into creating the new price.

7. We can create a table that will show the path of the prices by going to the Insert tab on the Excel command ribbon and selecting a line chart or a scatter chart. In general, we will not walk

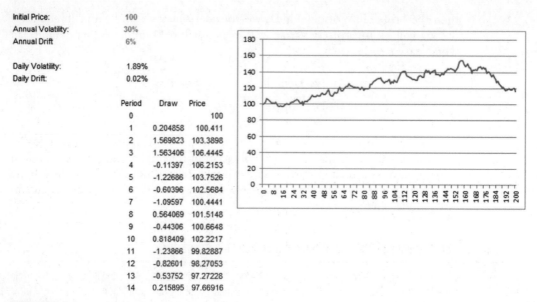

Initial Price:	100
Annual Volatility:	30%
Annual Drift	6%
Daily Volatility:	1.89%
Daily Drift:	0.02%

Period	Draw	Price
0		100
1	0.204858	100.411
2	1.569823	103.3898
3	1.563406	106.4445
4	-0.11397	106.2153
5	-1.22686	103.7526
6	-0.60396	102.5684
7	-1.09597	100.4441
8	0.564069	101.5148
9	-0.44306	100.6648
10	0.818409	102.2217
11	-1.23866	99.82887
12	-0.82601	98.27053
13	-0.53752	97.27228
14	0.215895	97.66916

FIGURE 6.1   Simulated asset prices with drift.

through the creation of these charts as they are not crucial for the creation of the model. Now we have completed a simple single-asset price simulator. See Figure 6.1.

If you are able to create the graph, iterate the path of the asset values a few times by pressing the F9 or Enter key. You can see that the scenarios created have a lot of variability. Play around with different drifts and volatilities to get a sense of what these numbers mean for the different scenarios that are generated.

MODEL BUILDER 6.2: Creating a Price Movement Simulation for a Pool of Assets

Drawing together methods that we used earlier in this book, we can begin to create a model of how we would expect defaults to occur in a portfolio of assets. We will build Model Builder 6.2 with a portfolio of five assets, but the process can be expanded to more assets.

1. Create a new workbook and name it MB_6.2_User. In C4:G6, we will enter price, volatility, and drift information for each asset. A complete version of this Model Builder can be found on the website.
2. In C13:G17, we will create a correlation matrix that will govern the correlation in price movements between each asset. Remember that the correlation is in asset price movements, not in asset prices. For risk-analysis purposes, practitioners may stress correlation by increasing the correlation levels above what is actually expected. In a long-only portfolio this will increase the value at risk for any confidence level.
3. In C20:G24 we will decompose the correlation matrix using the Cholesky decomposition function, which we first used in Chapter 3. For convenience (so we can use matrix multiplication later on when multiplying a row instead of a column), we will transpose the Cholesky matrix using a new transposeMatrix function:

```
Function transposeMatrix(inputMatrix As Range)

Dim cholMatrix, outMatrix() As Double
Dim matRows, matCols, rCount, cCount As Integer

cholMatrix = inputMatrix
matRows = inputMatrix.Rows.Count
matCols = inputMatrix.Columns.Count

ReDim outMatrix(1 To matRows, 1 To matCols)
For rCount = 1 To matRows
    For cCount = 1 To matCols
outMatrix(cCount, rCount) = inputMatrix(rCount, cCount)
    Next cCount
Next rCount

transposeMatrix = outMatrix

End Function
```

In order to use this array function, we will select an area equal in size to the Cholesky matrix (I20:M24). In the cell that is the upper left corner of the matrix (in this case I20) enter the formula "=transposeMatrix($C$20:$G$24)", and hold down Control and Shift and hit the Enter key. As you can see, the output is the Cholesky matrix immediately to the left, only inverted.

4. In 28, enter "=NORMSINV(RAND())" to get the normal distribution for our draws, which we will use to determine future price movements. Drag this to fill C28:G77. See Figure 6.2.

5. Now we will create the correlated variables by using matrix multiplication to recompose a string of price movements that have correlations that match our inputs. We will set this up in such a way that we can extend this matrix down for the number of periods that we want to forecast price movements. We will multiply the transposed Cholesky matrix by the random draws in each period. In H31 enter =MMULT($C28:$G28,I$20:I$24)". This number will be equal to the value in C28, since the first column of the transposed Cholesky matrix has a "1" in the first row and "0" in all other cells.

6. Extend this formula to the range I28:M77. This will give the values for matrix multiplication across a number of draws. In J28, for example, the value is determined by the equivalent of the formula "=C28*J20+D28*J21+0+0+0". You can test this by entering this formula into any open cell.

7. Now that we have the correlated draws complete, we can input what this actually means for the prices of the assets. First, we'll input the initial price for period 0. In O27 enter "=C4" and drag this across to S27. Below this, in O28, enter =O27*(1+C$9+(I28*C$8))", which is the formula we entered before, and drag this across to column S, and down to row 77. See Figure 6.3.

Now we have created a set of asset values that retain their correlation in the future. We have inserted a graph that tracks the asset movements. Again, if you are able to insert a graph to see how the asset prices move, as you refresh the worksheet you will get a sense of the outcomes that are possible using this setup.

Pooled Price Movements

	Asset 1	Asset 2	Asset 3	Asset 4	Asset 5
Initial Price:	100	100	100	100	100
Annual Volatility:	30%	100%	40%	25%	15%
Annual Drift	6%	2%	1%	7%	-3%
Daily Volatility:	1.89%	6.30%	2.52%	1.57%	0.94%
Daily Drift:	0.02%	0.01%	0.00%	0.03%	-0.01%

Correlation

	Asset 1	Asset 2	Asset 3	Asset 4	Asset 5
Asset 1	1	0.2	0.2	0.35	-0.1
Asset 2	0.2	1	0.15	0.22	-0.2
Asset 3	0.2	0.15	1	0.08	-0.1
Asset 4	0.35	0.22	0.08	1	-0.4
Asset 5	-0.1	-0.2	-0.1	-0.4	1

Cholesky {=Cholesky(C13:G17)}

1.00	-	-	-	-
0.20	0.98	-	-	-
0.20	0.11	0.97	-	-
0.35	0.15	(0.01)	0.92	-
(0.10)	(0.18)	(0.06)	(0.37)	0.91

Inverted Cholesky {=transposeMatrix(C20:G24)}

1	0.2	0.2	0.35	-0.1
0	0.979796	0.112268	0.153093	-0.18371
0	0	0.973343	-0.00738	-0.061
0	0	0	0.924126	-0.36502
0	0	0	0	0.905145

Random Variables

0	=NORMSINV(RAND())				
1	0.493215	-1.38982	0.429112	-0.65	1.07152429
2	-0.4447	-0.69824	0.336947	-0.82	0.11689946
3	-0.68289	0.293812	-0.18497	-0.132	0.03101329

FIGURE 6.2 Model Builder 6.2 after step 4. Market assumptions are on top, followed by correlation assumptions, the Cholesky decomposition matrix, and the random draws.

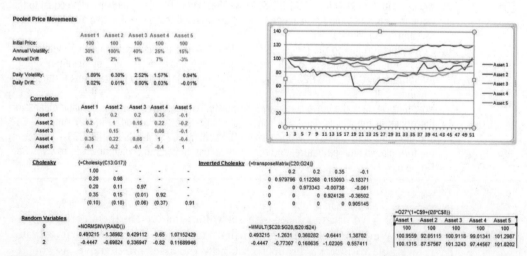

FIGURE 6.3 Model Builder 6.2 with a graph showing asset price movements.

VALUE AT RISK (VAR)

Price forecasting has a major role in risk management. There are a number of methods that portfolio managers and regulators will use in order to track the risk a portfolio runs due to sudden market movements. One method is scenario modeling, in which managers will use a specific scenario, either imagined or from the past (such as the credit crunch in 2008 or the oil shocks of the 1970s) and estimate what the impact on their portfolio would be in such a case. This is typically used to track response to certain exogenous events, but doesn't give much information about how the portfolio is likely to perform during most days or months. For this, a set of stochastic processes often referred to as "value at risk," or VaR, are often employed.

VaR is an estimation, over a certain time horizon and at a certain probability level, of what the minimum mark-to-market losses portfolio would be. A daily, 99 percent VaR of $1 million means that a portfolio manager would expect to have a 1 percent chance of losing $1 million or more in a day. It is important to notice that this does not say that in the worst 1 percent of performance that a portfolio will lose only $1 million. VaR is not a worst-case-scenario measure.

While there are an endless number of variations of how VaR can be calculated, a few conventions are generally followed in its reporting. Generally 95 percent VaR and 99 percent VaR are reported: what a portfolio's returns would be expected to exceed 19 out of 20 and 99 out of 100 times, respectively. VaR is generally calculated on a daily or monthly level. These calculations are done similarly to price and default forecasting: the correlation between different assets and their respective volatility are taken into account, and a number of scenarios are run via a Monte Carlo simulation and then evaluated. See Figure 6.4.

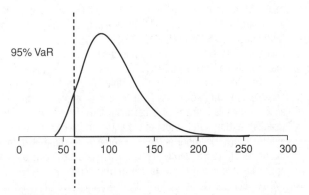

FIGURE 6.4 The dotted line represents the 95 percent VaR point. In 5 percent of scenarios, the asset value is below 65. Value at risk gives information about the loss expected at a certain probability level, but it does not give information about the worst-case loss for the portfolio.

The major differences between VaR calculations are in how the distribution of asset movements is calculated. Prices can be estimated as having movements that are normal or they can be forecast using nonnormal distributions, such as a lognormal distribution.

We will create a basic VaR calculation using one asset and assuming a normal distribution

MODEL BUILDER 6.3: Creating a Value at Risk Model

1. Create a new workbook and save it as MB_6.3_User. Again, a completed Model Builder is available on the website. We recommend that you have this model for reference and use the proxy data that is contained in the complete model. In B3:B6, insert the following labels for inputs:

> B3: "Asset Price"
> B4: "Daily Volatility"
> B5: "Confidence"
> B6: "Asset Drift"

In C3:C6, enter the values to use for the calculation: in this model we will use an asset price of 100, volatility of 25 percent (extremely high but we are using this for explanation purposes only) a confidence of 95 percent and a drift of 1 percent. Daily volatility can be taken either from historic volatility or from option implied forward volatility (often abbreviated to forward "vol"). "Confidence" is the probability level at which we want to calculate VaR, traditionally 95 percent or 99 percent. Asset Drift is the expected return on the asset; for most short-term applications it can be set to zero.

2. In B7, enter the label "Price at Confidence Level". Since we are assuming a normal distribution, the price that the asset will approach at the confidence level we are interested in can be calculated using the inverse normal function: "=NORMINV((1-B22),$C$3*(1+$C$6),($C$4*$C$3))".

3. Finally, to calculate VaR, we will find the difference between the current price and the price at the confidence level, "=C3-C7".

One basic criticism of this simple construct is that normal distributions are an unreasonable estimation of possible asset prices, since in reality the price cannot go negative. To account for this, we will also calculate VaR assuming that the asset values follow a lognormal distribution. While most of the equations necessary for our analysis are available in Excel automatically, it is important to have some understanding of this distribution. Lognormal distributions are used frequently in quantitative finance because if we assume that price movements are independent and follow the form of a geometric Brownian motion, we can prove that we will expect prices to be lognormally distributed. We will not prove this in the text, but interested readers are encouraged to read further. Basic lognormal probability distributions are described by equation 6.3:

$$ f(x, \sigma, \mu) = \frac{1}{x\sigma\sqrt{2\Pi}} e^{\frac{-(\ln x - \mu)^2}{2\sigma^2}} \tag{6.3} $$

In this formula, μ is the mean value (the current or expected value of the asset), x is the value after the movement, and σ is the standard deviation of the distribution's logarithm (the standard deviation of the asset price).

Unfortunately, there is no way to directly calculate the probability density function (pdf) for a lognormal distribution in Excel. However, using algebra we can rearrange to produce equation 6.4:

$$f(x, \sigma, \mu) = \frac{1}{x} \times \frac{1}{\sigma\sqrt{2\Pi}} e^{\frac{-(\ln x - \mu)^2}{2\sigma^2}} \tag{6.4}$$

This is the $(1/x)$ multiplied by the pdf of a normal distribution of the variable $\ln(x)$, which we can calculate in Excel automatically. While we will not exploit this fact in these calculations, we use this to create a graphical representation of the lognormal distribution in the spreadsheet.

4. Fortunately for us, there is an inverse lognormal function, called LOGINV, which is equivalent to the NORMINV function. In G7 enter the formula "=LOGINV(B22,LN($C$3*(1+$C$6)),$C$4)" to get the price at our confidence level assuming a lognormal distribution.
5. Finally, to calculate VaR in G9 we will find the difference between the current price and the price at the confidence level, "=C3-G7". See Figure 6.5.
6. In this model, it is helpful to view the distributions by graphing the distribution and marking where the VaR component is. Since this text is focused on simulation, we will not go through the process of building the graph, but the results can be seen in the completed model. Use an X-Y scatter plot when creating the graph.

While the lognormal distribution is considered to be a much better reflection of reality than the normal distribution, some analysts would rather not depend on a regular distribution

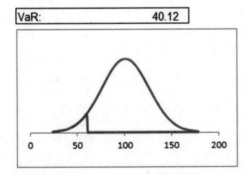

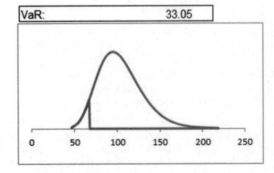

FIGURE 6.5 VaR calculated with normal and lognormal distributions.

concept at all. The "historical return" method for calculating VaR takes all historical daily returns and uses them as a basis for future projections of asset values.

7. In order to implement a historical return VaR, several years of price data is needed. We will take 30 years of IBM data for this example, pasted from J8 down. Note that this data is contained in the complete version on the website and ordered by newest date first.

8. Next to this we will calculate the daily returns. In K8 we will enter "=(J12-J13)/J13" and extend this formula down to K7596.

9. In K5 enter "=PERCENTILE(K12:K7596,1-C5)" to find the asset value change that is associated with the confidence level. We can transform this into a price in K7 by multiplying the current price by this value change. Enter "=C3*(1+K5)" into this cell. Finally, we calculate VaR in K9 with the formula "=C3-K7". Note we do not have a drift or volatility term in the historical VaR because the distribution characteristics are already captured in the historical returns of the asset.

VaR Calculations for Portfolios

Now that we have completed a simple VaR calculation for individual assets, we will do the same for portfolios. There are three general methods by which VaR is calculated: the historical method, the variance-covariance method, and the Monte Carlo method. The variance-covariance method is the fastest method, but as computing power has improved the need to emphasize speed has faded, while the need to account for nonnormal distributions and other idiosyncrasies has grown. We will cover the historical and Monte Carlo methods.

MODEL BUILDER 6.4: VaR Calculations Using the Historical Method

VaR calculated using the historical method is in many ways the simplest implementation, because the analyst does not have to choose any of the parameters, such as volatility, correlation, or drift. The only real decision that needs to be made is which time frame of historical values should be selected as the data set to use. In general, most applications use at least five years of data. Using more than this may be counterproductive, as the price movements of companies and the correlations between different assets may change over time. There is no hard and fast rule on the data set that should be used, but using price data from several economic cycles is generally encouraged.

1. To begin, create a new workbook and name it MB_6.4_User. Again, a completed Model Builder is available on the website. We have inserted proxy data in the complete version that can be used for this exercise. In your spreadsheet, start with inserting our portfolio (in our example, four assets, though it can be any number). In C6:F6, enter the names of four positions. In C7:F7, enter the number of units (shares, bonds, etc.) that make up the current portfolio.

2. Below these names, from row 9 on down, enter historical (proxy) prices. Be sure that the data accounts for any stock splits, as unadjusted numbers can artificially appear as huge losses! The data can be listed earliest-latest or latest-earliest; just be sure that the listings are consistent across all assets.

3. In H9, we will begin calculating what the historical daily profit or loss on the portfolio is. Enter "=(C9-C10)*C$7" into this cell, then extend to K9 and all the way down to your next-to-last row

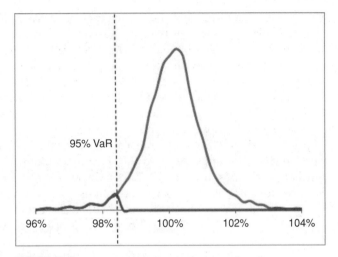

FIGURE 6.6 Historical VaR calculations often do not display normal curve characteristics. As concerns over normalcy assumptions mount, the historical VaR method becomes increasingly popular.

of price data (we cannot calculate the price data change on the first day of the data set because we don't know what the previous value was). Note that this is how the calculations are done for a one-day VaR calculation. For a two-day calculation, the formula would be "=(C9-C11)*C$7".

4. In M9, sum the total change in value for the portfolio by entering "=SUM(H9:K9)" and extending this down. In N9, we will calculate the initial value of the portfolio. For a one-day VaR calculation, we will multiply the previous day's value-per-unit with the number of units of each asset: "=SUMPRODUCT(C10:F10,$C$7:$F$7)". For a two-day VaR calculation, we would use C11:F11 instead of C10:F10.

5. Complete the calculation by calculating the percentage change in O9 as "=M9/N9" and extending this down. If we enter a confidence level of 95 percent in O2, the change in asset value at the confidence level is equal to the 5th percentile entry in our data set, which we can calculate by entering "=PERCENTILE(O9:O6554,1-O2)" into O3. The VaR is just this percentage applied to the current value of the portfolio. Calculate it as "=O3*SUMPRODUCT(C7:F7,C9:F9)" in O4. See Figure 6.6.

As you see, the main difficult with implementing a historical VaR model is in obtaining all the data that is needed. Finding and scrubbing data is the key to successfully using this method.

VaR Calculated Using Monte Carlo Simulation

Many VaR models are implemented using a Monte Carlo simulation instead of historical experience. The ability to simulate future asset price movements gives the analyst implementing the model a high degree of flexibility in estimating the potential losses a portfolio might take. However, the additional flexibility comes with the burden of making choices for each asset. Assigning a price distribution shape, a volatility, and a drift term are three choices that take important roles in the construction of the simulation. We also need to assign correlations between different asset price movements to capture the fact that asset prices are not totally independent from other assets. In Chapters 3 through 5 we covered many of the same issues with respect to debt modeling, and the same methods for estimating these variables can be used here.

Once we have values for correlation, volatility $[\sigma]$, drift $[\mu]$, and a distribution of price movements (we will assume a normal distribution for now), we can build our Monte Carlo simulation. We will generate random price movement R_i from a normal distribution using the "NORMSINV(RAND())" command combination we have used before. Then using a decomposed correlation matrix, we will weight the random draws so our price movements have a correlation that matches our inputs. Finally, we will calculate each period's price, using the formula

$$A_i = A_{i-1}(1 + \mu + \sigma R_i) \tag{6.5}$$

MODEL BUILDER 6.5: VaR Calculations Using Monte Carlo Simulation

Be sure to set the volatility and drift terms for the correct time intervals.

1. Create a workbook named MB_6.5_User. C6:F9 will have similar information to the same cells in 6.4. Row 6 has the asset's names, row 7 will have the number of units owned, and row 9 will have the most recent price for each asset. A completed Model Builder is available on the CD and the website. We have inserted proxy data that can be used for this exercise. Find the total value of the portfolio in H9 but entering "=SUMPRODUCT(C9:F9,C7:F7)". This Model Builder is very similar to 6.2, so if there is confusion it may be useful to review that Model Builder from earlier in the chapter.

2. In C16:F19, we will create a correlation matrix that will govern the correlation in price movements between each asset. Remember that the correlation is in asset price movements, not in asset prices. For risk-analysis purposes, practitioners may stress correlation by increasing the correlation levels above what is actually expected. In a long-only portfolio, this will increase the value at risk for any confidence level.

3. In C23:F26 we will decompose the correlation matrix using the Cholesky decomposition function, which we first used in Chapter 3. For convenience (so we can use matrix multiplication later on), we will transpose the Cholesky matrix using the invertMatrix function. In order to use this array function, we will select an area equal in size to the Cholesky matrix (H23:K26), enter the formula "=transposeMatrix($C$23:$F$26)", and hold down on Control+Shift and hit the 'Enter' key. As you can see, the output is the Cholesky matrix immediately to the left, only inverted.

4. We will initially create this model for a five-day (one trading week) VaR. In C31:F35, enter "=NORMSINV(RAND())". This will give us the normal distribution for our future price movements.

5. Now we will create the correlated variables by using matrix multiplication to recompose a string of price movements that have correlations that match our inputs in C16:F19. We will set this up in such a way that we can extend this matrix down for the number of periods that we

want to forecast VaR through. We will multiply the transposed Cholesky matrix by the random draws in each period. In H31 enter "=MMULT($C31:$F31,H$23:H$26)" and hold Control and Shift and hit the Enter key. This number will be equal to the value in C31, since the first column of the transposed Cholesky matrix has a "1" in the first row and "0" in all other cells, we are effectively entering the formula "=1*C31+0+0+0".

6. Extend this formula to the range H31:K35. This will give the values for matrix multiplication across a number of draws. In I31, for example, the value is determined by the equivalent of the formula "=C31*I23+D31*I24+0+0". You can test this by entering this formula into any open cell.

   Now that we have the correlated draws complete, we can input what this actually means for the prices of the assets. First, input the initial price for period 0 in N30 by entering "=C9" and then drag this across to Q30. Below this, in N31, enter "=N30*(1+($C$12+(H31*C$11)))", which is the formula 6.5. Copy and paste N31 over the range N31:Q35. Sum the total value of the portfolio in S31 with the formula "=SUMPRODUCT(N30:Q30,$C$7:$F$7)".

7. We're almost done setting this sheet up. Up in L8:L10, we will enter the number of iterations in L8 (enter 500, a very small sample), the time interval (in trading days) in L9, and we will show the final value of assets in L10 by entering "=OFFSET(S30,L9,0)".

8. Now that the sheet is set up, we will write a short macro to run through this sheet a number of times. The macro will first clear the area where the outputs are printed and read the number of iterations.

```
Sub iterateMC()

    Dim iterations As Integer, runNumber As Integer
    Range("U8:V50008").Clear

    Application.ScreenUpdating = False

    iterations = Range("L8")
```

Now that the macro is set to run, it loops through and determines asset values in the full set of simulation runs.

```
    For runNumber = 1 To iterations
        Calculate
        Range("V" &runNumber + 8) = Range("L10")
        Application.StatusBar = Int(runNumber /
        iterations * 100) & "%"
    Next runNumber
    Application.StatusBar = False
End Sub
```

9. When the macro runs, we can track the program's progress with the Application.StatusBar command. Once the number reaches 100 percent, the results of our runs will appear in column V. This code is clearly too slow. We probably need to run 20,000 iterations or more in order to get good results. We can work on speeding this process up by moving more of the calculations into VBA

10. Now that we have our distribution of potential outcomes, the VaR calculation is straightforward. In V2 enter the confidence level, and in V3 we can calculate the value of the assets at

this confidence level by entering "=PERCENTILE(V9:V50008,1-V2)". The VaR is this value subtracted from the initial value of the assets, "=H9-V3", which we can insert into V4.

Now we have a simple (though slow) Monte Carlo VaR model, which we can expand to a portfolio of up to hundreds of assets. When we cover some of the more advanced components of model building, we will optimize this model to run much more quickly.

Now that we are able to estimate the VaR for a portfolio of assets using Monte Carlo techniques, the next question is, "How accurate is this model?" At this point in our analysis we have to quantify the error in our predicted VaR value. Unlike the Hull-White tree model or the Black-Scholes solve, the error in this case is purely statistical. In a technical sense, systematic errors inherent in the model do exist and errors in the drift and volatility term can propagate into our final calculation; however, determining the contribution of these uncertainties would be extremely difficult. For our current application it would be much more efficient if we asked the question, given that we *know* our drift and volatility to be *correct* how certain can we predict the results with our model?

To answer this question, we must determine the mean and spread, or standard deviation, of the possible outputs of our model. The last Model Builder allowed the user to choose the number of iterations used to produce one VaR estimate. We can more robustly estimate the output by running the model, with the same number of iterations, N more times. We can take the mean and standard deviation of our N samples as our expected VaR estimate and its associated error. Notice that this process is analogous to the N-sided die example we built in Chapter 2 (Model Builder 2.6).

As a further reminder, we should note that if we decided to run 10 simulations with 100 iterations each, it is not the same as running one simulation with 1,000 iterations, or 5 simulations with 200 iterations. Increasing the iterations used will decrease the spread of the final result, and similarly increasing number of samples taken will get the overall mean closer to the actual mean of the distribution.

STRUCTURED PRODUCTS AND CDOS

Now that we have covered the basics of simulating general asset price pools, we will move to default analysis, in particular the structured finance world. The term *structured finance* covers a wide range of financial products that have been created to transfer risk differently than do traditional equity and fixed income investments. In general, structured products are created for one of three reasons: to provide/supply leverage, to allow investors to minimize exposure to regulatory or taxation rules, or to allow access to a particular type of risk while minimizing idiosyncratic or company-specific risks like a company's bankruptcy.

In the credit world, the most prominent classes of structured product are asset-backed securities. Asset-backed securities, or ABS, are debt and equity that

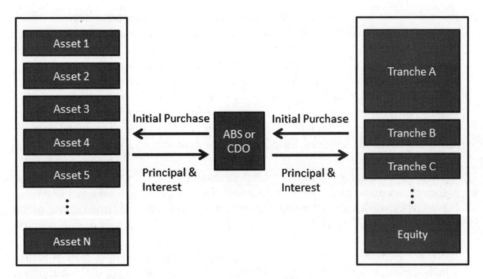

FIGURE 6.7 A generalized structure of CDO and ABS. Principal and interest payments are made by the assets in the CDO, then distributed to the holders of difference tranches according to a "waterfall."

are backed not by an operating company, but by a special-purpose entity whose sole assets are a portfolio of similar notes, such as trade receivables or auto loans (or in some cases the assets themselves, such as with airplanes).

One large set of structured products are collateralized debt obligations, or CDOs. CDOs, particularly ones that are backed by corporate loans, are usually considered separate from the rest of the ABS world, though they share many characteristics. Both ABS and CDO liabilities (bonds issued for different levels of debt often known as *tranches*) are supported by cash flow from the assets that are being held by a special purpose vehicle (SPV). The cash flow from these assets are assigned to the holders of different tranches through a "waterfall"; a priority of payments section spelled out in the documents that govern the working of the CDO or ABS. See Figure 6.7.

From the perspective of risk modeling, CDO and ABS bonds are modeled in different ways. For CDO bonds a simulation based on reduced-form models is typically used, whereas for ABS securities a transition matrix is the typical method to account for credit risk.

CDO and Corporate Basket Trade-Risk Analysis

CDOs can be structured in a number of ways, and different modeling approaches are required for these structures. The simplest CDOs are structures that obtain credit enhancement only from subordination. Typically, synthetic CDOs fit into this type of structure, as do the simplest cash CDOs. Structures such as "*N* to default" baskets, where an investor is buying incomplete protection on a pool of assets, is structurally similar as well and can be modeled in a similar way, though their portfolios are so small that they are often priced analytically instead.

CDO modeling applications are typically based on Monte Carlo simulations, which take into account the probability of each asset's default, the loss given a default (often abbreviated LGD), and the correlation between the different assets. Probability of default and LGD can be calculated in either a reduced form or structural method. Reduced form models are used more in practice due to their speed and tractability.

As a warning, the computational demands of a CDO or ABS model are higher than almost any other models used in finance. We will take steps to speed the analysis, making this model substantially more complex than most of the others in this text. We will create user-defined functions in order to minimize the complexity.

One user-defined function will be the Cholesky decomposition function, which we used previously. Two others will be creating a user-defined function that replaces the inverse of the standard normal cumulative distribution (NORM-SINV()) and a standardized pairwise correlation matrix.

MODEL BUILDER 6.6: CDO Monte Carlo Simulation

1. Create a new workbook named MB_6.6_User. Start building this sheet by inserting the inputs needed: the portfolio, the loan attributes, and the simulation/tranche information. Proxy data can be taken from the complete version on the website. In D3, enter a general correlation, which is a standardized correlation to be used between every pair of assets. We could instead use a pairwise correlation, specifying each correlation relationship, but in this example we will use a general number for simplicity.

2. In D4 enter the number of simulations we will run. (To start, keep the number fairly low, depending on the processing power of your computer. More than a few thousand runs may take a long time.) In D7 enter the number of tranches in the CDO that we are analyzing.

3. For a portfolio of 50 assets in our example, we will enter information about these assets in C9:E58. We will also enter the name of each asset in column B. In column C enter each asset's probability of default, in columns D the LGD, and in column E the size of the asset. Unfortunately, since we will be using a cumulative default probability later on, we cannot enter a 0 percent default probability, so if there are assets like cash with no risk, enter something sufficiently small such as .000000001 percent.

4. For a final set of inputs, we will enter the attachment points of tranches from G4 down and the detachment points from H4 down. The attachment and detachment points are the key structural components of a CDO or *n*-to-default basket. The position that takes the first loss has an attachment point of 0 percent. It has no subordination to absorb losses beneath it. A position with 3 percent subordination in a $100 million pool would start taking losses after the pool has lost $3 million. If the position has a detachment point (also known as an "exhaustion point") of

10 percent, it will have lost all of its value when the pool has taken $10 million of losses (10 percent of the pool).

5. Now that we have the key inputs, we will start building the rest of the spreadsheet around them. In D5, we will calculate the number of assets by entering "=COUNT(C9:C1000)", and in D6 we will sum the size of the pool of assets by entering "=SUM(E9:E1000)".

6. Restate the probabilities of default in terms of the cumulative default probability: in F9 enter "=NORMSINV(C9)" and drag this down to cover all the assets. We need to restate the percentages in terms of cumulative default probability for two reasons. One is that we need a random distribution with an average of zero so the decomposed correlation terms do not decrease default probabilities by pushing up the correlated draw summation. The other is that a bounded uniform distribution will give us results that do not make sense (such as probabilities above 100 percent or below 0 percent).

7. Next, we will create a correlation matrix in H9:BE58. While inserting a unique correlation for each pair of assets may give us more meaningful results, we may not have the data necessary for such a construction. So we will create a matrix based on a proxy pairwise correlation that we will apply to every pair of assets, except for each asset's correlation with itself. For a correlation of 25 percent, we will want a matrix of three assets' correlations in equation 6.6:

$$\rho = \begin{bmatrix} 1 & .25 & .25 \\ .25 & 1 & .25 \\ .25 & .25 & 1 \end{bmatrix} \tag{6.6}$$

In order to save time as we create this matrix, we will create the following user-defined function, pairwiseMat().

```
Function pairwiseMat(pairCorr As Range, numAssets As Range)

    Dim pCorr, pOutMatrix() As Double, p, q As Integer
    pCorr = pairCorr

    ReDim pOutMatrix(1 To numAssets, 1 To numAssets)
    For p = 1 To numAssets
        For q = 1 To numAssets
            If p = q Then
                pOutMatrix(p, q) = 1
            Else
                pOutMatrix(p, q) = pCorr
            End If
        Next q
    Next p
    pairwiseMat = pOutMatrix

End Function
```

To create the matrix, select the full area where the correlation matrix will be placed (H9:BE58). Enter "=pairwiseMat(D3,D5)", hold down Control and Shift and hit Enter. See Figure 6.8.

	A	B	C	D	E	F	G	H	I	J	K	L	M	N
1		CDO Monte Carlo												
2														
3		Pairwise Correlation:		20%			Attachment	Detachment	Prob Loss	average LGD				
4		# of Simulations:		1,000			0%	3%						
5		# of Assets:		50			3%	10%				Run CDO Monte Carlo		
6		Pool Size:		50,000,000			10%	40%						
7		Number of Tranches:		3										
8		Loan	Probability of Default	LGD	Position Size	Normsinv		**Correlation Matrix**						
9		Asset 1	5.00%	50%	1,000,000.00	-1.64		1	0.2	0.2	0.2	0.2	0.2	0.2
10		Asset 2	1.00%	50%	1,000,000.00	-2.33		0.2	1	0.2	0.2	0.2	0.2	0.2
11		Asset 3	4.30%	50%	1,000,000.00	-1.72		0.2	0.2	1	0.2	0.2	0.2	0.2
12		Asset 4	3.20%	50%	1,000,000.00	-1.85		0.2	0.2	0.2	1	0.2	0.2	0.2
13		Asset 5	1.00%	50%	1,000,000.00	-2.33		0.2	0.2	0.2	0.2	1	0.2	0.2
14		Asset 6	6.20%	50%	1,000,000.00	-1.54		0.2	0.2	0.2	0.2	0.2	1	0.2
15		Asset 7	1.20%	50%	1,000,000.00	-2.26		0.2	0.2	0.2	0.2	0.2	0.2	1
16		Asset 8	3.10%	50%	1,000,000.00	-1.87		0.2	0.2	0.2	0.2	0.2	0.2	0.2
17		Asset 9	2.30%	50%	1,000,000.00	-2.00		0.2	0.2	0.2	0.2	0.2	0.2	0.2
18		Asset 10	5.00%	50%	1,000,000.00	-1.64		0.2	0.2	0.2	0.2	0.2	0.2	0.2
19		Asset 11	4.90%	60%	1,000,000.00	-1.65		0.2	0.2	0.2	0.2	0.2	0.2	0.2
20		Asset 12	4.80%	60%	1,000,000.00	-1.66		0.2	0.2	0.2	0.2	0.2	0.2	0.2
21		Asset 13	2.40%	60%	1,000,000.00	-1.98		0.2	0.2	0.2	0.2	0.2	0.2	0.2
22		Asset 14	7.80%	60%	1,000,000.00	-1.42		0.2	0.2	0.2	0.2	0.2	0.2	0.2

FIGURE 6.8   Model Builder 6.6 after step 7.

8. Next, decompose the correlation matrix and create the Cholesky decomposition matrix (this function can be copied from previous Model Builders or from the complete one on the website). Select CB9:DY58 and enter "=Cholesky(H9:BE58)". Again, hold down Control and Shift and hit Enter. Now we have the decomposed matrix, similar to what appeared in Model Builder 6.5. For the simple 3 × 3 matrix we showed previously, the Cholesky matrix is shown in equation 6.7:

$$C = \begin{bmatrix} 1 & 0 & 0 \\ .25 & 0.97 & 0 \\ .25 & .19 & 1 \end{bmatrix} \qquad (6.7)$$

9. From here on out, we will be creating everything in code, with an eye toward maximizing the speed of the model. One key component to maximizing the speed will be to create our own 'NORMSINV' function, so we do not have to call the Excel function. Fortunately, available code is free of redistribution restrictions that match the Excel function (and the true distribution), so we can create a user-defined function. We have taken our function from one of the existing codes (with minor modifications for extreme values) and named it InverseCDF(). We recommend that you take the code in the complete model in the CD with this book and on the website, as derivation of this is far beyond the scope of this text.

10. Next, we will begin on the Monte Carlo code. We will try to follow good coding etiquette by defining our variables and reading all inputs first. We will place most of them into arrays due to the massive amounts of scenarios we will have to handle.

```
Sub monteCarloCDO()
    Dim pDefault(), assetSize(), LGD(), randMatrix(),
cholMatrix(), drawsMatrix(), fullOutput(), sumOutput() As Double
    Dim numSim, numAssets, counter1, counter2, counter3, counter4,
    numTranches As Long
```

```
      Dim corrDraw, attPoint, detPoint, poolSize, sumLosses,
      trancheProbLoss, trancheLGD As Double

      'Read sheet inputs
      numAssets = Range("D5")
      numSim = Range("D4")

   numTranches = Range("D7")
    poolSize = Range("D6")

    ReDim pDefault(1 To numAssets, 1)
    ReDim LGD(1 To numAssets, 1)
    ReDim assetSize(1 To numAssets, 1)
    ReDim cholMatrix(1 To numAssets, 1 To numAssets)

    For counter1 = 1 To numAssets
        For counter2 = 1 To numAssets
        cholMatrix(counter1, counter2) = Range("CA8").Offset(counter1,
        counter2)
        Next counter2
    Next counter1


    For counter1 = 1 To numAssets
        pDefault(counter1, 1) = Range("F" & 8 + counter1)
        LGD(counter1, 1) = Range("D" & 8 + counter1)
        assetSize(counter1, 1) = Range("E" & 8 + counter1)
    Next counter1
```

11. Now that we have read all inputs (save for the tranche attachment/detachment points), we will create all of the random numbers that we will use in the simulation. To make sure that the normal distribution is followed, we will use our "InverseCDF(Rnd())" command combination.

```
'create random number variables
ReDim randMatrix(1 To numAssets, 1 To numSim)
For counter1 = 1 To numAssets
    For counter2 = 1 To numSim
        randMatrix(counter1, counter2) = InverseCDF(Rnd())
    Next counter2
    Application.StatusBar = "Creating draws " & Int(100 * counter1 /
    numAssets) & "%"
Next counter1
```

12. Now we have reached the most complex part of the macro. We have one array full of random draws for each asset in each simulation. We also have an array that contains our Cholesky decomposition of the correlation matrix, which will govern the relationship between each asset's relative likelihood of defaulting. What we need to do now is to complete a very large

matrix multiplication, which will result in the correlated draws for each asset in each scenario. The multiplication is shown in equation 6.8.

$$\begin{bmatrix} 1 & 0 & 0 \\ .25 & 0.97 & 0 \\ .25 & .19 & 1 \end{bmatrix} \times \begin{bmatrix} -.67 & 1.00 & -1.99 & 0.08 & 0.17 \\ -0.01 & 0.07 & 1.02 & -1.98 & 0.15 \\ 1.30 & 0.51 & -0.77 & 1.91 & 0.98 \end{bmatrix}$$

Cholesky   Uncorrelated Draws

$$= \begin{bmatrix} -.67 & 1.00 & -1.99 & 0.08 & 0.17 \\ -0.18 & 0.32 & 0.49 & -1.90 & 0.19 \\ 1.13 & 0.77 & -1.07 & -2.27 & 1.05 \end{bmatrix}$$

$$(6.8)$$

Correlated Draws

Notice that the top row of the random draw and the correlated draw matrices are the same. This is the row for the first asset, where every column in the first row is multiplied by [1,0,0]. The later assets are "forced" to change by the decomposed correlation terms, which are now recomposed into sets of numbers that follow the correct correlation. The code for this is hard to follow, but keep this in mind as you look at it. We will also add in another Statusbar update to tell us where we are in the process.

```
'Create Correlated draws
ReDim drawsMatrix(1 To numAssets, 1 To numSim)
For counter1 = 1 To numAssets
    For counter2 = 1 To numSim
        corrDraw = 0
        For counter3 = 1 To numAssets
            corrDraw = corrDraw + randMatrix(counter3, couter2) *
cholMatrix(counter1, counter3)
        Next counter3
drawsMatrix(counter1, counter2) = corrDraw
    Next counter2
    Application.StatusBar = "Correlating Draws " & Int(100 *
    counter1 / numAssets) & "%"
Next counter1
```

13. Now we are ready to create the outputs. Our fullOutput() array will capture whether each asset defaults in each scenario. When it does, we will put the amount of loss (the asset size multiplied by the loss given default) in that cell; otherwise we will put 0.

```
'create outputs
ReDim fullOutput(1 To numAssets, 1 To numSim)
For counter1 = 1 To numAssets
    For counter2 = 1 To numSim
        If drawsMatrix(counter1, counter2) < pDefault(counter1, 1)
        Then
            fullOutput(counter1, counter2) = assetSize(counter1,
            1) * LGD(counter1, 1)
        Else
            fullOutput(counter1, counter2) = 0
        End If
```

```
        Next counter2
        Application.StatusBar = "Running Scenarios " &    Int(100 *
        counter1 / numAssets) & "%"
    Next counter1
```

14. Now that we are through the most difficult section, create a small array to sum up the losses in each scenario.

```
For counter1 = 1 To numSim
    sumLosses = 0
    For counter2 = 1 To numAssets
        sumLosses = sumLosses + fullOutput(counter2, counter1)
    Next counter2
    sumOutput(1, counter1) = sumLosses
Next counter1
```

15. Finally, we will create the tranche outputs and post them next to the tranche inputs. We will mark two outputs: the frequency with which a tranche takes a loss (how often losses are greater than the attachment point) and the LGD (which is the excess of loss over the attachment point divided by the size of the tranche, capped at 1). To finish we will turn off the Statusbar Updates.

```
For counter4 = 1 To numTranches
    attPoint = Range("G" & 3 + counter4) * poolSize
    detPoint = Range("H" & 3 + counter4) * poolSize
    trancheProbLoss = 0
    trancheLGD = 0
    For counter1 = 1 To numSim
        If sumOutput(1, counter1) > attPoint Then
            trancheProbLoss = trancheProbLoss + 1
            If sumOutput(1, counter1) > detPoint Then
                trancheLGD = trancheLGD + 1
            Else
                trancheLGD = trancheLGD + (sumOutput(1, counter1)-
    attPoint) / (detPoint-attPoint)
            End If
        End If
    Next counter1
  If trancheProbLoss = 0 Then
        Range("J" & 3 + counter4) = "N/A"
  Else
        Range("J" & 3 + counter4) = trancheLGD / trancheProbLoss
      End If
Next counter4
    Application.StatusBar = False
End Sub
```

This code can be used for a multitude of credit products, but it may be more important first to cover which products it is not appropriate for. While this can be used for certain asset-backed securities, it is not appropriate to use this for most resecuritizations, such as ABS CDOs or Re-REMICS. The problem with these assets is that the underlying loans are not on/off, pay/default type assets. Instead, the cash flow due from these assets can wax or wane depending on the performance of their underlying assets and their structural components.

Also, structures with cash flow triggers can be based on these Monte Carlo–type models, but the outputs cannot be stated as simply as a tranche loss due to defaults. Since excess interest and diverted cash flow make up a large part of the subordination for these assets, cash flow models must be built and tied into any Monte Carlo model. If you are unfamiliar with this process, we can recommend the first book in Keith Allman's Step-by-Step series: *Modeling Structured Finance Cash Flows with Microsoft Excel: A Step-by-Step Guide.*

Finally, as with our other topics, we should mention a bit about error. Quantifying errors in our CDO calculations is very much like quantifying the error in our VaR calculation in that, practically speaking, we can quantify only the statistical error. Any attempt to propagate the errors inherent in our input values, such as the correlation coefficients or the default probabilities, using Equation 2.17 would be extremely impractical.

TRANSITION MATRICES

The final subject we will cover in this chapter will be transition matrices. Transition matrices are representations of the likelihood that a credit will switch from one "state" to another. Transition matrices are useful when a large number of positions are held and there is little or no specific information about the fundamental drivers of performance. The major example of this is in consumer ABS assets like mortgage-backed securities (MBS) and auto loan securitizations, where there are potentially tens of thousands of individual loans that a noteholder may be exposed to. Due to privacy restrictions or just deficiencies with data, there may be limited information about the specific situation of most or all of the borrowers.

Another area where transition matrices can be used is with corporate credit pools such as CDOs. Typically, there is sufficient trading information about the assets in a widely syndicated deal that market information can be used to create default probabilities using a reduced form model for each asset. However, for small-business loans and other extensions of credit to small enterprises, market information may be impossible to obtain. As a result, for large pools, historical or projected transitions are likely to be a modeler's best bet to forecast the credit performance of the pool. And even for pools of larger credits, where ratings are available, many analysts use a rating transition matrix to include some differentiation between assets in their analysis.

In both of these situations, an expected transition matrix is built. The matrix is set up as a table where each row represents the current state, and the column represents the next possible state. To give an example, let's build a general transition matrix for a pool of mortgages. The potential states are "current" (mortgages that have paid in the last month), "1–30 days delinquent", "31–60 days delinquent", and "defaulted". Our generalized transition matrix will look as follows:

TABLE 6.1

FROM STATE		Current	TO STATE 1–30 days delinquent	31–60 days delinquent	Default
	Current	P(C,C)	P(C,1–30)	0	0
	1–30 days delinquent	P(1–30,C)	0	P(1–30,31–60)	0
	31–60 days delinquent	P(31–60,C)	0	0	P(31–60,D)
	Default	0	0	0	P(D,D) = 1

Note some of the general rules in the transition matrix. Loans can generally move one state at a time, from current to 1–30 days delinquent, from 1–30 days delinquent to 31–60 days delinquent, and so on. There is no way for a current loan to move to 31–60 days delinquent in one period (periods in this case being monthly), for example. Loans can move to current, however, if the borrowers make their full payments up, no matter how delinquent they had been previously. However, loans that have already defaulted are stuck as defaulted. The borrower cannot simply pay back the loan any longer, and the lender has already begun the process of repossessing the house. As such we state that the probability of staying in the defaulted bucket is 1.

One other additional rule is that the sum of probabilities across each row must add up to 1. We need to account for each loan and what will happen to it each period. We will use this as we estimate a "stationary" transition matrix. We call this stationary because it will be used across different periods. The same matrix is assumed to be an accurate estimation of transitions for all periods. More advanced models will sometimes use nonstationary matrices.

Our procedure for estimating transitions will be as follows. First, we will guess the initial transition matrix based on our data. Then, we will create an output table based on our results. Finally, we will adjust the estimation using the solver to minimize the sum of the squared errors.

MODEL BUILDER 6.7: Transition Matrices

1. Create a new workbook and name it MB_6.7_User. We have provided a complete version of this model-builder on the website available with this book. The complete version contains all of the proxy data that we will refer to in the text below.
2. Begin by entering the transition data table in C5:F24: in our example we have included 20 months of delinquency data broken down into "Current", "1–30 days delinquent", "31–60 days delinquent", and "Defaulted". Note that in each period in the sample data, the sum of the loans is equal to 1,000,000 in all cases.
3. In column G, track the newly defaulted assets by subtracting the current period's defaulted bucket from the previous period. In G6, enter "=F6-F5" and extend this formula down.

4. Now that we have entered the initial data, we will build the initial estimation of the transition matrix. Since there are four potential states in this matrix, the matrix will be 4×4 in size. Enter the following labels for the matrix. It is important to remember that the matrix rows represent the state the assets are from, and the columns represent the state the assets are going to:

> From
>
> J5: "Current"
>
> J6: "1–30 days delinquent"
>
> J7: "31–60 days delinquent"
>
> J8: "Defaulted"
>
> To
>
> K4: "Current"
>
> L4: "1–30 days delinquent"
>
> M4: "31–60 days delinquent"
>
> N4: "Defaulted"

5. We will create the estimates of the main transitions by comparing the total amounts of assets in each state over the life of the deal. This will not be exactly accurate but will help to give us an initial guess so we can use the Solver add-in to find the final amounts. L5 represents the transition from a Current asset to a 1–30 day delinquent asset. We will estimate this based on the sum of the current assets (excluding the last period, since we will not see the transitions from that period). In L5 enter "=SUM(D6:D24)/SUM(C5:C23)".

6. In M6 enter the similar transition formula from 1–30 days delinquent to 31–60 days delinquent. Enter "=SUM(E6:E24)/SUM(D5:D23)"

7. In N7 enter the estimate for the transition from 31–60 days delinquent to defaulted assets: "=SUM(G6:G24)/SUM(E5:E23)". Notice that we are using column G, the newly transitioned assets, instead of the full defaulted asset bucket. In addition, in N8 enter the transition from defaulted to defaulted assets, which is 100 percent.

8. Now that we have the major downward transitions (to later and later delinquencies), we need to estimate the upward transitions to current payment. To estimate the chance that a loan is current in the next period, we take advantage of the fact that the sum of each column must add up to 100 percent. This means that each loan ends in one of the four states.

   For current assets, a fair estimate of the number of assets that stay current is 100 percent minus the percentage of assets that will move to 1–30 days delinquent. In K5 enter "=1-L5". For assets that are moving from 1–30 days delinquent to Current, we enter a similar formula in K6: "=1-M6". For assets that are 31–60 days delinquent in K7, enter "=1-N7". Since no defaulted assets move to Current, enter "0" in K8. These are all of the allowed transitions, so in all of the remaining cells in the 4×4 matrix, enter "0".

9. The generating transition matrix (which can now be created) will be based on the initial estimate matrix before we use the solver to optimize it. Copy the first column of the initial estimate matrix K5:K8 and paste it in K13:K16. We are going to build the matrix again in the same columns only eight rows farther down.

10. Now use the fact that the entries in each row sum to 100 percent again in the other direction. We will calculate the percentage of assets in each state that experience downward transitions as the difference between 100 percent and the number of upward transitions. In L13 enter "=1-K13". In M14 enter "=1-K14". In N15 enter "=1-K15". And in N16 enter "100%".

Now enter "0" in all of the empty cells in the 4×4 matrix. You will notice that this matrix looks the same as the initial estimate matrix above. This is true at this point. We have simply set up this matrix to be simple to use with the Solver add-in.

11. Now that we have the generating matrix, we will generate data from that matrix to see what the delinquencies would look like if the matrix exactly represented what was happening in this pool of loans. In effect, we will be creating proxy data that will be similar to the data we input in C5:F24, only this table will be in Q5:T24. For the first row of the data, enter the loan-count that you see in the first period of the actual data. In Q5 enter "=C5". Copy and paste this formula right to T5.

12. Now use matrix multiplication (the MMULT function) to transform the previous period's delinquency data into the next period's delinquencies. Select Q6:T6 and in Q6 enter "=MMULT(Q5:T5,$K$13:$N$16)". This is an array function, so hold down Control and Shift and hit Enter. You will see that this period has taken the distribution of loan states in the previous period and adjusted it as prescribed by the generating matrix. Extend this formula down to row 24. You will see that the generated data follows a broadly similar pattern to the input data, but is markedly different.

13. With the generated data created, we need a measure to compare how similar the generated data is to the input data. In order to do this we will use the sum of squared errors, which can be calculated directly using the SUMXMY2 function. In K10 enter "=SUMXMY2(C5:F24,Q5:T24)".

14. Finally, we will use the Solver function to optimize the generating matrix. We will do this by using Solver to change the generating matrix to minimize the sum of squared errors between the generated matrix and the input data. Make sure that the Solver add-in is installed and open the tool. In "Set Objective", enter "$K$10". Hit the "Min" radio button so the Solver is minimizing the difference between the data and the proxy data. In the box under "By Changing Variable Cells:" enter "$K$13:$K$15". See Figure 6.9, then hit the "Solve" button.

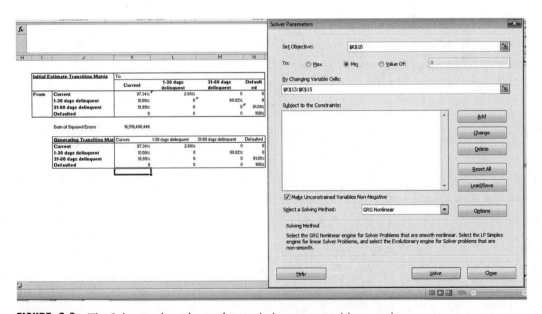

FIGURE 6.9 The Solver tool can be used to optimize your transition matrix.

The result of running the Solver is that the generating transition matrix produces an output that best matches the observed behavior of the loans. This can be used to forecast future transitions in the pool and to estimate future loses. More advanced analysis also takes into account the impact of tenor. Loans may be more likely to default either at the beginning of their life or at the end. These are typically nonstationary matrices or a set of different matrices that are applied during different points in the life of the loans.

KNOWING YOUR ASSETS

Simulating pools of assets is in some ways the most treacherous of the simulation techniques we cover in the book, since very little fundamental work is done on the underlying assets. Before beginning a simulation, analysts need to have confidence that they have some qualitative knowledge of the credits in the pool in order to temper confidence in the results.

However, despite shortcomings, simulation techniques are important tools for both pool analysis and risk management. Portfolios that grow extremely large are difficult to understand, and simulation techniques offer some simple metrics that can help an analyst grasp the risks being taken. However, before implementing the techniques in this chapter, analysts need to be confident they have clean, consistent, and accurate data. In the next chapter, we will cover issues with data and some basic techniques for improving data quality.

CHAPTER 7

Dealing with Data Deficiencies and Other Issues

At this point we have covered not only the basic mathematical components of a simulation, but also how to apply them to either a single asset or a pool of assets. We also have covered some steps to streamline and speed your analysis. However, if you are attempting to implement a new simulation, these concerns will probably require a minority of your time. The vast majority will likely be spent collecting, formatting, and debugging your data.

Having a dependable, complete data set from which meaningful statistical analysis can be obtained is of prime importance for a practitioner. While academics have the option of choosing what papers they will write based on the availability and completeness of datasets that are available to them, traders, portfolio managers, and risk managers have a limited ability to choose which types of assets they are going to allocate capital to or analyze, and even traditional assets such as bank loans may lack market or financial data that passes muster for full analysis.

Unfortunately, the research on methods for handling imperfect data is scant; data-handling issues have not occupied as central a role in the academy as they do in commercial applications. Most of the methods discussed in this chapter would likely be frowned upon by academics. However, they are tricks and methods that we have learned or developed over the years in order to overcome barriers to analysis. Handle them carefully. Fortunately, as the markets become more liquid and the world we live in becomes more attuned to the value of transaction information, the need for these techniques will hopefully diminish.

"GARBAGE IN, GARBAGE OUT"

Programmers and modelers frequently deal with data issues. In the financial world, there are several sets of issues that an analyst must take into account. The most obvious one is obtaining data. Models such as Merton or reduced form models force us to find equity or collateral default swap (CDS) market data. However, for many small private companies, such data is simply not available. In some cases where the data is available, it is deficient. Stock prices may not account for dividends and splits, which clearly should impact the trading level of the asset without necessarily impacting the risk of owning the stock. CDS and bonds may trade as infrequently as a few times a month. Whether illiquid markets actually tell us much about the riskiness of a security or company is a reasonable question to ask in these situations.

And even when full data sets are available, there are judgment calls that must be made in any analysis. Should we take historical equity returns from 5 years or 20? Should we weight the data equally or give greater weight to recent events? These choices have very real impacts on model results. These issues gained prominence due to the results of risk models in the 1990s. We understand that a number of models showed a sharp decrease in risk from one day to the next, despite the fact that portfolios had not changed. When investigated, it turned out that the stock market crash of 1987 had rolled out of their historical data set, and as a result these models suddenly projected the market to be a much safer place.

"Garbage in, garbage out," or GIGO, is programmers' shorthand for model results that are nonsensical on account of poor data quality. Frequently, models will give us results that are counterintuitive or do not make sense with our view of the world. In these cases, analysts should not simply throw out the results, but should instead take the time to understand why the results are different from expectations. Often an in-depth look at the model will lead to a change in assumptions or in the mechanics of the model. In other situations the model may be accurately forecasting the probability of a certain event that was not considered by the modeler. These situations are where the value of simulation modeling can be apparent.

INCONSISTENT DATA FORMATS

Inconsistent data formatting is not an issue with the data itself, but with how different sets of data are presented. The most common form of discrepancies comes in ordering data and in data frequency. Historical pricing data is typically recorded daily; however, some sources of data display the most recent trade date on top, while other sources list the information in an ascending-date format. Other data fields may be produced or provided on a weekly, monthly, or yearly basis. When aggregating source data to set up a model, typically a number of different sources of data are necessary, and organizing the data, even when all the data sets are of high quality, can be difficult. Most formatting issues can be handled by using sorting functions in Excel and by recording macros to implement them automatically. In the Model Builders for this chapter, we will cover techniques to deal with some common data-quality issues.

Dividends and Splits

Many companies increase the number of equity shares they have outstanding through either secondary issuances, stock dividends, or share splits. All of these will influence the value of the shares and need to be handled differently depending on the type of model that is being implemented. Splits are the most simple. In a stock split, shares are exchanged in a defined ratio that does not change the economic position of the shareholder. So, for example, a holder of 10 shares of a $5 stock, after a 2-for-1 stock split, holds 20 shares of a $2.50 stock. The split needs to be accounted for by dividing all price history for the stock previous to the effective date of the split, also known as the 'ex-dividend date', by 2. Typically, most available stock price data sets have already made this change.

Dividends, whether in stock or in cash, reduce the value of a stock after the stock trades ex-dividend. Note that the ex-dividend date is not the date that the dividend 'settles' or is received by the stockholder, it is the date that the stock begins to trade without the dividend included, typically a few days earlier. The component of the price move that is accounted for in the dividend may be included in the analysis or excluded, depending on the goal of the analysis. For a risk analysis, for example, the reduction in equity price due to dividends should be included. A dividend payment will increase the risk for a bondholder because money that could otherwise go to pay debt service has "leaked out" to equity. As a result, there are fewer assets available to make the required payments, and the risk increases accordingly. However, for a price movement analysis such as value at risk, or VaR, price movements due to dividend payments should not be included. A holder of a stock that pays dividends will see a decrease in the nominal value of the stock due to dividends, but the holder will be entitled to this cash outflow, so it is inappropriate to assume that such a payment will increase the holder's loss on the position.

Stock dividends are when corporations grant additional shares of stock to shareholders. These should usually be treated as splits, because effectively additional stock is being issued without any additional economic consideration being received by the holder of the security. However, in companies with complex capital structures and the possibility of meaningful dilution, a stock dividend should be treated as cash dividends with the value of the stock on the day of the dividend (since the new stock could be sold that day).

While accounting for splits and dividends appears to be straightforward, a number of complexities need to be taken into account, especially if historical percentage changes in price are the desired output. The most accurate way to do this is to start with a single share of the stock at the beginning of the time period, and add dividends and extra stocks received (or fractional stocks lost in a reverse split). While this gives the most accurate historical view of the day-to-day returns on a position, it is difficult to implement in a VaR scenario because at a certain point the previously paid dividend stops being part of the basis on which we calculate percentage change.

This is a difficult concept, so we will walk through an example. Let us suppose we held 1 share of stock XYZ that was marked on March 31, 2009, at $4/share. Assume XYZ had previously announced that it would pay a $1/share dividend with an ex-dividend date of April 1, 2009 (the next day). The stock then closed trading on April 1 at a value of $3.12.

If we naively calculated the change in asset value as the difference in the closing prices, we would calculate that the change in price was equal to ($3.12 − $4.00)/($4.00) = −22 percent, a sizable loss! Of course, this isn't an accurate picture of the change in our investment's value, since we have received a $1 dividend (we will not discount the future dividend payment for simplicity). Including the dividend, the value of our investment will be $3.12 + $1.00 = $4.12, which translates to a gain of ($4.12 − $4.00)/($4.00) = 3 percent.

However, imagine that one month later, on April 30, the stock was marked at $2.50 and closes at $2.25. This is a drop of ($2.25 − $2.50)/($2.50) = −10 percent. However, if we are considering the long-term value of the investment and include previous dividend payments by adding $1.00 to the price before and after (since a long-term holder of the investment on April 30 has one stock worth $2.50 and $1.00 of paid dividends), we would say the change in the value of our investment in XYZ, "all-in," was from $3.50 to $3.25, or about −7.14 percent. Additionally, marking the bonds at $3.25 will cause an inaccurate weighting when we calculate the value at risk in a portfolio, as we will overweight the value of high-dividend stocks compared to low-dividend stocks.

A simpler estimation is to start with the current stock price and to adjust the previous stock value for any splits or dividend payments. We will do this for a VaR implementation in Model Builder 7.1.

MODEL BUILDER 7.1: VaR with Splits and Dividend Payments

1. Create a new workbook and name it MB_7.1_User. While we have provided versions of each Model Builder on the website, we believe that to understand the material it is best for readers to use these as guides off of which they will build their own models. For the purposes of this and other Model Builders, we have used proxy data that can be copied from the files on the website.

2. In B4, put the most recent date for which there is a stock price available. In C4, enter the price for that date—in the complete version of the model we use 12/8/2010. Then enter the historical prices and dates below this for the entire period from which data is being used.

3. In F4, enter the date of the most recent stock split, reverse split, or dividend. Enter dates of previous splits or dividends that occurred during the period in question. In G4 (and below this for subsequent splits or dividends), enter the amount of the dividend for each share. We have to remember that dividend data usually does not account for splits, so we will build this into our adjustments.

4. In H4 and I4, we will enter any information about stock splits. In column H we will list the shares before the split, and in column I we have the number of shares after the split. For a 3:1

split, in which the number of shares triple, we would enter 1 in column H and 3 in column I. For simple dividends without a split, enter 1 in both columns.

5. Once the required data is entered, we will start on the VBA code that will correct our data. First, we will define variables and collect data from the worksheet.

```
Sub correctPrices()
    Dim stockPrices(), dividendsSplits(), cumDividendsSplits()
    As Double
    Dim i, j, numDays, numDiv As Integer

 'collect raw stock info
    Range("B4").Select
    Range(Selection, Selection.End(xlDown)).Select
    numDays = Selection.Rows.Count
    ReDim stockPrices(1 To numDays, 2)
    For i = 1 To numDays
        stockPrices(i, 1) = Range("B3").Offset(i, 0)
        stockPrices(i, 2) = Range("B3").Offset(i, 1)
    Next i

    'collect raw dividend and split info
    Range("F4").Select
    Range(Selection, Selection.End(xlDown)).Select
    numDiv = Selection.Rows.Count
    ReDim dividendsSplits(1 To numDiv, 3)

    For i = 1 To numDiv
        dividendsSplits(i, 1) = Range("F3").Offset(i, 0)
        dividendsSplits(i, 2) = Range("F3").Offset(i, 1)
        dividendsSplits(i, 3) = Range("F3").Offset(i, 2) / Range("F3")
        .Offset(i, 3)
    Next i
```

We are creating two arrays, stockPrices() and dividendsSplits(), which will contain all of the information from the sheet. We use the "Range(Selection, Selection.End(xlDown)).Select" method to select the full set of data, no matter how many days of price data or dividend payments/splits there are.

6. Next we will begin the calculations. The key calculation for us is to track the cumulative impact of dividends and splits, which we will calculate in the cumDividendsSplits() array. Remember that in a stock split, we do not need to correct the stock price just on the day before the split, but we also need to adjust the previous stock prices all the way back to the beginning of the period for which we are using data.

```
ReDim cumDividendsSplits(0 To numDays, 2)
j = 1
cumDividendsSplits(0, 1) = 0
cumDividendsSplits(0, 2) = 1
For i = 1 To numDays
  If stockPrices(i, 1) = dividendsSplits(j, 1) Then
        cumDividendsSplits(i, 2) = cumDividendsSplits(i-1, 2)
```

```
* dividendsSplits(j, 3)
cumDividendsSplits(i, 1) = cumDividendsSplits(i-1, 1)
+ dividendsSplits(j, 2) * cumDividendsSplits(i, 2)
j = j + 1
 Else
        cumDividendsSplits(i, 2) = cumDividendsSplits(i-1, 2)
        cumDividendsSplits(i, 1) = cumDividendsSplits(i-1, 1)
 End If
Next i
```

In this segment of code, we are tracking dividends in column 1 of the array, and splits in column 2. We expand the array to "0 to numDays" (most of our arrays start at 1, current day, and track back as we move down the array) because we want to be able to account for splits or dividends that may have happened today. We then go backwards through the days, and when a date matches the date of a split or dividend (which is tracked in dividendsSplits() column 1, we enter an adjustment. For a split, we take the previous factor and multiply by the inverse of the split. A 3:1 split reduces the factor of the stock before the split to one-third. This is because if we hold one stock today, it is the equivalent to holding one-third of a share before the split.

For the dividends, we sum together the paid amounts on the ex-dividends dates, but we again must adjust for the splits. We multiply the amount of the dividend by the cumulative split factor.

7. Finally, we use the cumDividendsSplits() array to adjust the stockPrices() array and give us corrected prices for a VaR implementation. For each date, we will multiply the raw price of the stock by the cumulative split factor and then subtract dividends that are paid between that date and now. See Figure 7.1.

```
'adjust prices for splits and dividends
 For i = 1 To numDays
stockPrices(i, 2) = (stockPrices(i, 2) * cumDividendsSplits
(i, 2))-cumDividendsSplits(i, 1)
 Next i

'print
Range("K4").Select Selection.Resize(numDays, 3).Select
 Selection = stockPrices

End Sub
```

Illiquid Products

Additional data issues come from illiquid securities. Certain assets, typically securities issued by smaller or closely held entities, do not trade frequently. This can cause analysis problems, in particular when a full set of data is needed to estimate the volatility or the historical VaR of a security.

With illiquid products, one key qualitative decision that an analyst must make is whether the information provided by the market is enough to result in

A	B	C	D	E	F	G	H	I	J	K	L	M	N
	7.1 Equity Adjustment Worksheet for VaR												
	Original Data Set				Date	Dividend	Original # Shares	Final # Shares			**Corrected Data Set**		
	12/8/2010	5.18			11/10/2010	$0.05	1	1			12/8/2010	5.18	
	12/7/2010	5.13			9/3/2010	$0.00	1	2			12/7/2010	5.13	
	12/6/2010	5.16			8/10/2010	$0.10	1	1			12/6/2010	5.16	
	12/3/2010	5.07			5/10/2010	$0.10	1	1			12/3/2010	5.07	
	12/2/2010	4.98			2/10/2010	$0.10	1	1			12/2/2010	4.98	
	12/1/2010	4.9			11/10/2009	$0.10	1	1			12/1/2010	4.9	
	11/30/2010	4.84			8/10/2009	$0.08	1	1			11/30/2010	4.84	
	11/29/2010	4.86			5/11/2009	$0.08	1	1			11/29/2010	4.86	
	11/26/2010	4.91			2/10/2009	$0.08	1	1			11/26/2010	4.91	
	11/24/2010	4.91			11/10/2008	$0.08	1	1			11/24/2010	4.91	
	11/23/2010	4.83			8/11/2008	$0.08	1	1			11/23/2010	4.83	
	11/22/2010	4.87									11/22/2010	4.87	
	11/19/2010	4.88									11/19/2010	4.88	
	11/18/2010	4.86									11/18/2010	4.86	
	11/17/2010	4.81									11/17/2010	4.81	
	11/16/2010	4.82									11/16/2010	4.82	
	11/15/2010	4.94									11/15/2010	4.94	
	11/12/2010	4.92									11/12/2010	4.92	
	11/11/2010	4.96									11/11/2010	4.96	
	11/10/2010	4.9									11/10/2010	4.85	
	11/9/2010	4.92									11/9/2010	4.87	
	11/8/2010	4.86									11/8/2010	4.81	
	11/5/2010	4.71									11/5/2010	4.66	
	11/4/2010	4.77									11/4/2010	4.72	

FIGURE 7.1 Model Builder 7.1. Note that the correction for the 11/10/2008 dividend decreases the value of previous quoted stock values.

meaningful analysis. The assumption that markets give us useful data about the risk of a security is predicated on the existence of a wide base of investors who are informed about the security and are driving the security's price toward a fair value with some level of efficiency. If this is not the case and stock prices are dominated by the relationships between a few stakeholders, then pricing information is not useful in the determination of risk, and the analyst should treat the security as if there were no pricing data available.

If the determination is made that there is enough data to begin an analysis, there is a question as to how summary data can be obtained from the incomplete data sets. A security that trades only every other day may appear to have a lower volatility than a liquid security, since days with extreme price movements may not have included a trade that is listed in the data set. Additionally, since transaction costs are typically larger for illiquid securities, the net capital received in the sale of an illiquid security may be meaningfully less than the gross selling price.

The more conservative way to create matching datasets is '*Pairwise Deletion*'. In this method, all data that is available for only one security is deleted; only the dates when there is data available for both securities do we use price information. This allows the analyst to compare volatilities on an apples-to-apples basis and to

Date	Security 1	Security 2
12/8/2010	5.18	22.9
12/7/2010	5.13	23.12
12/6/2010	5.16	N/A
12/3/2010	5.07	N/A
12/2/2010	N/A	N/A
12/1/2010	4.90	22.30
11/30/2010	4.84	21.56

Date	Security 1	Security 2
12/8/2010	5.18	22.9
12/7/2010	5.13	23.12
12/1/2010	4.90	22.30
11/30/2010	4.84	21.56

FIGURE 7.2 In pairwise deletion, only dates where data is available for all securities are included.

calculate correlations between assets, but it has the downside of eliminating much useful data. See Figure 7.2.

MODEL BUILDER 7.2: Implementing Pairwise Deletion for Illiquid Securities

1. Create a new workbook and name it MB_7.2_User.xls. We will be using this sheet for the next two Model Builders, so we recommend that you go through this Model Builder patiently and refer to the complete version on the website if there is any confusion.

2. We will be doing analysis on one liquid security (a security for which we have pricing for every day in the period in question) and one illiquid security (a security for which there are gaps in the pricing). Ideally, we will want to use securities that are as similar as possible (with a high correlation). The proxy data we are using is included in the complete version on the website.

   In B4 enter the most recent date for the liquid security, and in C4 enter the price for that day. In our proxy data, the most recent date is 12/8/2010, and the most recent price for the liquid security is 5.18. Enter the dates and prices in descending order below this. In F4 enter the most recent valuation date for the illiquid security, and in G4 enter the price. In our example, the most recent date is 12/8/2010 and the most recent price is 22.90. Again, enter dates and prices for this security in descending order. Since the illiquid security does not trade every day, there are going to be gaps between dates.

3. We will generate some summary statistics so we can see how complete or deficient our illiquid data set is. In J4, to see how many prices we have for the liquid security, enter "=COUNT(C4:C3000)" (this will work for securities with fewer than 3,000 price entries, of course). In J5, do the same for the illiquid security, by entering "=COUNT(G4:G3000)". And in J6, we will calculate the percentage of dates where the illiquid security has data by entering "=J5/J4". If this value in J6 is high enough for comfort (we will use 75 percent as an arbitrary threshold), then we proceed to creating a set of pairwise deleted prices.

4. To begin, we will write code to gather the data on this worksheet and define a number of arrays where we will complete calculations. In illiquidPrices() we will put all pricing data on the dates where we have prices for the illiquid security. In illiquidReturns() and fullReturns() we will put return information for the two securities so we can calculate the correlation between them.

```
Sub estCorrelation()

    Dim fullPrices(), illiquidPrices(), fullReturns(),
    illiquidReturns()
    As Double
    Dim i, j, numfullpricedays, numIlliquidDays As Integer

    'collect full price info
    Range("B4").Select
    Range(Selection, Selection.End(xlDown)).Select
    numfullpricedays = Selection.Rows.Count
    ReDim fullPrices(1 To numfullpricedays, 2)

    For i = 1 To numfullpricedays
        fullPrices(i, 1) = Range("B3").Offset(i, 0)
        fullPrices(i, 2) = Range("B3").Offset(i, 1)
    Next i

    'collect illiquid price info
    Range("F4").Select
    Range(Selection, Selection.End(xlDown)).Select
    numIlliquidDays = Selection.Rows.Count
    ReDim illiquidPrices(1 To numIlliquidDays, 5)
    ReDim fullReturns(1 To numIlliquidDays-1, 0)
    ReDim illiquidReturns(1 To numIlliquidDays-1, 0)

    For i = 1 To numIlliquidDays
        illiquidPrices(i, 1) = Range("F3").Offset(i, 0)
        illiquidPrices(i, 2) = Range("F3").Offset(i, 1)
    Next i
```

5. Now we will go through the pricing information for the liquid security and pull out the dates that have both prices for it *and* the illiquid security. We will do this using a For loop that goes through all liquid security trade dates (I = 1 to numfullpricedays) and compares the dates to the illiquid price days. We use the counter "j" for the illiquid price days; once we find a date that both securities were priced, we move to the next date that the illiquid security was priced (j = j + 1).

```
    'Only take days where there are prices for both securities
    j = 1
    For i = 1 To numfullpricedays
        If fullPrices(i, 1) = illiquidPrices(j, 1) Then
            illiquidPrices(j, 3) = fullPrices(i, 2)
            If j <> nullliquidDays then
                j = j + 1
            End If
        End If
```

6. In order to get the correlation in price movements, we will enter the returns between periods by calculating returns in two arrays. This is a little bit unusual because there are not consistent time intervals between the data points. Fortunately, correlation does not require a time component (as opposed to volatility, which we will get to shortly)

```
'Calculate changes in price
For i = 1 To numIlliquidDays-1
    illiquidReturns(i, 0) = (illiquidPrices(i, 2)-illiquidPrices
    (i + 1, 2)) / illiquidPrices(i + 1, 2)
    fullReturns(i, 0) = (illiquidPrices(i, 3)-illiquidPrices(i +
    1, 3)) / illiquidPrices(i + 1, 3)
Next i
```

7. In order to finish this macro, we will print out the prices that remain after the pairwise deletion, as well as the correlation and estimated volatilities (standard deviations of return) that we have found in the data. Since the intervals are not constant and the different interval lengths are not accounted for, these estimates are not true volatility numbers. However, they do offer us some information, and we will use this information to help us if we are going to try more aggressive strategies to work with our deficient data, so we will produce these numbers anyways, being mindful of their limitations.

```
'print
Range("J11").Value =
Application.WorksheetFunction.Correl(illiquidReturns, fullReturns)
    Range("J12").Value =
    Application.WorksheetFunction.StDev(fullReturns)
    Range("J13").Value =
    Application.WorksheetFunction.StDev(illiquidReturns)
    Range("L4").Select
    Selection.Resize(numIlliquidDays, 4).Select
    Selection = illiquidPrices
```

While the previously mentioned process is useful, we are eliminating a lot of very useful data, which is why many modelers use more aggressive data techniques. *Imputation* is the practice of inserting additional data to complete a data set. It is used in the social sciences via a number of different methods, and not without controversy! When there is relative confidence that the data available is complete (a data completion standard might be that there is price data for 75 percent of the dates in question, or a minimum of 500 holders of the security, or some other measure of liquidity or information), then we will impute data to allow us to use our models on securities with incomplete datasets.

In finance, there are two general methods by which data is imputed: using an expectation-maximization algorithm, and using a partial proxy. We will cover a partial proxy methodology here. This is a practitioner's attempt to make do with an incomplete dataset without running through a processing intensive procedure. We will build off of the estCorrelation() subroutine that we were working with previously.

1. Continuing with the sheet that we used for the estCorrelation() subroutine, we will enter the Cholesky() function that we had developed in Chapter 3. We will use this to attempt to keep the correlation in asset movements similar to what we have experienced previously (or we can

7.2 Data Deficiency Worksheet for Illiquid Securities

Data From Liquid Security		Data From Illiquid Security		Summary Data		Pairwise Deletion Set		
12/8/2010	5.18	12/8/2010	22.9	Full Data Set Count:	489	8-Dec-10	22.9	5.18
12/7/2010	5.13	12/7/2010	23.12	Deficient Data Set Count:	428	7-Dec-10	23.12	5.13
12/6/2010	5.16	12/1/2010	22.3	% of Dates with Data:	87.5%	1-Dec-10	22.3	4.9
12/3/2010	5.07	11/30/2010	21.56			30-Nov-10	21.56	4.84
12/2/2010	4.98	11/29/2010	21	Estimate Correlation		29-Nov-10	21	4.86
12/1/2010	4.9	11/26/2010	22.65	From Pairwise Deletion		26-Nov-10	22.65	4.91
11/30/2010	4.84	11/22/2010	22.75			22-Nov-10	22.75	4.87
11/29/2010	4.86	11/19/2010	23.05	Estimated Correlation:	83.00%	19-Nov-10	23.05	4.88
11/26/2010	4.91	11/18/2010	23.24	Liquid Security Vol:	4.66%	18-Nov-10	23.24	4.86
11/24/2010	4.91	11/17/2010	22.82	Illiquid Security Vol:	5.39%	17-Nov-10	22.82	4.81

FIGURE 7.3 Model Builder 7.2: Boxes on the left indicate dates when both securities are priced. These dates are included in the final dataset on the right.

stress a portfolio by increasing the correlation between the assets). Our correlation will not be precisely the same as what we are projecting since we will respect the actual data points that we have for the illiquid security, but the correlation should be close.

2. We will need to add a few values and change some names, but in general the section of the code where we take values from the worksheet will look similar.

```
Sub imputeValues()

    Dim allPrices(), allReturns(), trueVol(), estLiqVol, trueLiqVol,
    estIlliqVol, registry(), cholesky1, cholesky2 As Double
    Dim i, j, numfullpricedays, numIlliquidDays As Integer

    'collect full price info
    Range("B4").Select
    Range(Selection, Selection.End(xlDown)).Select
    numfullpricedays = Selection.Rows.Count
    ReDim allPrices(1 To numfullpricedays, 3)
    ReDim registry(1 To numfullpricedays, 3)
    ReDim allReturns(1 To numfullpricedays-1, 3)
    ReDim trueVol(1 To numfullpricedays-1, 1)

    For i = 1 To numfullpricedays
        allPrices(i, 1) = Range("B3").Offset(i, 0)
        allPrices(i, 2) = Range("B3").Offset(i, 1)
    Next i

    'collect illiquid price info
    Range("F4").Select
    Range(Selection, Selection.End(xlDown)).Select
    numIlliquidDays = Selection.Rows.Count
    j = 1
    For i = 1 To numfullpricedays
        If Range("F3").Offset(j, 0) = allPrices(i, 1) Then
            allPrices(i, 3) = Range("F3").Offset(j, 1)
            registry(i, 1) = i
            j = j + 1
        Else
```

```
            allPrices(i, 3) = 0
            registry(i, 1) = registry(i−1, 1)
        End If
    Next i
```

One important array that is new that we need to track is the registry() array. In this macro, when we are collecting price information in the allPrices() array, we are not deleting liquid security pricing. Instead, we are taking all of the liquid security prices and matching them up with illiquid security prices. Where we do not have illiquid security prices, we are leaving a blank space (specifically, the lines "Else allPrices(I,3) = 0"). When we do not have a price for the illiquid security, we want to track what period the next price will be in. We are tracking this in the registry() array in column 1 (remember, since we are going back in time as we go down the array, period i − 1 is the period *after* period i.

3. Next, we are going to go "backward" and look at the allPrices() array from bottom to top to find the previous price for each period when the illiquid security does not have price information. When the security does have info, we will enter the current period into column 2 of the registry() array.

```
    'Create Returns for Illiquid Security
    'Create registry of 'previous price points'
    For i = 2 To numfullpricedays
        If registry(numfullpricedays + 1−i, 1) =
        numfullpricedays + 1−i Then
            registry(numfullpricedays + 1−i, 2) =
            registry(numfullpricedays + 1−i, 1)
        Else
            registry(numfullpricedays + 1−i, 2) =
            registry(numfullpricedays + 2−i, 2)
        End If
    Next i
```

4. Next, we are going to use the information in the registry() array and the price points we already know to create average values for the dates when we don't have prices for the illiquid security.

```
    'create mean prices for missing dates
    For i = 1 To numfullpricedays
        If registry(i, 1) = i Then
            registry(i, 3) = allPrices(i, 3)
        Else
            If registry(i, 2) = 0 Then
                registry(i, 3) = registry(i−1, 3)
            Else
                registry(i, 3) = allPrices(registry(i, 1), 3) +
                ((i−registry(i, 1)) / (registry(i, 2)−registry
                (i, 1)) * (allPrices(registry(i, 2), 3)−allPrices
                (registry(i, 1), 3)))
            End If
        End If
    Next i
```

The key line in this section of code is repeated here for further analysis:

```
registry(i, 3) = allPrices(registry(i, 1), 3) + ((i−registry(i, 1))
/ (registry(i, 2)−registry(i, 1)) * (allPrices(registry(i, 2), 3)−
allPrices(registry(i, 1), 3)))
```

What we are doing, for dates without a price, is creating a price based on the previous and next dates for which we have illiquid security prices. "Registry(i, 1)" is the next date when a price is available, and the value of that price is obtained by searching for that period in the allPrices() array via the command "allPrices(registry(i, 1), 3)". Then we will fractionally increase this price so it is linearly moving toward the price at the previous value we have in our dataset, a process known as linear interpolation. So if we have a price in period 6, and the next price is in period 2, we determine the prices for periods 3, 4, and 5 through equations 7.1, 7.2, and 7.3, respectively, which are represented in this code.

$$P_3 = P_2 + [(3 − 2)/(6 − 2)] \times (P_2 − P_6) \tag{7.1}$$

$$P_4 = P_2 + [(4 − 2)/(6 − 2)] \times (P_2 − P_6) \tag{7.2}$$

$$P_5 = P_2 + [(5 − 2)/(6 − 2)] \times (P_2 − P_6) \tag{7.3}$$

5. Now we have created a price for each period, but the values between each true price point are not realistic. They are just linear interpolations of the nearest prices. This means that the price movements will not necessarily have the appropriate correlation with our liquid security, and the price movements will certainly not have a realistic volatility! Remember that when we project prices, we generally do so by using a drift term, μ (mu) and a volatility term σ:

$$P_{i+1} = P_i \times (1 + \mu + (\sigma \times Draw)) \tag{7.4}$$

In order to use this formula, we must find the volatility of the illiquid security. As discussed previously, analysts usually do this in two ways: by taking the historical volatility of the stock, or by using option prices to estimate future volatility. Unfortunately, we do not have daily historical volatility (if the stock traded daily, we would have no need for this exercise in the first place), and it is likely that there will not be a liquid options market for an illiquid stock. Instead, we will use the limited historical volatility that we determined using the dataset that incorporated pairwise deletion, and then we will take the relationship between the liquid stock's estimated volatility and its true volatility, and use that to calculate a daily volatility for the illiquid stock.

As we do this, we will also create and decompose the correlation matrix for the two securities. Since there are only two securities, we will only have to create a 2 × 2 matrix in I22:J23. In I22 and J23, we enter the number 1, in the cells not on the diagonal (J22 and I23) we enter "=J11" to take the previously estimated correlation. Below this we will create the Cholesky decomposition of this matrix by selecting I26:J27, entering "=Cholesky(I22:J23)" and holding Control and Shift and pressing Enter.

The resulting decomposed matrix in I26:J27 is what we would use to forecast the movements of correlated securities, as we did in Chapter 6. However, here we have a slightly different goal—we want to take the already observed movement of the liquid stock and use that to generate the missing prices for the illiquid security. To do this, we will take the second row of this matrix and make I27 the liquid security's factor. We will assign the variable name "cholesky1". J27 will be the factor assigned to the illiquid security's uncorrelated draw, which we will call "cholesky2".

```
'Collect Vol and correlation info and Estimate Volatility
For i = 1 To numfullpricedays-1
    allReturns(i, 1) = Range("B3").Offset(i, 0)
    allReturns(i, 2) = (allPrices(i, 2)-allPrices(i + 1, 2)) /
    allPrices(i + 1, 2)
    trueVol(i, 1) = (allPrices(i, 2)-allPrices(i + 1, 2)) /
    allPrices(i + 1, 2)
Next i

cholesky1 = Range("I27")
cholesky2 = Range("J27")
trueLiqVol = Application.WorksheetFunction.StDev(trueVol)
estLiqVol = Range("J12").Value
estIlliqVol = (Range("J13").Value * trueLiqVol) / estLiqVol
```

6. Now we are ready to create the missing prices for the illiquid security and impute them. Where we have an actual price from the dataset (we track this as registry(i, 1) = i, which means the next true price we have is the current one) we will use it. When we do not have a price, we will create one.

```
'add in error
For i = 1 To numfullpricedays-1
    If registry(i, 1) = i Then
        allPrices(i, 3) = registry(i, 3)
    Else
        allPrices(i, 3) = registry(i, 3) * (1 + estIlliqVol *
        (cholesky1 * Application.WorksheetFunction.NormDist
        (allReturns(i, 2), 0, trueLiqVol, True) + cholesky2 *
        Application.WorksheetFunction.NormSInv(Rnd())))
    End If
Next i
```

When we do not have a price, we will start with the mean price and then add on a correlated draw. However, we will not actually create a draw for the liquid security, because we already have a real return for each period. Instead, we use the volatility and the actual return, and we use that to figure out what draw would have resulted in that return. To do this we use the NormDist worksheet function, which is the inverse of the NormSInv function we used heavily in Chapter 6 for our Monte Carlo simulations.

7. Once the calculations are done, we print the outputs to complete the Model Builder.

```
'print
Range("J18").Value = trueLiqVol
Range("J19").Value = estIlliqVol
Range("P4").Select
Selection.Resize(numfullpricedays, 4).Select
Selection = allPrices
End Sub
```

LACK OF DATA

Finally, there are securities for which pricing history is completely unavailable. Real estate, asset-backed securities, private equity investments, and complex derivatives are all types of investments for which meaningful market data is effectively unavailable.

In these situations, the general approach is to find a similar, "proxy" security or portfolio of securities that match the payoff structure and risk of the position in question. Emanuel Derman, in his book *My Life as a Quant: Reflections on Physics and Finance*, wrote, "I believe that you can summarize the essence of quantitative finance on one leg.... If you want to know the value of a security, use the price of another security that's as similar to it as possible. All the rest is modeling. Go and build."

CHAPTER 8

Advanced Topics and Further Reading

In this book, we have covered the basics of financial simulation across a number of asset classes. Instead of focusing on a single asset class, we have touched on equities, corporate and government debt, derivatives, interest rates, and even illiquid products such as structured credits and private equity. We have implemented reduced form and structural models, simulated prices and rates using Hull-White and Monte Carlo simulations, and introduced basic stochastic concepts such as Brownian motion and log-normal distributions.

However, all of this serves as only an introduction to the world of financial simulation and practical methods for modeling. Journals devoted to quantitative finance and simulation go into much further depth and cover topics similar to what is in this text, only in much greater detail. The reader is encouraged to think of this text as the starting point to a much wider world of simulation and quantitative analysis.

In this chapter, we will briefly cover some more advanced topics and considerations that are built into more advanced models, as well as topics that are commonly discussed in the quantitative finance community. These topics range from data mining to programming to mathematical modeling questions.

VBA AND OTHER LANGUAGES: DIFFERENT PROGRAMS FOR DIFFERENT USES

One component of this text that differentiates it from other simulation texts is the use of Visual Basic for Applications (VBA), which is an object-oriented language appropriate for working with Excel for smaller, simpler macros. VBA's main advantages are in its simplicity and its ability to use worksheet and application objects to manipulate the output, which is usually (but not always) also an Excel worksheet or object. For shorter, ad hoc projects and when flexibility is valued over computational horsepower, VBA is generally as easy to work with as other languages, and the ability to have calculations done in the Excel worksheet and then read by the code can save a massive amount of programming time.

However, VBA is considered by many to be insufficiently powerful for Monte Carlo simulations due to its speed and persistent questions about random number generation. In general, we believe that random number generation in the 2010 version of Excel does not have the same problems seen in previous versions of Excel. But the speed question is still an issue for modelers working in real time.

As a result, a large proportion of Monte Carlo–related models are done in C++, a general-purpose programming language. C++ programs can be built to handle extremely large amounts of data and calculations and can be integrated effectively into Excel workbooks. The main issues with C++ are the amount of time it takes to program and most finance professionals' unfamiliarity with the language, whereas many financiers have some knowledge of VBA and many are very familiar with Excel.

In practice, most of the work done in finance is handled through these two languages or in languages that are proprietary to individual firms. VBA is generally used for applications that either do not need to be in real time or smaller projects where the computational needs are secondary to the ability to change the way things work quickly.

In 2010, the Securities and Exchange Commission proposed in release 33–9117 that most issuers of asset-backed securities (ABS) make code available to investors so that the buyers of the securities could simulate future cash flows themselves. The SEC proposed:

> [T]o require the filing of a computer program (the "waterfall computer program," as defined in the proposed rule) of the contractual cash flow provisions of the securities in the form of downloadable source code in Python ... would be required to allow the user to programmatically input information from the asset data file that we are proposing to require as previously described. We believe that, with the waterfall computer program and the asset data file, investors would be better able to conduct their own evaluations of ABS and may be less likely to be dependent on the opinions of credit rating agencies.

The SEC chose Python because it is an open-source language (meaning that the code can be accessed by anyone). Python is a general-purpose language, and in this way it is much more similar to C++ than it is to VBA. However, we do not believe it has been widely used in finance applications. While the SEC proposed this rule in 2010, no requirements for the filing of a program had been instituted in the United States at time of publication.

QUASI–MONTE CARLO AND COMPUTATIONAL TIME

While the most direct ways to reduce the computational time of a model are to speed up the processing or write the program in a faster language, there are additional methods that can be used to reduce the number of runs that need to be done to get meaningful results. Speed can have a real impact on the ability to react to changing market conditions and execute trades. In some markets, minutes or seconds can be crucial in the capturing the value from news or new pricing data.

Most of the work on speeding up models that we will cover relates to Monte Carlo simulations, and the methods of analysis using these methods are called quasi–Monte Carlo methods. In these methods we take sequences of numbers for our draws that would appear to be random but that are in fact not random. The sequences are specifically designed to appear random and to be more efficient at covering a range of possible outcomes than a random sequence.

The simplest of these methods is the Halton sequence. The Halton sequence is constructed by choosing a prime number as a base, and then creating nonrandom draws up to the desired number of runs. Draws can also be across multiple dimensions; price, interest rates, the state of the economy, and the recovery rate of a bond may all be simulated together. However, Halton sequences are generally not used for more than five or six variables at a time due to loss of some of the properties of randomness.

EFFICIENT MARKET HYPOTHESIS AND ITS WEAKNESSES

More important than the programming language chosen to implement the model, however, is the reasoning behind the model itself. Many simulation models, particularly those which gather probabilities of future price movements from the markets, are based to some level on the efficient market hypothesis (EMH). EMH, which exists in several forms, states that market prices reflect all available information. This means that while market prices are not static and solely driven by new releases of information, it is very difficult to "beat the market" since any information that may lead one to buy or sell a security has already had an impact on that security, so investors will not be able to consistently outperform.

This concept and initial popularization of EMH are often ascribed to Eugene Fama, a professor at the University of Chicago. EMH has been heavily dissected since it gained popularity in the 1960s, and any number of criticisms point to anomalies in performance that contradict some of the premises of the hypothesis. Value investors typically point to data indicating that stocks with a lower price-to-earnings, or P/E, ratio outperform other stocks (Dreman & Berry 1992). Behavioral economists point to predictable irrationalities and errors in human reasoning that indicate investors are unlikely to act in accordance with EMH (Kehneman & Tversky 1979). And the entire field of technical trading effectively exists in defiance of EMH, claiming to be able to predict price movements based on sentiment indicators or previous movements of certain stocks.

Certain models presented in this text, such as the reduced-form model for debt defaults, draw heavily on EMH rationale in their derivation. When the market fails to accurately capture all of the information that may impact the pricing of a security, that will cause the results of the model to be skewed. For example, if a bankrupt entity holds a large position of company ABC's loans and is forced to sell that position quickly, in a thin market it may push down the price of ABC's loans substantially by flooding the market. Our models will show a substantial increase in the likelihood that ABC will default. However, nothing has fundamentally changed about ABC (other than it will need to find different buyers for its loans in the future).

Other market actions that can cause substantial impact to EMH-based models include short squeezes, rating changes that force the selling of an issuer's debt, and changes in tax law or other regulations which may drive trading. All of these are "technicals": drivers of pricing that are not related to the fundamental value of the security or underlying business. Modelers are wise to stay abreast of such major technical issues, which may influence the pricing of securities over a short period.

DISTRIBUTIONS: NASSIM TALEB AND NORMALCY

One assumption that is commonly used in quantitative finance and in simulations is the normal, or Gaussian, distribution. Normal and lognormal distributions are related to the concept of Brownian motion (which we covered in Chapter 2). These concepts make assumptions about the relative likelihood of a price moving up or down, and the size of such a movement. Unfortunately, these assumptions are not exact representations of the how prices *actually act* much of the time. Extreme price movements have been observed to occur with a higher frequency than a normal distribution would lead us to predict.

After the mortgage meltdown of 2008, the use of normal distributions in finance was roundly criticized. One especially prominent voice in the denouncement of models using these distributions was Nassim Taleb, a highly regarded derivates trader and professor. Taleb is best known for his book *The Black Swan: The Impact of the Highly Improbable,* which was first published in 2007 and argued, among other things, that the statistical methods used in finance were dangerous because they led managers to think they knew more about potential outcomes than they actually did. This situation encourages certain actors to take (or allow) more risk than is prudent. Central to this argument is that extreme events are more likely than forecast in a normal distribution (a "fat-tail" or "heavy-tail" distribution may be more appropriate), and these extreme events have such massive effects that they make models that underestimate their likelihood useless, even dangerous. While many readers took this to mean that the occurrence of the mortgage meltdown was an example of a black swan event, Taleb actually specified in the text that the collapse of the major government-sponsored mortgage firms was foreseeable and that he would not consider their collapse to be outside of previous experience.

Indeed, the central fallacy that Taleb identifies is what he terms the *ludic* fallacy, from the Latin word for *game*. Financial modeling typically assumes that consistent rules govern future states, whereas in actuality the rules of the game are not known and are subject to change. Taleb's criticisms touch on many of the qualitative questions that risk managers and traders must ask themselves and that they must ask of their models (and modelers). How do we estimate future correlations or distributions? How do we build a portfolio that is robust to our errors or to unforeseen events? How do we account for the potential magnitude of loss we may incur?

Almost by definition we do not have rich-enough data on rare events to determine probability with confidence. From a practitioner's standpoint, a number of methods can be used to try to account for these events, but they all have shortcomings. This simplest method is just to stress the volatility of the potential returns of an asset by increasing the volatility of returns. The advantage of this is that it is generally simple to implement and intuitive to understand. And though a simple increase of 10 percent does not seem like it would have a large impact, the probability of a "five-sigma" event in the stress case is almost 10 times what it is in the standard case.

While this holds appeal (and keeps all of the models we have built internally consistent), it does not truly account for the possibility of very extreme events. There is an entire subbranch of statistics known as Extreme Value Theory (EVT), which tackles the subject of dealing with tail events. Several distributions are used in modeling extreme events; probably the most important of these are "power law" distributions, in particular the Pareto distribution.

But the true spirit of Taleb's criticism is that we live in a world in which we cannot understand or forecast with precision what will happen, in particular events that have a very small probability of happening. Further, our attempts to define probabilities and possibilities make us, and the financial system in general, prone to instability and crashes as we become more overconfident and take risks that we do not fully understand.

This critique is important because our recently observed financial history offers evidence not only that our models do not properly account for extreme events, but that we as a financial system have not built enough safeguards into our institutions to account for this. Unfortunately, there is no simple solution to this, especially as an investor or risk manager. A concerted effort to understand new risks and to build portfolios that account for every contingency we can possibly think of is the best that most of us can do. Recognizing the limits of our models is an important part of successfully using them.

NEW FRONTIERS OF ECONOPHYSICS

One new frontier in simulation modeling is the interface between the natural sciences and markets. Financial modelers have long looked to the sciences for ideas on how to model financial phenomena. The Black-Scholes Model itself is based on a heat-diffusion equation. However, as new questions arise, financial modelers look to different fields for inspiration on how to best model markets.

One of the more prominent names in this field is Didier Sornette, a professor at ETH Zurich. He previously held an academic position as a geophysicist and has dedicated some of his research work to exploring econophysics: applying models built originally for physics that may have applications in finance of economics. One application that has gained some following is that of a "regime change," that sudden events like the bursting of asset bubbles are like earthquakes. There is a build-up of pressure and then there is a sudden movement. After the bubble or earthquake, the strain is gone and the asset or seismic activity would be expected to follow a different pattern. Along these lines, in a recent paper in the *Journal of Economic Behavior & Organization* titled "Bubble Diagnosis and Prediction of the 2005–2007 and 2008–2009 Chinese Stock Market Bubbles," the authors claim to have predicted the date of two crashes with 80 percent probability within one month of the highest closing price.

The tool that this research team believes has the ability to reveal the date of a large change in securities pricing is the log-periodic power law (LPPL). The LPPL model is also claimed to be able to predict "bottoms" with a high level of accuracy as well.

WORKING WITH IMPERFECT MODELS

Regardless of how effective a model may be, an important point to remember is that our models are all simplifications of reality based on our understanding of it. Inevitably, simplifications in our simulations will leave out inputs or information that can help inform investment and risk decisions. It is important to remember this when evaluating model results: Our simulations are created to help guide us, not to dictate our actions. A good modeler is confident in the model's results but is conscious of the model's shortcomings and is willing to consider information that the model may not take into account.

Partial Differential Equations

The foundation for many interest rate and derivative pricing models in finance starts with a partial differential equation (PDE). To understand how a model, such as the Black-Scholes Model, is formulated, one must first understand what a partial differential equation is and what is meant by a "solution" to such an equation. This text will assume the reader already has some familiarity with basic calculus. Furthermore, we will not go into extreme detail on the various methods by which a PDE is solved. This is a very complicated process, and entire mathematical books are written to deal with this specific problem. Instead we will only introduce the concept of "equation" and "solution" so that the meaning of these terms is clear when discussing financial theory.

PARTIAL DERIVATIVES

Introductory calculus covers derivatives and integrals. You may remember that derivatives measure the change of a function relative to a change of its underlying variable, that is, the slope of a function. *Partial* derivatives, on the other hand, may not be something everyone is familiar with. In a basic sense a partial derivative is a regular derivative but taken within the context of a function with multiple variables. For a simple refresher, let's take the derivative of the following function (equation A.1):

$$f(x) = 4x^2 \tag{A.1}$$

For those who still remember how to take derivatives, the answer to this is trivial. However, we will take the rigorous approach and do this step by step. We start by applying the Chain Rule (equation A.2):

$$\frac{df(x)}{dx} = 4\frac{d(x^2)}{dx} + x^2\frac{d(4)}{dx} \tag{A.2}$$

175

Now, "4", the second term, is a constant so its derivative is zero. The first term can be quickly evaluated using the Power Rule (equation A.3):

$$\frac{df(x)}{dx} = 4(2x^{2-1}) = 8x \qquad (A.3)$$

Now imagine that equation A.1 had a second variable, y, associated with it (equation A.4):

$$f(x, y) = 4yx^2 \qquad (A.4)$$

With two variables, it would be necessary to measure the change of $f(x,y)$ relative to x while keeping y fixed, and vice versa. And indeed, this is how a partial derivative is defined. So what does all this mean? Let's take the partial derivative of equation A.4 with respect to x (equation A.5):

$$\frac{\partial f(x, y)}{\partial x} = 4y\frac{\partial(x^2)}{\partial x} + 4x^2\frac{\partial y}{\partial x} + yx^2\frac{\partial(4)}{\partial x} \qquad (A.5)$$

First off, notice that when doing partial derivatives, the notation changes from d to ∂. You may also notice that by using the Chain Rule we have added a new term, the partial of y with respect to x. Recall that when taking the partial derivative of a function, f, with respect to x, all other variables are remained fixed. Practically speaking this means they can be viewed as constants, much like "4" is a constant, and is reduced to zero. Equation A.5 can be simplified to equation A.6.

$$\frac{df(x)}{dx} = 4y(2x^{2-1}) = 8yx \qquad (A.6)$$

To complete our example, we will now take the partial with respect to y (equation A.7).

$$\begin{aligned}
\frac{\partial f(x, y)}{\partial y} &= 4y\frac{\partial(x^2)}{\partial y} + 4x^2\frac{\partial y}{\partial y} + yx^2\frac{\partial(4)}{\partial y} \\
&= 0 + 4x^2(1) + 0 \\
&= 4x^2
\end{aligned} \qquad (A.7)$$

Conceptually what we just determined is the slope along the x and y direction respectively.

ORDINARY DIFFERENTIAL EQUATIONS (ODE)

The next step to understanding partial differential equations (PDE) is to understand an ODE, or ordinary differential equation. But before we can even discuss that, let us first review "equations" in general and their "solutions." Suppose we were given the following equation (equation A.8):

$$x^2 + x = 12 \qquad\qquad (A.8)$$

The solution(s) to equation A.8 is the value that x can take that satisfies the equality. In this example, there is only one solution, and that is $x = 3$. We employ a similar concept when dealing with ODEs. However, instead of trying to determine a set of values a variable can take to satisfy the equality, we are trying to find a *function* that, when its derivates are taken, satisfies the given differential equation. An ODE deals strictly with regular derivatives, and as we saw in the last section, this means they only operate on functions with one variable. In their simplest form, ODEs look something like equation A.9:

$$df = 4dx \qquad\qquad (A.9)$$

The solution to this equation is any function, $f(x)$, that when its derivative with respect to x is taken, produces 4 (equation A.10).

$$\frac{df(x)}{dx} = 4 \qquad\qquad (A.10)$$

You may notice that equation A.10 is just a rewrite of equation A.9. Ultimately the solution to this particular problem is fairly simple. We can either use our intuition and make a guess, or we can do this formally and integrate the equation to get our answer via equation A.11.

$$\int df = 4 \int dx \qquad\qquad (A.11)$$

We will not go through the details of discussing integrals, but it is still helpful to see the process. At this point we can state that the answer if $f(x) = 4x$. You can prove this to yourself by taking its derivative and seeing that it does indeed satisfy equation A.10.

At this point you may be wondering why we are even talking about differential equations. Differential equations are extremely important in all fields of science, including finance, because we are usually always trying to quantify how an instantaneous change in one variable relates or causes an instantaneous change to another variable. For example, bond returns, and hence their pricing, are affected by how the interest rates change. If the rate is a constant, then the price, P, is just a simple equation, $P(r)$. However, in real life interest rates do not remain fixed but change continuously through time. Now the relationship between the price, P, and rate, r, is not so simple. When working with a model where the rate is always changing, dr, we have to quantify how that would affect a change in the price, dP. The relationship between the two is the differential equation, and the solution to this relationship tells us the overall effect on the price.

BOUNDARY CONDITIONS

Let's return to equation A.9 and examine its solution more closely. We determined that the solution to this particular equation is $4x$ because the derivative of $4x$ is indeed 4. However, is this the full story? Recall that the derivative of a constant is zero. Therefore our *general* solution must be of the form in equation A.12:

$$f(x) = 4x + C \qquad (A.12)$$

where C is a constant. What does this mean, and why do we need to complicate matters even further? Moreover, how do we even figure out what C is, given that at this point it could be anything! We will discuss its importance a little further on, but C is determined by the *boundary condition,* or initial condition, of the system. This means that to determine C for equation A.12 we must first know the value of $f(0)$.

I realize this all sounds very strange, so let's take as a real-life example, something that we are all familiar with. This example should also convey the importance of what a boundary condition is in a very physical sense. Just as in the discussion about Brownian motion, let's look at bond values that accumulate with a constant interest rate. At any time, t, its value will be (equation A.13):

$$B(t) \propto \exp(rt) \qquad (A.13)$$

Now we ask ourselves, if we were to invent a toy model, just for demonstration purposes, that were to relate dB, the differential of B, to dt such that its solution took the form of equation A.13, what would it look like? Let us make the following guess in equation A.14:

$$dB = r\,B\,dt \qquad (A.14)$$

By using some algebra and basic calculus we can solve this equation (equation A.15):

$$\int \frac{dB}{B} = r \int dt$$
$$\ln(B) + C_1 = rt + C_2 \qquad (A.15)$$
$$\ln(B) = rt + C_2 - C_1$$

Notice that since both Cs are constants, the difference of the two is still a constant (equation A.16):

$$\ln(B) = rt + C$$
$$B = e^{(rt+C)} = e^C e^{rt} \qquad (A.16)$$
$$B = B_0 e^{rt}$$

The only bit of trickery we did here was simply redefining e^C as the constant B_0, which we are free to do since both are constants and can be easily "renamed." Furthermore, notice that B_0 is the constant associated with the solution to the ODE. And as we discussed before, this constant is determined from the boundary condition of the system, which, in the context of our example, is the bond. Equation A.16 should be familiar to everyone as the value of a bond at time, t, with a *starting value* of B_0. Boundary conditions may sound abstract and complicated, but in reality it just defines either the starting or ending point of a system we are dealing with.

PARTIAL DIFFERENTIAL EQUATIONS

Finally, what is a partial differential equation? After all the buildup, the answer is quite anticlimactic. Very simply, PDEs are to ODEs as partial derivatives are to ordinary derivatives. PDEs are differential equations in which the answer, the function you are trying to find, depends on more than one variable (equation A.17):

$$dr = \sigma dW + \mu dt \qquad (A.17)$$

I understand that the notation is inconsistent, but the differentials in PDEs are typically written just as they are in ODEs. Equation A.17 essentially states that our variable, r, is now a function of both the time, t, and a process, W. Since dW is a Weiner process and by its definition is a stochastic variable, equation A.17 is actually a special type of PDE. PDEs with stochastic elements are called, not surprisingly, stochastic differential equations (SDEs), which we will discuss next.

STOCHASTIC DIFFERENTIAL EQUATIONS

In the prior section, we discussed partial differential equations and we have seen previously that we can use random walks to model financial processes. Here we will try to bring both concepts together by introducing stochastic differential equations. Much like with regular ODEs, we will not discuss the mathematical peculiarities of stochastic calculus or the complex methodologies by which these equations are solved. Instead we will try to attain a conceptual understanding of a differential stochastic process by understanding their numerical properties. (We saw these equations in action when exploring the Black-Scholes and Hull-White models in Chapter 4.)

In the financial world of derivatives and option pricing, the interest rate is king. Trading strategies typically pair stocks with bonds in an arbitrage-free market, and as such, the rate on the bond becomes the driving force of how stocks are traded. Hence, stochastic differential equations are commonly used to model interest rates that are then applied toward a specific trading strategy. The most simplistic interest rate model, and the basis for the Ho-Lee Model, is given by equation A.18.

$$dr = \sigma dW + \mu dt \qquad \text{(A.18)}$$

Conceptually speaking, it is pretty clear what "dt" means. Most everyone who has a watch or a calendar can imagine incremental changes in time. However, what does "dW" mean? What does it mean to take the derivative of a Weiner process? Recall from basic calculus that differentiating a function with respect to a variable, in this case we'll take that to be the time, t, is defined to be the following (equation A.19):

$$\frac{df(t)}{dt} \approx \frac{f(t_i) - f(t_{i-1})}{t_i - t_{i-1}} = \frac{\Delta f}{\Delta t} \qquad \text{(A.19)}$$

The relation in equation A.19 is exact in the limit that Δt becomes infinitesimally small. Since it is technically impossible to observe rates in such an ideal manner, all applications of this relationship will result in a solution that is only an approximation of the actual solution. With this limitation in mind, we can rewrite equation A.18 in a more friendly manner (equation A.20):

$$\Delta r = \sigma \Delta W + \mu \Delta t \qquad \text{(A.20)}$$

We saw that the value of a Weiner process at time t is a random number drawn from a normal distribution with mean 0 and standard deviation of sqrt(t/T) (equation A.21),

$$W_T(t) = N\left(0, \sqrt{\frac{t}{T}}\right) \qquad \text{(A.21)}$$

We also know that where the process ends up in the next step, $t + 1$, depends only on its current location at time t. The fact that the future state of the process is independent of its past allows us to make an argument that will greatly simplify our problem. Imagine if at time $t = 0$ I were to take a step in a random direction. Then at time $t = 1$ I were to take another step in an arbitrary direction that was completely independent of where I was at $t = 0$. At that point, practically speaking, it is as if I just "started" off at $t = 1$ and the step that would take me to $t = 2$ would just be my "first" step. In effect I am reinitializing my frame of reference to be the starting point at each new time step. I can do this because once I've taken that step, where I was *before* is completely irrelevant to where I will be *next*. With this view in mind, we can represent ΔW as $W_T(1)$ where $T = 1$ (equation A.22), that is:

$$\Delta W = W_1(1) = N(0, 1) \tag{A.22}$$

Substituting this into equation A.20 and expanding out the Δs, we get equation A.23

$$r_{i+1} = r_i + \mu(t_{i+1} - t_i) + \sigma N(0, 1) \tag{A.23}$$

We see here that dW is nothing more than a randomly drawn number with a normal distribution! Also, notice that we have discovered a way to iteratively solve equation A.18 without actually finding the formal analytical solution. This iterative method of numerically solving an SDE is known as the Euler Scheme. In technical jargon, it is valid only to the first-order approximation when expanding out the SDE using Ito's Lemma. In other words, there is a slight cost in accuracy since we are approximating a continuous differential of infinitesimally small step sizes to a more realistic differential with discrete observable time steps.

Newton-Raphson Method

The Newton-Raphson Method is an iterative procedure used to determine the root of an equation. In some simple situations the root is easy to find. Consider the following equation (equation B.1):

$$f(x) = x - 3 \tag{B.1}$$

Clearly the root of $f(x)$, the value of x such that $f(x) = 0$, is when $x = 3$. A slightly more complicated example is a generic quadratic equation (equation B.2):

$$f(x) = ax^2 + bx + c \tag{B.2}$$

where the solution is the quadratic equation in the form of (equation B.3):

$$x = \frac{-b \pm \sqrt{b^2 - 4ac}}{2a} \tag{B.3}$$

However, what happens when we need to compute the root of an arbitrary function that does not have an analytical solution? For example, how would we find the root of the following function (equation B.4)?

$$f(x) = x^{\frac{5}{6}} + e^{x^2} \tag{B.4}$$

The answer in this case is not so easily determined. The simplest solution is to guess a possible range that might contain the answer and then step through each value until the answer is found. This brute-force method, however, is highly unreliable and extremely slow. A more robust and faster solution is to use the Newton-Raphson iterative method.

The method requires the analyst to start with a guess, x_o, and then the process iterates through successive values of x until the root is found. The step size of the

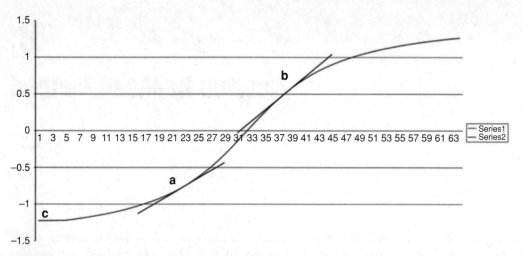

FIGURE B.1   Point *a* would cause a jump forward, while point *b* would cause a jump backward. Point *c* is unstable because the slope is nearly 0.

guess and the direction of the step are determined not only by the value at *f(x)* but also by its slope, or derivative. The derivation of the method is simple, but it provides deep insight into how the process works. To begin, we can write the definition of a derivative (equation B.5):

$$\frac{df(x_n)}{dx} = f'(x_n) = \frac{f(x_n) - 0}{x_n - x_{n+1}} \tag{B.5}$$

The zero in the numerator is there because we are trying to arrive at the root, with a value of zero and with the hope that this happens at x_{n+1}. This equation can be rewritten to give the formal definition of the Newton-Raphson procedure (equation B.6):

$$x_{n+1} = x_n - \frac{f(x_n)}{f'(x_n)} \tag{B.6}$$

The reason why this equation doesn't just "work" is that a *true* definition of a derivative is an instantaneous change in *x*. If x_n is too far from the root, then the slope as computed by equation B.5 would not be a very accurate representation of the derivative. In other words, there is too much error in the representation, and an iterative process is required to converge onto the right answer.

Figure B.1 provides a graphical view of how the iteration works. At point *a*, the slope is positive but the value of the function is negative. Thus the next step in the iteration would result in an increase in x. At point b, the slope is still positive but the value is also positive, resulting in a decrease in x. Point c is an illustration of how crucial the starting guess, x_0, is regarding the stability of the iteration. Notice at point c that the slope is effectively zero and would cause the second term in equation B.6 to effectively "blow up." When applying this method, care should be taken to not start off in this region.

References

Baxter, Martin, and Rennie, Andew, *Financial Calculus: An Introduction to Derivative Pricing.* Cambridge, Cambridge University Press, 1996.

Bharath, Sreedhar, and Shumway, Tyler, "Forecasting Default with the KMV-Merton Model." Working paper, University of Michigan, 2005.

"Corporate Default and Recovery Rates, 1920–2008," Moody's Investors Service, Special Comment, February 2008. www.dbresearch.com/PROD/DBR_INTERNET_EN-PROD/PROD0000000000183612.pdf

Deutsche Bank Research, "How Do CDS Spreads Relate to the Probability of Default?" accessed April 2, 2011.

Hull, J., and White, A., "Using Hull-White Interest-Rate Trees," *Journal of Derivatives* (Winter 1996).

Hull, J., and White, A., "Numerical Procedures for Implementing Term Structure Models I: Single-Factor Models," *Journal of Derivatives* 2, No. 1 (Fall 1994a), 7–16.

Löffler, G., and Posch, P., *Credit Risk Modeling Using Excel and VBA.* New York, John Wiley & Sons, 2007.

Merton, Robert C., "On the Pricing of Corporate Debt: The Risk Structure of Interest Rates," *Journal of Finance* 29 (1974), 449–470.

"Sovereign Defaults and Recovery Rates 1983–2007," Moody's Investors Service, Special Comment, 2008.

Taleb, Nassim N., *The Black Swan: The Impact of the Highly Improbable.* New York, Random House, 2007.

FURTHER READING

Dreman, D., and Berry, M., "Overreaction, Underreaction, and the Low-P/E Effect," *Financial Analysts Journal* 51 (July–August 1995), 21–30.

Jiang, et al., "Bubble Diagnosis and Prediction of the 2005–2007 and 2008–2009 Chinese Stock Market Bubbles," *Journal of Economic Behavior & Organization* 74 (2010), 149–162.

Kahneman, D., and Tversky, A., "Prospect Theory: An Analysis of Decision under Risk." *Econometrica* 47, No. 2 (March 1979), pp. 263–292.